D1559908

A "POLIO" FINDS HIS WAY

A "POLIO" FINDS HIS WAY

My Father's Remarkable Journey

SUSAN CLOUGH WYATT

A "Polio" Finds His Way: My Father's Remarkable Journey

Cover Design by
Nathan McClintock and Kate Winter

Book Design by
Kate Winter

Library of Congress Cataloging-in-Publication Data

Wyatt, Susan C. (1943-   )
A "Polio" Finds His Way: My Father's Remarkable Journey
By Susan C. Wyatt—First Edition

All photos from author's collection.
Cover photo: Kezar Stadium, San Francisco, 1933

Published by Asbury Press
www.susancwyatt.com

1. Clough, Forrest Weldon (1909-1983) — poliomyelitis — biography
2. Poliomyelitis — United States — history — Texas — vaccine — global
eradication efforts 3. Wyatt, Susan Clough — Poliomyelitis — Postpoliomyelitis
Syndrome 4. Southern Methodist University Mustang Band — history
5. Early radio in Texas

Printing History
First Edition: March 2020

ISBN: 9798632687997

Printed in the United States of America

for

Maggie Johnson Clough, mother
and
Mildred Wyatt Clough, wife

Loving caregivers who helped make
Forrest's life as successful as it was
in an inhospitable era

Also by Susan Clough Wyatt:

Arabian Nights and Daze: Living in Yemen with the Foreign Service
Thirty Acres More or Less: Restoring a Farm in Virginia

CONTENTS

AUTHOR'S NOTE

Regarding manuscript wording and style:

Because many polio survivors refer to themselves as "polios," I've chosen to use this term without quotes throughout, except in the title which introduces a moniker for a polio survivor that most are not familiar with. Survivors also used the words "able-ism" and "normals," which I have included as well, also without quotes.

Many words common to my father's era, such as "Negro" or "squaw," are no longer acceptable today, since we now view them as racist and demeaning. However, I have retained these words when quoting or paraphrasing directly from original material in order to reflect the actual discourse of the day. This not only reveals how ingrained such thinking was, but also how far we have come.

Likewise, words used 80 to 100 years ago to describe people with disabilities, such as "cripple" or "handicap," are seen as insensitive or disrespectful today. Thus, "disability" is preferred in lieu of "handicap" to acknowledge this sensitivity. Along with his contemporaries, my father referred to himself as a cripple, or crippled, or handicapped, and never used the word "disabled." I use his words interchangeably in this book when quoting directly or paraphrasing from original sources.

I use trumpet and cornet interchangeably.

In citing materials from any of the seven scrapbooks, I use the generic term Scrapbook with a capital letter.

A bird came hopping on my shelf
with one good foot—a stump the other.
It hurt my heart to see so maimed
a feathered brother.

Yet when he spread his wings to go
He seemed to launch himself with laughter,
as though to shame my sorry thoughts
that fluttered after.

For though he could not perch so well,
nor strut, nor swagger any longer,
His wings were strong as any bird's—
Or were they stronger?

THE CRIPPLE
Karle Wilson Baker
(1878-1960)
Nacogdoches, Texas

PREFACE

Life was challenging for victims of poliomyelitis and their families in the first half of the twentieth century. Commonly known as polio, the crippling disease often had lasting effects on all parts of the body, especially limbs, lungs, and the motor neurons of the brain that control movement.

People born after the late 1950s routinely receive their polio vaccine and typically have little knowledge of the disease. They do not understand how the threat of polio pervaded everyone's life during the first half of the 20th century and spread fear and helplessness among the population. Many feared polio more than the AIDS virus of the 1980s, likely because it hit the population so randomly, attacking both rich and poor.

There were many starts and stops along the way as medical researchers tried to determine the nature and progression of polio, how to treat the paralysis when it occurred, and how to prevent the disease. Solving this major public health crisis took over sixty years from the time of the first US epidemic in Vermont in the mid-1890s until the Salk and Sabin vaccines in 1955 and 1962 respectively were successful and licensed for use. Were it not for the powerful influence of President Franklin Roosevelt, it might have been many more years before a cure was found. With the vaccines, the disease was eliminated in Western societies. Except in a few countries mired by strife in Asia and Africa, eradication of the disease worldwide is close at hand. Yet, getting there has not been easy.

Before the vaccines, the two-to-three percent left seriously paralyzed had few physical, legal and social resources available to them. Many victims became the total responsibility of their families. Some were relegated to institutional care for much of their lives. Like others with disabilities, many polio victims in the early years lived in isolation. They were often openly shunned or devalued in subtle ways and taught to believe they must work toward the ideal of able-ism if they were to be accepted in society.

Simi Linton in *Claiming Disability* maintains that the individual and collective voices of the disabled were simply not heard, nor was much written about them.[1] However, she claims the disabled were always a distinct minority of over fifty million Americans rather than the isolated individuals they believed they were.

Initially, in the United States the numbers of polio survivors were relatively small. Between 1915 and 1942 the United States witnessed the number of polio cases per year as well under 10,000, with the exceptions being 1916 (27,363), 1927, 1931, and 1935. Between 1943 and 1956, the numbers ranged from 10,827 to 57,874, with nine of those years registering 25,000 and above.[2] By the 1940s and early 1950s the number of afflicted families and polio victims was so great that society could no longer avoid them. Something had to be done.

During the presidency of Franklin D. Roosevelt (FDR) in the 1930s, New Deal legislation offered some limited assistance to the disabled. For the first time, the Social Security Act provided financial aid to the states for "medical treatment and rehabilitation" of the mentally and physically disabled. Appropriations were divvied up according to the numbers of crippled, especially children, in each state, but nothing was provided to educate them. In 1939 the Pepper-Boland legislation corrected that shortcoming and gave states financial support to create "educational facilities and programs to fit the needs of crippled children." Under this legislation "91,000 children became eligible for benefits."[3]

Exhibiting Linton's concept of a larger group consciousness, by mid-century the disability rights movement had gained momentum and forced the government's hand. Polio victims contributed to the groundswell. Following historic civil rights legislation of 1964 and 1965, Congress passed several pieces of legislation to help protect and support the disabled: the Architectural Barriers Act of 1968, the Rehabilitation Act of 1973, as amended (Rehab Act), the Individuals with Disabilities Education Act of 1975 (IDEA), the Americans with Disabilities Act of 1990 (ADA), and the Americans with Disabilities Act Amendments Act of 2008 (ADAAA). (See

Appendix A for details.) This landmark legislation not only lowered structural barriers and granted certain rights and protections, it also admitted these once isolated and marginalized people, including polio survivors, into society's mainstream. It granted them equality with their normal, able-bodied peers.

Once the vaccines eradicated polio in the Western world, little was heard about polio or its survivors. As a result, young people today have no first-hand knowledge of this public health crisis or of the impact it had on American families. Those who contracted the disease in the 1940s and 1950s will not be around much longer to remind younger generations of this scourge that once plagued our society.

Anne Gross, author of *The Polio Journals: Lessons from My Mother*[4] that is based in part on her paraplegic mother's diaries, says:

> *The personal stories of those affected are becoming more of a rarity . . . these first-person accounts . . . enable us to understand not only what the disease meant medically, but how it acted on all aspects of an individual's life: from childhood, to marriage, parenthood, to career. Personal polio narratives also provide valuable lessons in history, as over time individuals faced different cultural responses to their minority status . . . as people with disabilities trying to fit into society.*

Believing like Gross in documenting polio disability stories before they are lost forever, I initiated this project about my father over 20 years ago. I wanted to describe the extraordinary life he created for himself despite the ravages of paralytic polio in the pre-legislation era.

Originally, I had no plans to tell my story in this book. It was simply to be a tribute to my father as a successful polio survivor in the early-mid-20th century. Now it covers my polio story as well. Contracting the disease during the 1952 epidemic, I managed to avoid paralysis, unlike my father. Although he left me many useful legacies, there were certain consequences of having been raised by a disabled parent. After many years of gestation, this has become a family memoir that spans more than 100 years of a father-daughter relationship cemented by a common disease.

My father, Forrest Clough, contracted spinal and bulbar poliomyelitis at four months of age in 1909 in Fort Worth, Texas. Called infantile paralysis at the time, the disease left him a paraplegic with additional muscle loss in both arms. Had it not been for the wonderful care and support from his able-bodied family and friends, his life might have ended at several points during his early years.

In addition to his personal story, this narrative reveals aspects of American social history covering the first half of the twentieth century. Woven through the threads of his life are glimpses of early polio history and treatments; the contributions of polio survivor Franklin Roosevelt; economic and political events leading up to World War II and social issues prevalent at the time; college football of the 1930s before the sport became a major commercial enterprise; national entertainment in the form of vaudeville and Big Band era stars; and the evolution of transportation, the movies, radio and television. After my brother and I were born in the forties, this story focuses more narrowly on our family of four, my father's later years, and my retrospective comments about his life. An epilogue documents the current international campaign to eradicate polio worldwide, and the two appendices describe key disability legislation passed since the 1960s and my late effects of polio (i.e., post-polio sequelae or syndrome—PPS).

Forrest's remarkable story is drawn from several materials that document his life from birth through 1940: a hand-written autobiography crafted at age 22 for a college sociology class; a year's collection of his articles and editorials for his journalism class published in *The Semi-Weekly Campus* newspaper of Southern Methodist University (SMU); a four-page Colorado travelogue written in 1925 as well as a 16-page handwritten travelogue of the family's two-month vacation in New York City in the summer of 1929; seven scrapbooks compiled between 1927 and 1940—herein referred to as *Scrapbook* or *Scrapbook I, II,* etc.; several musical compositions, with at least one copyrighted; an eight-page hand-written autobiography of his life put together in 1967; and an assortment of news clips about him.

Interviews with family and friends primarily conducted between 1992 and 2003 helped fill in some gaps: my mother, Mildred; Forrest's sister-in-law, Adele; Floyd Patterson and Joe Rucker, who were colleagues in the

SMU band; and Johnny Smith and Dave Naugle, who worked with him at KFJZ Radio. All are deceased now. I also include reminiscences of Forrest's younger sister Margaret, my brother George, my cousin Mike, and other living family members and friends.

My father rarely mentioned in his writings the disease's emotional consequences for him, and I have had to guess at what those might have been. I have attempted to interpret his feelings and behaviors with the help of narratives written by other polios, of family members, and my own memories. I have also tried to interpret them against the historically challenging backdrop of the era in which he lived.

Forrest Clough's story is noteworthy for its day. He was, in fact, a polio pioneer before national attention began to focus on the disease and the great challenges that he and people like him were up against. Despite his disability, Forrest created a full and satisfying life for himself. However, because he was heavily dependent on others for his care, he could never forget his disability. That fact shaped everything he did or aspired to do.

Our family's journey may resemble other multi-generational stories about caring for the disabled, but hopefully A "Polio" Finds His Way will contribute its unique spin to the collective history of the pre-disability-legislation era. May it help keep alive the narratives of some remarkable people who defied the odds of this devastating disease with little public support, especially after the last of us who contracted the disease are gone. Finally, may it provide inspiration for today's physically disabled, for their families, and for those working with them.

Susan Clough Wyatt
Eugene, OR
February 2020

EARLY LIFE: 1909-1929

CHAPTER ONE

GROWING UP AS A POLIO SURVIVOR

No one expected Forrest Weldon Clough to live beyond the age of four months. Born at home in Fort Worth, Texas, on June 28, 1909, Forrest was the first child of George and Maggie Clough. He was a sweet little boy, bald at birth with a big round face, who would one day look like his father in all but one respect: He could not walk and would spend his life on crutches or in a wheelchair. Looking back at age 22, he wrote:

> When I was four months old, one of the most dreaded of all diseases attacked me. It was that disease known as infantile paralysis [polio]. The doctors said that the nearest such case was in New York City, so naturally, it seems that the germ or whatever it was, just decided to pick on me.

New York City had some of the early polio epidemics in the United States, including 2,000 cases reported in the summer of 1907.[5] Forrest was apparently the only child in Fort Worth to have contracted the disease in the fall

CHERUBIC FORREST (BEFORE POLIO)

1

of 1909. What was this strange disease that caused such fear throughout this country and the Western world?

Polio's Early History. The poliovirus has been endemic—a wild virus, natural to or characteristic of a location or people—throughout the world since prehistory. Archeologists found an Egyptian mummy dating from 3700 BC and a stone carving from 1400 BC that show otherwise healthy people having withered limbs characteristic of polio deformities.[6] Hippocrates, the Greek father of medicine, and the Roman physician Galen five centuries later were both familiar with congenital deformities of the lower extremities and with acquired "clubfoot," many cases caused by paralytic poliomyelitis.[7] Roman Emperor Claudius likely had polio as a child and forever walked with a limp.[8] As an infant Sir Walter Scott was afflicted in 1773 with a fever of three days that resulted in a lame right leg—perhaps the first recorded case of polio anywhere.[9]

The term poliomyelitis comes from the Greek: "polios" or gray, "myelos" or marrow (referring to the anterior matter or marrow of the spinal cord), and "itis" or inflammation—an inflammation of the gray marrow of the spinal cord.[10] It was first described clinically in medical literature in 1789 by London physician Michael Underwood whose second edition of a book titled *Diseases of Children* referred to the disease under the heading "Debility of the Lower Extremities."[11] A number of expanded investigations of the disease by medical doctors and researchers followed in the 1800s, particularly by Europeans. These investigations were of isolated cases involving small numbers of patients.

"Infantile paralysis," among many terms used over the years, including "Heine-Medin disease" named for two 19th century researchers, Jacob von Heine and Karl Medin, was an early label given to the poliovirus because it struck mostly young children. When older children, adolescents and some adults began contracting the disease, it was more commonly called "poliomyelitis" or simply "polio."

German orthopedist Jacob von Heine, after treating a number of polio patients, published the first rigorous, systematic study of the disease in an 1840 monograph and concluded that the disease affected the central nervous system's spinal cord.[12] He also maintained the disease was contagious and recommended "exercise, warm baths, and the use of braces."[13]

In 1870 French neurologist Jean-Martin Charcot and colleagues confirmed through autopsies of paralyzed individuals that the anterior horn cells or motor neurons in the gray matter of the spine were damaged with lesions. Dr. Mary Putnam Jacobi, the first woman to achieve an MD degree in the United States, published a well-regarded 50-page summary of the disease up until 1886 in Dr. William Pepper's *System of Medicine*. She had studied in France at Charcot's clinic and brought to the States this new concept of damage to the motor neurons of the spine. She wanted to supplant a current notion that it was an inflammation and pressure of the fluid surrounding the spinal column that caused paralysis.

Swedish physician Karl Oskar Medin added another theory from the 1887 Stockholm epidemic of 44 cases. The disease involved two bouts of fever, the first only making the patient feel sick, the second paralyzing him when the central nervous system became affected.

Dr. Charles Caverly, physician and health officer of his state, kept careful records of the 1894 polio epidemic of 132 cases in Rutland, Vermont, the largest ever reported in the world at that time. He realized that a quarter of the patients were older than six, not just infants, and a majority were male. It eventually became clear that as epidemics increased, the ages of those affected grew higher. Caverly's biggest contribution to the understanding of polio was the determination there were likely abortive and non-paralytic cases with minor symptoms who recovered quickly.[14] Still, he did not detect the disease was contagious.[15]

Finally, Dr. Ivar Wickman, Medin's student, resurrected Heine's 1840 theory that the disease was contagious after studying a 1905 epidemic in another part of Sweden. He concluded that mild cases of polio, without spinal lesions and paralysis, occurred more frequently than anyone realized and that mild cases were just as contagious as the severe cases. He also determined that the incubation period from time of exposure to onset of minor illness was three to four days.[16] The second or major illness or paralytic phase did not occur until eight to ten days later. His keen observations showed that the disease was not fully a disease of the central nervous system but spread primarily through subclinical infections.[17]

Soon after Wickman's study, in 1908 the direction of polio research turned from clinical observation to laboratory or experimental research and remained there for years following a discovery in Vienna. Three scientists, renowned bacteriologist Robert Koch and his colleagues Karl Landsteiner and Erwin Popper, determined the disease was caused by a filterable virus when they successfully transmitted human polio "agents" to Old World monkeys and discovered lesions on their spinal cords. "By late 1909 almost the whole microbiological world had accepted the viral etiology of poliomyelitis."[18]

About the same time, Dr. Simon Flexner, director of the prestigious Rockefeller Institute founded in 1902 in New York City, was able to spread polio from one animal to the next, thus allowing researchers to study animals in the laboratory.[19] Flexner was the leading polio researcher in the country whose opinions most medical professionals respected. He continued to focus on animal research in the laboratory for the next 20-30 years, turning away from looking at the human disease. He also insisted that the disease was airborne and entered the body through the nasal passages, another theory that turned out to be erroneous and misdirected research for many years.

In 1909, Forrest's birth year, everyone, including Maggie, George, and likely their doctors, was puzzled as to why these outbreaks occurred and how the disease was transmitted. Only a year earlier they had learned it was a virus. Despite severe odds, Forrest survived the illness primarily due to the determination of his mother, Maggie. During the infectious stage of the disease, Forrest was unable to cry or swallow. So, Maggie force-fed him breast milk, using an eyedropper and massaging his throat to make the milk go down. To test whether he was still breathing, she put her forefinger to his nostrils in search of a faint stream of air. It must have been frightening for this first-time mother to see her baby in such a precarious state.

Maggie and George (or G.O., for George Obadiah, as most people called him) had moved to Fort Worth just before Forrest's birth. G.O. had accepted a position there as head of the physics department at Jennings Avenue Junior High School so that Maggie would have support for her new baby. Her parents, Sam ("Popee") and Mary Johnson, had moved to Fort Worth from East Texas in the early 1900s. Founded in 1849 as a US Army outpost following the Mexican-American War, Fort Worth, with a population of 70,000 by 1910, had become a center for the ranching and oil drilling industries.

Initially, Maggie and G.O. sought whatever help local specialists could provide to treat Forrest's paralysis. At the time, there was much confusion about how the poliovirus caused paralysis, and knowledge of therapy and rehabilitation were limited.

Early Treatments. One can only imagine the kinds of treatments these specialists recommended based on traditional methods used in the 19th century. For example, in an 1835 outbreak of four cases in England, physician J. Badham used calomel, "cold applications to the head, blisters to the spine" and poultices to the affected limb.[20]

For the aftercare of his polio patients, Jacob von Heine in 1840 preferred "exercise, baths, and various simple surgical procedures," followed by braces rather than the typical "purges, emetics, blisters, and bleedings"[21] so common to his era. Heine was far ahead of his time and the methods he used would not become common practice for another hundred years.

Traditional practice was hard to abandon. Dr. Mary Jacobi in the 1870s and 1880s applied ice as well as mercury ointment to the spine, injected ergot to bring blood to the surface of the skin, and administered iodides followed by electrical treatment after the first week.[22]

Dr. Samuel D. Gross, a distinguished surgeon in Philadelphia, described the disease as an inflammation that puts pressure on the sheaths of the nerves causing the paralysis. He then went on to recommend "bleeding, either by leeches or cut cups, and blisters..." and stated the "best and most efficient means of treating the disease is...with a red-hot iron, a good issue [a discharge of blood...from the body generally induced by an ulcerous lesion] over the affected spot." For physical therapy he suggested the "muscles must be rubbed and shampooed, and steadily exercised with the battery [electrotherapy]..." He recommended application of mercury ointment over the entire spine and the backs of the limbs twice a day, then "wring the end of a towel out of cold water, and with it strike the entire surface of the body, quite smartly, until the skin is reddened." This was to be continued for one month.[23] Author Heather Wooten added to this list of painful 19th century treatments: injections of "smallpox vaccine, adrenaline, silver nitrate, strychnine, horse, goat, and monkey serum, and convalescent serum extracted from recovered polio patients."[24]

Such were the treatment methods for paralytic polios before the medical doctors knew what they were dealing with, with some of these methods continuing into the 20th century. Medical professionals used the spinal tap as the primary means throughout the polio years to diagnose suspected poliomyelitis. Increased white blood cells and protein levels were often indicative of polio. Because they were still confused about "how the poliovirus caused paralysis," physicians used the limited "medical therapy and rehabilitation" they had available but also "prescribed plasters, pills, and injections, some with devastating effects."[25] In general, medical treatment for the handicapped, including polio victims, during the early years of the 20th century was inadequate, ineffective, and grim.[26]

TWO YEARS OLD (AFTER POLIO)

Despite consulting local specialists, Maggie and G.O. found nothing to restore Forrest's afflicted muscles in either upper or lower body. For later illnesses, Maggie put mustard plasters on Forrest's chest and hung asafetida bags (lumpy, acrid gum resin to calm the bowels) around his neck. Perhaps Maggie might have been open to experimental treatments for polio had they been available in 1910.

The Cloughs soon expanded their family, for Maggie was already over thirty years old and Fort Worth was a good place to raise her young children.

In October of 1911, my brother, Ancel, was born. It seemed as though the good Lord knew what I needed most—a brother, one who could be big and strong in order to help me about as we both climbed the long ladder of life.

Over the years the two brothers became best buddies. As they grew older, Ancel served as Forrest's legs much of the time—pulling his older brother to and from school in a little red wagon and later carrying him up and down stairs to help Forrest get to his college classes.

Therapy in St. Louis. In 1910 a number of US and European scientists confirmed that antibodies found in the blood of recovering polio patients could neutralize or inactivate live poliovirus. [27] This discovery also encouraged people to believe that a vaccine might be possible. However, a vaccine to prevent the disease was over forty years in the making with many diversions along the way. So researchers and clinicians had to find other ways to deal with this debilitating disease and its paralyzed victims.

In August 1912, G.O. took Forrest to St. Louis, Missouri, to check out L.C. McLain Orthopedic Sanitarium for Cripples at 936 Aubert Avenue, one of 15 to 20 such facilities scattered around the country. Although there is no record of the quality of accommodations or of Forrest's treatments at McLain's, an ad in a January 1922 *Cosmopolitan* magazine gives the testimony of a man who had walked on his toes for 33 years due to polio. He claimed he was able to walk flat-footed after five months of treatment at McLain's. Earlier ads such as this may have intrigued the Cloughs to check the place out.

Hugh Gallagher, author and polio survivor, states that these facilities were "often . . . depressing places—dark, gray piles indistinguishable from asylums or prisons." [28] "Treatment was spartan and severe" in such institutions "and purposely so: fresh air in all seasons; windows open at all times; no central heating; basic institutional cooking . . .; strict rules and firm discipline." Because of an underlying attitude that the handicapped were outwardly inferior and morally weak, the medical profession believed treatment should "have a punitive quality to it."[29]

Whether or not G.O. carefully surveyed the facility, officials there persuaded him that the sanitarium could help Forrest. When he wired Maggie that he was going to leave Forrest at the hospital for treatment, Maggie quickly wired back that she and 10-month-old Ancel would arrive by train in two days. Perhaps Maggie had heard about the notorious rehabilitative orthopedic hospitals for children that provided harsh treatment with punitive rules. She certainly would have wanted to keep a keen eye over Forrest's experiences there and make sure he was not ill-treated. And she knew how frightened Forrest would be if left all alone in strange surroundings. She was not about to abandon her young child to what may have been a depressing asylum-like place.

It must have been wrenching for Maggie, who was probably still nursing Ancel, to split up the family. But bottle feeding had been around since the mid-1800s, so she sent G.O. and her baby back to Fort Worth. She rented a place for her and Forrest and thus had control over Forrest's care and was able to accompany him to all his treatments, whatever they entailed. As in later years, Maggie was on the scene to ensure her son's safety and well-being, even though this time it meant leaving her infant son and extended family for almost a year. Forrest lamented:

> It was impossible for mother to carry me to my treatments, give me my exercises on the mechanical devices in the treatment room, and take care of little brother.

Back in Fort Worth, G.O. rented out the family home for that school year and moved in with Maggie's parents about ten blocks closer to downtown. This move made it easier for Grandmother Johnson to care for Ancel while G.O. was teaching at the nearby junior high school. The boys' grand-father Popee ran a grocery store on West Seventh.

MAGGIE AND FORREST IN ST. LOUIS, 1912

No family story remains about what must have been a lonely time for Maggie and Forrest. Despite rumors to the contrary about places like McLain's, the therapy provided in St. Louis gave Forrest a new lease on life and better tools for coping with his disability. Forrest was fitted with his

first braces and crutches and taught how to use them. When he and his mother returned to Texas, he had a surprise for his family:

> None of them knew I could take slow, faltering steps, so one can . . . imagine their surprise when I showed them that I could walk. The first night, I think I made three or four dollars from my relatives. Grandfather offered me a dollar to walk across the room, then Dad offered me one to walk back to the other side, and so on until far into the night!

Forrest must have truly mastered his crutches during the ten-month sojourn in St. Louis, as those were the same slippery hardwood floors in the house at 2208 Fairmount Avenue I visited in 2008, almost a hundred years later. He also developed a great deal of upper body control, not to mention

IN FORT WORTH, 1913

determination. Since four dollars was a lot of money in 1913, the family must have been very impressed with Forrest's accomplishments.

By 1913, 25,000 cases of polio had been documented in every state and province in the United States and Canada.[30] Texas's first polio outbreak of 60 cases occurred that year in the northeastern part of the state.[31] A year later, when he was five years old, Maggie and Forrest returned to St. Louis for further treatment. Although he was likely fitted to larger braces and taught to walk on them, how long they stayed or what they experienced on this second trip is unknown.

1916's Big Polio Outbreak. The large epidemic in New York City and more dispersed parts of the country sent authorities frantically racing to stop the disease's spread. The public health officials tried traditional methods learned from other epidemic diseases to no avail. They cleaned up garbage, quarantined affected individuals in their homes or sent them to hospitals, restricted travel among the boroughs, killed 72,000 cats, suspected flies, mosquitoes and other insects. Many blamed immigrants who lived in filth as the carriers. Wealthier families shipped their children to relatives out of the city.

Before it was over in November 1916 the virus had affected almost 9,000 and killed 2,448 in New York City alone. According to the 1960 annual statistical review of the National Foundation for Infantile Paralysis (NFIP), the number of polio cases nationwide in 1916 was 27,363 and 7,179 died, with no indication of the number of paralytic cases.[32] Eighty percent of those stricken were children under the age of five.[33]

Authorities learned from this epidemic that insects, animals, and poor sanitation did not spread this highly contagious disease, that far more people are carriers of the virus than was clinically evident, and that an epidemic such as this one immunizes the population and the "epidemic declines spontaneously."[34] However, they continued to believe the disease to be transmitted airborne through the respiratory tract.

Forrest's Family. As a backdrop for his 1931 "Trails of Happiness" autobiography written for a college sociology class, Forrest introduced his parents and grandparents:

> My father, George Obadiah Clough, was born in Ben Wheeler, Texas, February 10, 1878, the son of Ancel Cicero and Mary [Belcher] Clough . . . . His grandfather, George Washington Clough, came [to East Texas in 1842] from . . . Alabama with his life-long friend, Mr. [Ancel] Heard . . . seeking happiness and prosperity . . . .
> My mother [Maggie Llewellyn Johnson] was born in Nacogdoches, Texas, on January 19, 1880, the daughter of Samuel McBride and Mary Ross Johnson. Her father . . . was born in South Carolina . . . . When he was about ten years old, his family moved to East Texas by . . . means of a pioneer wagon train . . . .

Maggie Johnson and George Clough were married in Cleburne, Texas, a small town southwest of Fort Worth, on August 24, 1904, while George

MAGGIE AND G.O., 1904

was studying at the University of Texas. Graduating with a BA in 1908, George began his career in education, teaching in rural schools in Ellis and Leon counties until their move to Fort Worth in 1909.

Forrest's own words sum up his early days and provide the motto he was to live by for dealing with what he termed his "affliction:"

This one little sick-spell of three short days, during which time I had very little fever, was the fundamental shaping element of my life for all my years on this earth . . . . I was to be a cripple, one who would have to get about on crutches, or in wheelchairs, the rest of my days. Through all the years, I have endeavored to keep on 'Keeping On.' What is the use of meeting an uncontrollable condition with a frown and a bad philosophy? Just keep on smiling, and the world will smile with you!

He further acknowledges all the sacrifices made on his behalf:

Immediately after the paralysis attack . . . Mother and Dad—DEAR OLD MOTHER AND DAD—started taking me to all types of specialists in an attempt to bring relief . . . . I know that through all my life things have revolved around me. I was always the center of my people's interest; they were unselfishly doing all in their power for my . . . comfort; . . . Mother and Dad, relatives, neighbors, and dear friends . . . . I shall always be appreciative of their . . . many kindnesses . . . .

Early Schooling in Corsicana. By the time his mother and he returned from St. Louis in June 1913, Forrest was better able physically to deal with his handicap and to enjoy 2-year-old Ancel's company. In fact, he bought a Shetland pony from his grandfather Popee for the "outstanding bargain price of five cents." Popee hitched that pony to a small buggy and the boys took many enjoyable rides together.

In 1914, the family moved to Corsicana, Texas, a town of about 10,000 people 65 miles southeast of Fort Worth, where G.O. became principal of Corsicana High School. Founded in 1848 by José Navarro whose family hailed from the isle of Corsica, the town provided Forrest his first opportunity for some "school training" as he called it, even though he had to wait three years to get it.

> The doctors thought it best to keep me out of school until I was ten or twelve years old. They seemed to think that if given time, my body would develop some strength and become well.

Finally, convincing his parents he was ready to be like other kids, go to school and have friends, he attended public school for one full year in 1917-1918.

> I wanted to go to school so badly that when I was eight years of age my parents, upon the consent of the doctors, decided to let me enter . . . .

Author Hugh Gallagher notes that in the early days of the 20th century, doctors were guided more by a "lingering primordial fear, unspoken but nearly universal, of the crippled." [35] They were not allowed into the mainstream of public education. Sheltered workshops run by charitable organizations that trained cripples to do handicrafts were all that were available to most disabled children in the 1910-20 period. [36] Forrest was fortunate to have been born into a middle-class, educated family, who would make every effort to create a normal life for him—despite the hesitancy of his doctors. He would not be marginalized by his family. To ensure her son's welfare that first year of public schooling, Maggie took a job in the school cafeteria.

If there was ever any sort of harassment or discrimination against Forrest, he never mentioned it in any of his writings. By all accounts folks were always considerate, helpful and generous toward the family. G.O.'s position as high school principal may have been one reason for this acceptance. He was a respected educator wherever they lived, and it would have been socially unacceptable to shun the family. Also, Forrest had an outgoing, friendly personality and positive self-image, which his strong-willed mother, his teachers, and other adults around him helped instill. People liked him. And, students in this small, conservative Southern town were well-mannered and probably did not act out against their classmates, especially a disadvantaged one.

Forrest's first schoolteacher was Miss Sallie Evans, "a loveable [sic] old lady . . . hard to forget." In a 1978 eight-page life summary, Forrest wrote:

> *Everybody has a first day of school and mine came in September 1917. I started in the second grade because mother taught me at home the first year. The second grade class was on the 2nd floor of the school in Corsicana.... It was too hard for me to be carried upstairs to the...class, so I was given second grade work while rooming with the first grade class on the ground floor . . . .*

The children in Forrest's class were "nice" to him and pulled him "around at recess time in a little red express wagon." It was the first time he experienced "true comradeship" with playmates other than his brother Ancel.

Several incidents that happy year stuck in Forrest's memory. One was the class' Christmas celebration on the last day of school before the holiday recess. His classmates decorated a tree and eagerly awaited a visit from Santa Claus. What fun they had with Old St. Nick, who delivered a present to each of them. It was another five or six years before Forrest learned that his mother had played Santa that memorable day—probably about the time he and Ancel discovered the truth about Santa Claus.

Another incident occurred when "all the little fellows started going barefooted." Wanting to be just like the rest of the boys, Forrest did not wear any leg braces to school for several days: "What a great feeling it was to be like the other fellows." However, he could not run around to get his feet dirty, so he figured out another way to blacken them. His classroom seat was on the far side of the room, in the row right next to a "huge soot pipe" coming down the wall from the second floor. "At last, an idea...!" He surreptitiously drew his feet back and forth on the sooty floor and achieved the desired result. "Of course . . . that didn't last very long!" His teacher must have put a quick stop to that.

> I went to school in this wonderful surrounding for only one short year. I hated to leave my school chums and most of all I hated to leave my dear old teacher, Miss Sallie Evans. The students gave me a farewell party at the close of the year . . . . We went to a park in the city, and had a picnic lunch with all the fixin's 'n' everything.

A small clip from the *Corsicana Daily Sun* describes his farewell party. Two of his classmates went to the local newspaper office and declared to the editor:

> Today is Forrest Clough's birthday. He is nine years old and is going to move to Fort Worth next Saturday. He is one of the smartest and best boys in our school . . . . Each one in Miss Sallie's room will make a donation of money . . . and Forrest will present . . .[it] to the Red Cross.

Forrest was "double-promoted" to the third grade at the end of this first year of public schooling. His report card of straight A's contained Miss Sallie's handwritten comments:

> To Forrest's teacher, We are sending you a brilliant little pupil. He has a wonderful mind. I am sure that you will be very proud of him. He is a lovable child. We are all sorry to give him up.

His beloved teacher wrote this personal note at the end of school:

> How dearly I love you and how sweet and smart I know you to be . . . you are going to make a fine noble man . . . . You are the bravest dearest little fellow in all the world . . . . Goodbye darling little child. Miss Sallie.

What crippled child could receive greater affirmation than that!

Return to Fort Worth. In June 1918 G.O. was named assistant principal and teacher of math and physics at Jennings Avenue Junior High School in Fort Worth, where he had taught before. Forrest described the move back to his birthplace, which by then had increased in population to 100,000:

Mother was indeed very happy to be back in Fort Worth, for her parents lived there. Grandfather ran a large vegetable wagon, and, of course, Ancel and I . . . got to see our granddad every day as he passed our house on his daily run.

By that time Forrest was getting around nicely with his crutches and braces. "Bud"—his nickname for Ancel—was always on hand to help him and "became quite strong" from carrying his older brother around. Once again, living in Fort Worth proved advantageous for whatever continued treatment Forrest needed. With the end of World War I, the returning lame and maimed veterans required more facilities and better treatment. Perhaps Fort Worth had an orthopedic specialist familiar with current treatments. As he grew in size, Forrest needed new braces and crutches as well as the physical therapy to train him how to use the larger, more cumbersome iron and leather devices. No mention was ever made of how often he got new braces (and shoes, probably yearly) as he grew or what kind of physical therapy (PT) he required.

The two brothers entered the Alexander Hogg Grammar School, Forrest starting in the low (fall semester) third grade and Ancel in the low first. Forrest used a new conveyance, modern for the time, to get around:

Instead of my trusty little red express wagon, this time I rode around in a better flivver—a ball-bearing roller coaster wagon. All the school boys were very kind to me; the teachers were good to me; my grades were all right, and everything went off so smoothly from day to day that I never thought much about my having to walk on crutches.

Forrest reminisced about those halcyon days and, in particular, about his fourth grade buddy, Vernon Carter, who carried Forrest from their classroom to the little coaster wagon at recess time and pushed him along the sidewalks. As a way of thanking his friend, at Christmas 1919 Forrest gave him a baseball and bat that made Vernon "extremely happy."

The family received a scare in late 1919 when "that dreaded disease of paralysis" entered their neighborhood again.

Two cases . . . occurred in the short space of two weeks. One case proved fatal. . . a little ten-year-old girl . . . took the disease and died within a very short while.

About a week after the fatal case, a girl by the name of Frances Guthrie, living next door to us, took it.

Frightened that polio had struck so close to them, the family prayed Ancel would be spared. But, nine days after Frances became ill, Ancel got sick. The doctor gave Ancel a "preventive serum," similar to one given Frances after her case was discovered but not before "paralysis had already begun to creep up her limbs." Such a preventive was not available when Forrest "took paralysis in 1909." Fortunately, Ancel's sick spell proved only to be a cold.

Although the serum given to Ancel is unknown, it was likely akin to the immune serum therapy first used in France in 1915 and tried during the New York polio epidemic in 1916. Spinal serum from a recovering, and thus immune, polio victim was given within 48 hours of the disease's onset to a patient whose own spinal fluid was positive for polio—the sooner the better.[37] To prevent the spread of polio in its contagious stage to family members, in the 1920's doctors were still trying serum therapy. Hoping to force the development of immunity, they took fluid from the spinal columns of convalescing polios and injected it into the spine or a muscle of someone who had not yet been exposed to the virus. Used into the late 1930s with mixed results, this therapy was strictly experimental. After many years of trial and error, doctors determined serum therapy did not prevent people from contracting polio. Scientifically controlled clinical trials did not become the standard for evaluating efficacy until mid-century.

By the 1920s and 1930s polio was hitting communities with increasing frequency. Polio replaced tuberculosis as a primary public concern for finding a cure.

Tyler, the Heart of East Texas

We moved to Tyler, Texas [about 100 miles east of Fort Worth], in August of 1920 when Dad was elected Superintendent of the Tyler Public Schools. We hated to leave Ft. Worth . . . . It was not long, however, until we were enjoying our new home immensely.

Soon after their move to this East Texas town of 12,000, the family transferred its church membership from Central Methodist Church of Fort

Worth to Marvin Methodist of Tyler. There they made new friends and acclimated quickly. Forrest joined the Sunday school class and met a "great bunch of fellows" who became his buddies during grammar and high school.

The family's home in Tyler was on South Broadway, at the edge of town, five or six blocks from the Smith County courthouse and square. Built on an acre or so with a few hills and a winding stream, the house had numerous trees surrounding it. The setting was ideal for exploring what the two brothers called the "great out-of-doors." Their nearest friend, Jimmy Fitzgerald, lived about 400 yards north of their home. The three "little fellows had one glorious time from day to day."

> A new vim and vigor was added to our 'Happiness Days' when . . . a friend living across the street, gave us a . . . billy goat. Dad bought a big goat wagon . . . so we could drive the goat from place to place. We got a good . . . harness . . . . Over hills, across streams . . . everywhere, that high-powered goat pulled us . . . plenty of . . . fun and amusement!

A story passed down from Ancel to his son Mike concerned this billy goat. On one occasion, to encourage the goat to move faster, Ancel put a cocklebur under its tail while the goat was tethered to the wagon with Forrest sitting in it. The goat disliked that spiny burr and took off rapidly, dumping Forrest out, then running into the barn door and tearing it off. Although Ancel was disciplined for this prank, Forrest never mentioned it in his writings.

In the fall Forrest entered the fifth grade at Gary Grammar School about three blocks from their home. Since Ancel was in the third grade in the same building, he usually pulled Forrest over the unpaved roads to and from school in the coaster wagon. Occasionally, however, Ancel hitched the goat to the big wagon and the brothers traveled in elegant style to their classes. Forrest formed friendships with eight male buddies. They all had "grammar school sweethearts," believing they "were in love," but "those ideas were only thoughts and nothing else."

Since athletics was out of the question for Forrest, Maggie, knowing he loved music, decided it might be something he could excel at. If she pointed him in a direction where his creative talents would shine, then, she hoped people would not be too disturbed by his disability.

Maggie bought him a 12-inch foreign-made silver cornet for twenty dollars, believing he would be able to manipulate the instrument. (A cornet is a brass, valved wind instrument distinguished from a trumpet by its conical bore, more compact shape, and mellow tone quality. Forrest used the terms interchangeably.) Forrest's disabilities included not only two useless legs but compromised arms and hands. A strong upper right deltoid muscle permitted him to move his arm up and down and hold his trumpet with a gnarled and relatively limp right hand. His left shoulder muscle was mostly useless, but his left forearm and hand were perfectly formed and strong, which allowed him to play the valves on his trumpet. Although trumpets were made for a right-hander, he manipulated the valves by reaching the fingers of his left hand across the top of the half-inch-wide metal tubing. Whether or not he was predisposed to use his dominant left hand, he was forced to write and do anything that required intricate finger manipulation as a lefty.

Mr. J. F. (Doc) Witt, Forrest's music teacher and director of the Tyler Municipal Band, told Maggie it was always best to start a beginner on a cheap instrument. If he showed signs of improvement and great appreciation for the instrument's type of music, only then would it be advisable to buy a more expensive instrument.

> For all the wonderful experiences I have had in . . . music, I owe my most sincere and heartfelt thanks to my Mother. She is the one . . . responsible for my entering the field of music . . . which has given me . . . many hours of genuine happiness and satisfaction.

Forrest began taking lessons at age 12 in January 1922 and made rapid progress with his trumpet. After only two and a half months, Doc Witt asked him to join the Tyler High School Band that was just being organized.

Forrest vividly remembered his first band practice: he was given a chair in the second or third cornet section, handed a piece of music, and told to play when the time came, which was "not an exaggeration." He did not know how he managed to finish that first practice, but he quit playing when the rest of the boys did, making him "feel good."

For the rest of that year and through the sixth grade he went from grammar school to band practice at the high school two times a week. Ancel had joined the band with his clarinet, and the two brothers were happy to get out of school a little early on band days and go dashing down to the practice in Forrest's coaster wagon.

Forrest reflected on his musical career to date:

> During my nine years experience on the cornet and trumpet, I have not only learned to love my instrument, but music has gotten a firm and everlasting grip on my life. I appreciate the great message which good music brings to one's soul— that ever necessary comforting message which . . . conveys the Divine Word of God to mankind. A Dean of a certain university in the North said: 'Let me write the songs of a people, and I care not who makes the laws, I shall govern them.'

Corrective Surgery. In June 1922, just as he was turning thirteen, Forrest went from Tyler to Dallas's Baylor University College of Medicine for planned surgery on his right hip. Established in 1903, Baylor was one of two medical schools in the state. According to author Heather Wooten, in 1920 there were only four orthopedic surgeons in Texas. One of them, Dr. William Beall Carrell, had been a doctor in the American Expeditionary Force in Europe in WWI and practiced in Dallas, dedicating his life to helping polio patients.[38] Only a year and a half after Forrest's surgery, Carrell was instrumental in establishing the Hella Temple Children's Hospital that morphed into the Texas Scottish Rite Hospital for Crippled Children in May 1926. He was its long-time director as well as a driving force in getting the Gonzalez Warm Springs Rehabilitation Center established in Ottine, Texas, in 1937.

Whether Dr. Carrell or someone else performed the surgery, lowering a muscle about two inches alleviated some of Forrest's scoliosis and allowed him to sit up straighter. When he came out from under the ether's influence, Forrest found himself in a plaster of Paris cast from his chest to his knees. He had to remain in that cast, flat on his back, for at least four weeks.

Corrective surgery for treating polio-caused disabilities was first tried in Germany in the 1830s, but it was not until the introduction of "antisepsis and anesthesia" and the great developments in corrective surgery in the late 19th century that real progress was made.[39] Immobilization in body casts before and/or after such surgery was a common treatment for paralyzed polio survivors in the 1920s and 1930s. Often elaborate systems of frames and pulleys were erected over hospital beds and patients' legs were splinted regardless of whether or not the person was actually paralyzed.[40]

Daniel Wilson in his mid-century interviews with polio survivors of the thirties and forties states that body casts with "turnbuckles" (to be rotated a little each day to straighten the body) were used both pre- and post-surgery, often for months, for spinal fusions to correct scoliosis. Turnbuckles (or "racks" as some referred to them) usually caused extreme pain to the patients as they were tightened each day.[41] One polio victim facing surgery was put in a body cast with turnbuckle and "tied to a canvas supported by a heavy wooden frame for several months."[42] These "pieces of iron, cage-like equipment and frames—painful and ugly—were used to prevent increased deformity caused by growth and muscle imbalance."[43] Other polio survivors mentioned months of stretching and torture in body casts before or after surgery. In severe cases doctors made the disastrous recommendation for amputation of the useless limbs. Fortunately, most doctors believed a properly braced limb performs better always than a false one.

It is unknown whether, in the early twenties, Forrest's body cast had a turnbuckle on it. He never mentioned experiencing any pain during his monthlong confinement. Whether Forrest had to wear a body brace to help him sit upright and prevent further deformity once he returned home is also unknown.

Five days after the operation, Forrest was moved to a room across the street from the hospital, presumably a rehabilitation facility. Determined to amuse himself while confined to bed, he began to "make some plans." His first was to read, and read he did—a lot. His next plan was to blow his cornet. His mother claimed he learned to play "Dixie" while he was in the cast. If not for his music, Forrest would have spent "many a lonesome hour" during that period of confinement away from family and friends in Tyler.

In April 1923 a baby girl, named Margaret Louise after her mother Maggie, arrived. The name "Louise" was pulled from a hat just like Forrest Weldon's two names were, whereas Ancel McBride's names came from forbearers. G.O. had wanted to name his daughter Bonnie, but his wife's choice prevailed.

At age 42, it was a difficult pregnancy for Maggie. Doctors, fearing for her health, wanted to take the baby, but Maggie refused. Arriving prematurely at seven months, Margaret weighed only four pounds with her clothes on. To allow her to gain strength she was placed in a box for some days at the hospital with warm water bottles and blankets surrounding her. A happy surprise for her parents and two older brothers, Margaret miraculously survived. When the tiny bundle finally came home from the hospital, Ancel exclaimed to his parents, "Is that it?!" In fair health today at age 96, Margaret has long outlived her parents and her brothers.

In September 1923 Forrest's class from Gary elementary, along with classes graduated from three other feeder schools, entered Tyler High School. By then, Forrest had a brand new and "ultra-modern means of transportation" to go from one class to another: namely, a wheelchair with rubber tires, three wheels, and no brakes. As was common in the 1920s the chair was likely large, bulky and made of wood and wicker.[44]

Forrest found the students and teachers to be "cordial, friendly, and most helpful" in getting him initiated into high school. He took English, history, mathematics, Latin, and mechanical drawing his first semester and his grades were "all right."

> I was advanced to first cornet in the high school band, and . . . pleased with my schoolwork and activities. Mother and Dad presented me with a gold-plated Martin trumpet on Christmas of that year, and . . . that added much to my satisfaction.

Life-Threatening Appendicitis. Toward the latter part of February 1924, acute appendicitis brought Forrest down, and he had to have a leap-year operation on February 29. His case proved critical because the appendix burst five hours prior to surgery.

I wish to commend the courage and spirit of my mother for she had a man-sized responsibility upon her shoulder . . . . Brother and Margaret were sick in bed at the time, and Dad was in Chicago at the National Educational Association [meeting]. How mother held up under this trying situation is a wonder to me! Dad reached home two days after the operation.

Friends visited the hospital, sent flowers, and did what they could to be helpful. According to Forrest, "The world's greatest blessing is a friend!" However, he did not seem to be improving:

I was in the hospital, and, my, what a time I was having! Pain! Pain! And more Pain! The pain that I suffered was terrible, but I kept on hoping for the best. After three weeks of this intense suffering, with no relief whatsoever, I began to think that my time had come. It was a terrible feeling!

Complications set in and his condition grew steadily worse. The doctors gave him up, saying there was only a slim chance for his recovery, and asked Dr. H. R. Coats, a noted osteopath in Tyler, to go to the Clough home at once. Dr. Coats looked him over and agreed Forrest's chances of survival were slim, but said he would try to pull him through using "standard osteopathic practices of the day."

According to Dr. Norman Gevitz, Andrew Taylor Still founded osteopathic medicine and opened a training school in the early 1890s in Kirksville, Missouri. Doctors of Osteopathy (DO's) of the Still tradition believed displacements of vertebrae along the spinal column were the main cause of disease. These "lesions" interfered with nerve and blood supply and were responsible for disordered physiology in the body. To diagnose, D.O.'s placed patients on their sides and carefully ran their hands over the spinal column from the base of the spine to free up nerves or muscles or a bone out of line. They often used the lever technique, applying "pressure in one part of the body to overcome resistance in motion elsewhere," i.e., "twisting the patient's torso in certain directions while maintaining a steady hold on the point...to be influenced." Traditionally, DO's who were "lesionists" and disdained the use of drugs relied primarily on spinal manipulation to remove symptoms of pathology elsewhere in the body. However, after 1930 osteopathic manipulation therapy (OMT) began a steady decline as increasingly contentious DO's and MD's wrangled with each other for years over education and licensing issues.

Although osteopaths primarily treated for chronic ailments, a few administered OMT in cases of acute infectious disease and/or after surgery, believing "this treatment would prevent blood stasis and speed lymphatic absorption." They usually administered three treatments a week on a patient until improvement occurred, but Dr. Coats must have felt far more was needed to cure Forrest's infection. Whatever Coats did in the spring of 1924—whether he was a "lesion osteopath" or a "broad osteopath" who used whatever means would best help the patient, including drugs[45] —he saved Forrest's life.

After the first treatment, Forrest got three hours of sleep—the first he had had in forty-eight hours. Dr. Coats continued the treatments three times a day for twenty-one days. His ministrations worked wonders and soon Forrest was able to sit in a wheelchair and be pushed about the house.

> I shall never forget the day they rolled me out on the front porch of our house on Mary Street. The trees were green, the flowers were in bloom, and the little birds in the trees were chirping and singing merrily. It was like a new world to me, one of gladness . . . and thanksgiving . . . .

Happy to be alive, Forrest returned to school on May 2. His parents too sang praises for the heroic efforts of Dr. Coats, who had spent painstaking hours treating Forrest not knowing what the outcome would be.

Following his recovery, Forrest finished three of his courses with excellent grades. He dropped the other two classes, completing them the following year.

September 1924 found him pulling his "school supplies out of the closet and preparing for a new school year."

> After my long sick spell, I had a renewed appreciation for friends and life, and I re-entered school with the strong determination to show my school friends that I really appreciated their kindnesses to me during my illness.

To Forrest's great pleasure, Doc Witt promoted him at age fifteen to first chair solo cornet in the high school band. Forrest also became a key member of the Marvin Sunday School Orchestra. In every respect, the 1924-25 school year was "deeply satisfying" after his near-death experience. His feeling at the time: "All's well that ends well."

The Call of Colorado. Colorado State Teacher's College at Greeley invited G.O. to teach during the first six weeks of the 1925 summer term. The family piled into their Dodge touring car and drove to northeastern Colorado—Forrest's first overland trip of any importance. He was eager to "see all the wonders of the great Silver State."

In his journal, Forrest began the description of his Colorado adventure with a poem by his "good friend," Charles Bowman Hutchens, "world famous naturalist and bird man." Also a fine oil painter, Hutchens was a member of the Boulder Art Association and lectured for universities, national parks, and Chautauqua audiences everywhere. Forrest must have met him at one of those events. The first three stanzas of Hutchens's poem set the stage for a memorable family summer vacation:

> Come up where the mountain air
> Is scented with the pines;
> Come and climb our lofty peaks
> And share our happy times.
>
> Come to Colorado, come
> And spend your summer days
> Where the mountain bluebird wings
> And water ouzel plays.
>
> Here the snow-capped peaks stand guard
> O'er vale and fruited plain.
> Summer in the Silver State
> And you'll come back again.

Arriving in Greeley in mid-June, the Cloughs rented an apartment large enough for their family of five to live comfortably. G.O. relished the teaching, making new friends and enjoying the company of other teachers from Texas whom the family already knew. On weekends the Texas party journeyed to the mountains about 30 miles to the west, experiencing a love affair with Colorado that many Texans have long felt—enamored with the spectacular scenery and cool mountain air that eclipses the sweltering heat and humidity of their home state.

One late June weekend the family left the Greeley prairie and stopped in Boulder to join friends before venturing to the mile-high city of Denver.

The group toured "notable sights" there before visiting Lookout Mountain, 14 miles west of Denver:

> The scenery . . . [was] beautiful beyond all description. The views from the tavern atop the mountain looked as though they had been painted on a great canvas. What wonders! . . . . Here on the mountain rests the remains of that famous cowboy . . . William F. Cody (affectionately known as Buffalo Bill).

A few weeks later, they traveled 49 miles west to Estes Park and Rocky Mountain National Park. For this flatlander family, the drive up Fall River Road and crossing the Continental Divide were thrilling. One wonders how much Forrest could partake in these sightseeing adventures. Most likely, he rode shotgun so he could see as much as possible. And, by then, Ancel was a strapping teen strong enough to lift him into his wheelchair.

The family made their last weekend trip with a party of 20 Texans, who formed a motorcade of late-model Fords, Chryslers, and General Motors cars to Fort Collins and Poudre Canyon. Riding on winding roads up this canyon to an elevation of 9,173 feet, they found placid blue Chambers Lake, snuggled in the heart of towering snow-capped peaks covered in pine and fir trees.

When the six-week term at Greeley finished, the Cloughs drove 600 miles farther north to Yellowstone Park. Entering the park's east entrance through the Shoshone Canyon, Forrest described:

> . . . . this great monument to God and His Supreme Power. Beautiful lakes . . . gorgeous waterfalls . . . soul-gripping canyons, famous geysers, and other wonders . . . all seemed to whisper the Divine Story of God—Father of All.

Making their way back to Texas in time for school's opening in September, they traveled through Colorado Springs and climbed a narrow gravel road to the top of "awe-inspiring" Pike's Peak. A small detour to the Cave of the Winds ended their refreshing summer's stay in Colorado. This adventure whetted 16-year-old Forrest's appetite for further travel beyond Texas, but, at this time, he could not imagine the opportunities that lay ahead.

⁓⁓

Forrest's last two years of high school were filled with "happy experiences" because it was during that time he decided what he "would do for his life's occupation." Making a practical, logical choice, Forrest decided to capitalize on his keen interest in the humanities and choose a profession that would not be limited by his physical shortcomings.

> Handicapped as I was always to be, I . . . felt . . . I should do something [that] did not require much getting about from place to place. I had thought about becoming an architect, but . . . finally gave that idea up [because] . . . my physical condition could not compete . . . . Having always been fond of history, literature, and kindred subjects, I felt . . . such a liking would help me in a legal profession. I made up my mind to become a lawyer.

Music continued to keep Forrest company. He played regularly in the high school band, and, during two basketball seasons, he often directed the band from his wheelchair in its concerts. Pleased when Doc Witt asked him to join the City Band, Forrest played two summers with that group as well.

In June 1926, just as Forrest was preparing to enter his senior year, G.O. was invited to go to Southern Methodist University in Dallas as Dean of Men and Professor of Education. Reluctantly turning down the offer, G.O. likely did not want to prevent Forrest from finishing his senior year in Tyler. He also had just been named President of the newly organized Tyler Junior College, which he had played a major role in founding. He felt his place, at least for the near future, was in Tyler as Superintendent of the Public Schools and President of the Junior College, which stayed under the school board's jurisdiction until 1946. He wanted to see the college get off the ground.

And that it did—quite successfully. "G.O. Clough pioneered with vision and assumed the risk of promoting a junior college in the 1920s . . . a time when many of the general public considered junior colleges to be a new, and possibly expensive, luxury."[46] In 2001 G.O.'s grandchildren and daughter Margaret attended the 75th anniversary celebration of Tyler Junior College (TJC), which honored its founders and past presidents. Today TJC is one of the oldest and largest community colleges in Texas with approximately 12,000 two-year-degree students (full- and part-time). The college's website indicates it offers two bachelor's degrees (in healthcare fields), 78 associates degrees (some of which can be online degrees) and 43 certificate options in diverse fields. G.O.'s vision had come true.

At the beginning of his senior year, Forrest signed up for courses that would help him in his newly chosen career: American history, English, public speaking, mathematics, economics, and civics. Two months after school started, fellow students and faculty advisers elected him assistant editor of the *Alcalde*, the Tyler High yearbook. Spending many hours of "enjoyable labor" in the *Alcalde* office, Forrest felt the experience helped him hone writing and editing skills that he would need in the legal profession.

That year, Forrest also took his first step into the art of debating, thanks to the constant urging of a capable debating supervisor and some of his fellow students.

> *Resolved: That there should be a Department of Education in our National Government." My, . . . what great possibilities for some . . . constructive thinking! I had never had any debating experience before, but somehow I had good luck . . . . Out of some ten or twelve students competing to uphold Tyler High's honors in the County and District meets, Israel Smith and I were selected . . . . Quite an unexpected honor it was!*

FORREST AND ISRAEL SMITH WITH DEBATE TEAM, 1926

Israel and Forrest began work immediately, getting their arguments, both affirmative and negative, into final form. This question was not resolved in the affirmative for another 26 years. In 1953 the Federal Security Agency and its Office of Education were morphed into the Department of Health, Education and Welfare. Then, in 1979 it became the cabinet-level Education Department.

In mid-April Israel and Forrest won the county debate meet in a unanimous decision. They moved on to the district meet held in Nacogdoches, about 75 miles southeast of Tyler. The two seniors won two consecutive debates in the afternoon, both by unanimous vote, thereby gaining the right to enter the finals against Athens High, whose boys had made a similar record in their afternoon debates. After the final contest was over, Athens had wrested the decision away from them by a count of 7-2. Forrest and Israel consoled themselves, lamenting that not everyone can win. *Scrapbook* offers no evidence that Forrest ever participated in a formal debate again but this brief exposure gave him some idea of the critical thinking and oral argument skills a legal career would require.

The high school auditorium was packed for graduation exercises in May. As the band played the processional march, the graduates, in cap-and-gown, slowly filed down the aisle to their seats.

> *What a feeling . . . I had gone through high school in a wheelchair, and I was about to receive my diploma from the same old faithful conveyance. I was on the stage sitting in my chair.*

The ceremony included a quartet number called "In the Garden of Tomorrow" played by

HIGH SCHOOL GRADUATION, 1927

a saxophonist, two clarinetists, and Forrest on trumpet. He appeared later on the program in a trumpet solo titled "O, Thou Sublime Sweet Evening Star," followed by that old favorite, "Annie Laurie." Tyler's mayor delivered the commencement address and the president of the Tyler school board presented graduates their diplomas.

CHAPTER TWO

COLLEGE, MUSTANG BAND, AND NEW YORK

In the summer of 1927, soon after Forrest's graduation, G.O. finally accepted a position as Professor of Education at Southern Methodist University (SMU). Toward the latter part of August the family moved to Dallas, which boasted a population of approximately 230,000 and was located 30 miles east of their old home in Fort Worth. Everyone seemed happy about being nearer their Fort Worth and Ennis relatives and having access to "big-city opportunities."

Although Forrest never heard it spoken, he always assumed his father accepted the position the second time it was offered because Forrest would be entering SMU as a freshman. He would need family support and a place to live. The previous year when the position was first offered, G.O. may have affirmed his interest and requested a one-year delay in accepting the appointment. He knew Forrest could not live on his own and attend college classes.

It is also quite likely that Maggie was a powerful force behind the decision to move to Dallas to support her son. In no way would Forrest have survived or been as successful as he was without his mother's constant attention and devotion. Maggie was formidable, determined, persistent. Forty years later, she might have gone to college to become a lawyer or the leader of some cause she believed in. Instead she was active in the church, quilting circles, the mother's club at SMU, the women's temperance movement, and Eastern Star. An excellent seamstress, she took in sewing in the early years of her marriage when finances were tight.

Initially, the family lived in a couple of rental houses before buying a two-story yellow brick on Asbury Street, just a block west of the SMU campus. They inhabited the main floor (three bedrooms and one bath) and rented out the top floor as well as an apartment in the two-story frame garage behind the house.

Southern Methodist University. SMU was a natural choice for the family. G.O., prominent in Texas education circles and also a Methodist, had most likely been watching with keen interest for some years the development of Southern Methodist University. Between 1870 and 1910 the population of Texas had quadrupled to almost four million. Nationwide the number of Methodists had grown 400 percent in the same period to almost 600,000, over 45 percent of them in Texas.[47] The population growth in Texas convinced leading Methodists of the need for a school of theology west of the Mississippi. Vanderbilt in Tennessee was simply too far away.

Although several Methodist colleges in Texas vied for the theology school, Dallas was selected as the site, and Southern Methodist University was chartered in 1911. The city granted Dr. Robert Hyer and others approximately 662.5 flat acres of Johnson grass with no houses or trees six miles north of downtown Dallas on which to build the university.[48]

Hyer, a scientist who had worked on ether waves before Marconi and built the first wireless station in Texas, taught at Southwestern University, served as its president, and was the leading Methodist educator in the state. As the new president of SMU, Hyer and his team began raising money to build the campus. This took longer than hoped. The college did not open its doors until September 1915 after two buildings had been completed. Some 706 students, rather than the anticipated 300, showed up to enroll that first year, the second largest opening enrollment, next to the University of Chicago, at a new college in US history.[49]

In 1920 Hyer retired from the presidency to return to teaching his beloved physics. In 1924 Charles Selecman, minister of First Methodist Church in Dallas, was chosen as the new president. Although lacking a BA degree, Selecman had the backing of prominent businessmen and began a large building program, setting the university on a course of growth, particularly in athletics.

When Selecman arrived, Dallas Hall still housed all 36 classrooms for the College of Arts and Sciences, the School of Theology, and the School of Music, as well as the administrative offices, the library, the bookstore, and the chapel.[50] However, the student body had increased by 300 percent to 2,500 and everyone was clamoring for space. By the time G.O. and Forrest arrived as professor and student respectively in 1927, the campus had expanded in three short years to four buildings plus McFarlin Auditorium, Ownby football stadium, a gymnasium, a men's dorm, and two women's dorms.

A School of Law, which piqued Forrest's interest, and a School of Engineering had both been established in 1925. Due to increased national interest in professional training for teachers, the school of education was established within the arts college in 1926. Under the leadership of Dr. C.A. Nichols, the department expanded its course offerings and faculty members at a phenomenal rate. [51] This rapid growth—plus G.O.'s statewide prominence and his friendship with Dr. Nichols—is probably why he was first approached in 1926 and then hired in 1927 as a professor of education with only a master's degree. Searching widely, President Hyer had managed to recruit PhD's as 40 percent of the original core faculty.

By 1934 SMU's downtown night school, Dallas College (DC), had grown into a residence credit college. G.O., who had earned his PhD in 1931, was elected by SMU's Board of Directors as DC's first Director of Extension, where he served until his retirement in 1948. By the advent of World War II SMU could accommodate 3,000 students and had finally built a library and a School of Business Administration, along with five professional schools within the College of Arts and Sciences. Father (a professor from 1927 until 1948) and son (a student from 1927 until 1936) would both be caught up in SMU's first growth spurt that spanned the years from 1925-1940.

Soon after moving to Dallas in 1927, the Cloughs joined the newly dedicated Highland Park Methodist Church adjacent to SMU's campus on the northeast corner of Hillcrest and Mockingbird Lane. Forrest attended the Social Service Sunday School class, an organization devoting much of its time to helping unfortunate communities around the city of Dallas.

Dr. [H.K.] Taylor, a most wonderful Christian gentleman and worker, has been a stupendous influence and help to me during my college days. I shall remember

*him always by his great Christian work, his happy and cheery smile, and his
magnetic personality and influence over the young people whom he meets . . . .*

September came quickly and Forrest began preparing for his new adventure.
First, he called on the university's band director, Cyrus Barcus, who was
"very receptive." Barcus asked Forrest to attend an open-air concert the
band was giving on Friday night prior to the school's opening the following
Monday.

> *I went to this concert, met the band director, and numbers of the boys, and from
> that time on I have been a member of the famous Mustang Band. My relation
> with the band has meant much to me during my stay on the campus, and, as I
> proceed with this paper [his 1931 autobiography] I hope that I am able to show
> what it has really meant to me.*

Forrest stopped his musings at this point and paid tribute to his
wheelchair that had become his primary mode of transport. He still used his
crutches, but traversing great distances was too tiring and time consuming.

> *My wheelchair had carried me through high school, so I thought I'd better use the
> chair in college because it made getting around much easier. I shined up the old
> three-wheeled hack, gave it a few lessons on collegiate etiquette, and told it to
> take me around with plenty of speed. It has behaved wonderfully!*

Anxious on registration day about what courses to take, Forrest finally
matriculated into the College of Arts and Sciences. He signed up for English,
public speaking, mathematics, Spanish, and government, the latter a
fundamental prerequisite for law school.

Forrest's enthusiasm for his life as a college freshman was enhanced
further by his membership in the band. Aside from home games, the band
made trips to College Station (Texas A&M), Waco (Baylor), and Fort
Worth (Texas Christian-TCU).

> *Football season and all its wonders—Collegiate crowds, all tense with anxiety for
> the outcome of the game, waving gayly [sic] colored college pennants, and
> shouting themselves hoarse for the old Alma Mater! What a thrill I had upon
> seeing my first collegiate football game, and as a member of the Mustang Band it
> made the event even more exciting!*

On January 8, 1928, a feature article titled "Makes Classes in Wheel Chair" appeared in a Dallas newspaper. Situated below a large photo of Forrest in his wheelchair, the story began by citing Forrest's philosophy for the past 18 years: "Laugh and the whole world laughs with you, cry and you cry alone." The article continued: "Clough is a freshman at Southern Methodist University . . . rolls himself around campus with a grin as big as a 7-year-old in an ice cream factory and a hearty 'hello' to everybody; even the most blasé sophomore returns the greeting . . . . He came to SMU from Tyler High School where he was an honor graduate in a class of eighty-seven."

A few days later the Tyler newspaper shared its take on the former resident who "Rides Wheel Chair Through Law School." Mentioning Forrest's family's ties to Tyler, his "total paralysis," and his desire to obtain an AB and an LLB degree, the article also gives us a glimpse of how Forrest got around and related to his fellow students:

> A jovial fellow, he has won the admiration of every student on the campus. Never is it necessary for him to yell 'Hey, taxi' when he wants to go from building to building or floor to floor for his classes. There is [sic] always several fellow students ready to grab the wheel chair and race up or down the steps as Clough jokes with them.
> 'A little thing like that can't stop a fellow from getting something out of life,' Clough said, glancing at his helpless legs. In his public speaking classes, he wheels himself to the front of the room, gets his speaking 'stance' and makes a forceful delivery. His professors believe he will make a successful lawyer despite his handicap.
> Clough is a familiar character at all home football games. It is now a campus custom to see that he is carried to the sidelines and his wheel chair placed with the SMU band.

Although only a freshman, Forrest's musical talent as well as his affable manner must have influenced his invitation to join the SMU Light Opera Club on its ten-day tour of West Texas. Leaving soon after mid-term finals on February 1, 1928, the group visited several towns including Breckenridge, Abilene, and Sweetwater. Forrest was the only trumpet player in the ten-piece orchestra accompanying a 37-member chorus that presented two Biblical dramas, "Esther" and "Ruth." Forrest enjoyed the fellowship with club members, writing. "Especially did I appreciate being with my pal, Cornell Goerner [a bass singer and member of the SMU band], a true Christian young gentleman . . . . Our tour proved entirely successful."

Likely Goerner lifted Forrest onto and off of buses for this trip. Someone certainly did. And someone had to carry his crutches and/or his wheelchair up and down steps, help him into people's homes and onto stages. Forrest rarely acknowledged publicly the logistical service provided by those who aided him on the many band trips he made. Like other disabled polios of his day, he did not want to call attention, even in his autobiography, to his disability and the fact that he required far more physical help than the normals he associated with. Certainly he thanked each assistant at the time, and in his autobiography he did give generic appreciation to the many friends and family who had helped him over the years.

Forrest was honored that Paul von Katwijk, dean of the SMU School of Music and conductor of the Dallas Symphony Orchestra, asked him to participate in the SMU Oratorio Society's Easter season performance of "Elijah" by Felix Mendelsohn-Bartholdy. Performing in SMU's McFarlin Auditorium, Forrest played one of two trumpets in the 47-piece orchestra that accompanied 109 members of the chorus.

At the end of the year those band boys who had proven dependable and had passed enough courses received SMU Band sweaters as a thank you for their efforts. Forrest was particularly proud of his for it was the first reward he had ever received for "services to his school."

After an uneventful summer, in fall 1928, his second year at SMU, Forrest continued his course prerequisites for an AB/LLB degree. He especially liked a physics class taught by former president Robert Hyer, "a man loved and appreciated by everyone on the campus."

One had to be in Dr. Hyer's class before he could really appreciate his great character . . . . He [sic] lectures were thrilling, gripping, and . . . intense . . . so . . . interesting and instructive that many times I . . . wished . . . the[y were] three hours long instead of one. A wreath of sorrow hung over the hearts of all his friends when, on the 28th of May, 1929, Dr. Hyer passed away.

SMU-Army Game in West Point, NY. The headliner for the 1928 football season was the journey to New York City (NYC) and West Point for the SMU-Army match on October 6 in Army's Michie Stadium. A Dallas businessman helped raise the $5,000 needed to send the band on the trip. Forrest was one of the "lucky band boys" selected to go, his first trip to New York and his first time out of Texas following his 1925 Colorado summer.

With his usual attention to detail, Forrest wrote in *Scrapbook*:

Four special trains left the Union Terminal, ten minutes apart beginning at 3:30 p.m. on Oct. 3, 1928 . . . routed over the MKT (Katy) lines to St. Louis. Upon arrival in St. Louis on Oct. 4 at 11 a.m., the Katy engines and diners were exchanged for Baltimore and Ohio engines and diners and the trains were routed over the B and O to New York City. We certainly had a wonderful time the first night. All the band boys were nice to me and helped me around as though they had been doing it all their lives . . . .

Friday morn, Oct. 5 in the beautiful Harper's Ferry country in the Allegheny and Cumberland Mountain regions of West Virginia and Maryland, I rode on the observation car . . . for 3 hours. Each turn of the track brought new wonderful scenes . . . [including] a ten minute stop in Washington . . . . We arrived in NYC, Friday afternoon . . . . Baltimore and Ohio Motor Coaches took forty tired and weary band-boys from the B&O Station in Jersey City to the Hotel McAlpin in downtown NYC. Later we were sent up to the Hotel Endicott on Columbus Ave. at 81st for official headquarters.

The next day the steamer *Alexander Hamilton* carried this group of 1,000 enthusiastic Mustang ball players, band, and fans fifty miles up the Hudson from Manhattan to West Point. They marveled at the fall foliage of golds, reds, and oranges so much more spectacular than what had greeted them along the miles of track from Texas. The band boys spotted the SS *Leviathan* and other transport vessels used during WW I—about 36 in all—"shoved up the Hudson River out of the way."

At West Point, Forrest declared he had ridden from the parade grounds to the stadium in the Army football truck, one unusual way he got around at "away games" and other events. Army barely beat SMU 14-13, which so impressed US Secretary of War, Dwight Davis, that he spent his one-hour stopover in Dallas later that year at the SMU campus. Even in 1928, having a good football team was a clever marketing tool. A relatively young college, SMU was eager to gain national prominence.

Back in NYC after the game, the band strolled down Fifth Avenue, visited Grand Central Station and Grant's Tomb, and attended Paramount Theater's variety show featuring Ben Black and the theater's stage orchestra. Ben Black, composer of "Moonlight and Roses" among others, was music director of four Paramount Theaters across the country. The visit to the Paramount was Forrest's introduction to big-time theatrical and vaudeville stage music, an experience he would be eager to repeat. Again, no mention of how he maneuvered around the many inaccessible theaters he visited over the years.

For the return to Texas, the band ferried back to Jersey City, New Jersey, passing the Statue of Liberty en route, and boarded the B & O train for Dallas. This exciting trip far eclipsed the remaining two games of SMU's football season in Texas. Forrest was hooked on these broader band adventures and could hardly wait for the next one.

Spectator as well as performer, Forrest followed the best of the Big-Band-era musicians and likely sought to emulate their style to some extent. He tried to attend all jazz band productions that came to Dallas, usually at the state fairgrounds. He always had to convince someone to take him, so for Forrest having a wide circle of friends was an essential survival skill.

In November 1928 he accompanied someone to see Paul Whiteman's orchestra, one of the most popular dance bands in the United States during the twenties and early thirties. Referred to by Duke Ellington as the "King of Jazz," Whiteman commissioned George Gershwin to write and give "Rhapsody in Blue" its inaugural performance. He signed on Bing Crosby as one of the Rhythm Boys, thereby launching the famous crooner's career.

Perhaps Forrest—or some of his band buddies—would one day get an opportunity to play with a Big Band. The Clough family's upcoming 1929 summer adventure would give this Texas lad incredible insight into the New York music and entertainment scene and expose him to career options outside the legal field.

For Christmas 1928, Maggie and G.O. presented their son with a fine trumpet made by Frank Holton & Co., one of the most influential instrument makers in the first half of the twentieth century. This gift made the annual mid-winter tour for Forrest even more enjoyable.

As far as anyone knows, Forrest traveled with his Mustang Band on winter tours during 1928, 1929, 1930, and 1934. Despite the inclement weather of rain, mist, snow and ice, the February 1929 tour was successful. The group's itinerary took them to ten northern and northeast Texas towns, including Ranger, Wichita Falls, and Longview. As on other band trips around the state, the students were fed and housed overnight in homes of local citizens, a requirement to make these trips financially feasible.

At the end of the spring 1929 term the boys were again rewarded sweaters for their band participation. Forrest's now had a second stripe on the left sleeve.

New York City before the Crash.
G.O. spent the spring term of 1929 working toward his PhD degree in education at New York University (NYU) in Manhattan. In June, the family drove overland in their Dodge sedan to the metropolis. They would be with G.O. for two months while Ancel worked a summer job for the Penn Mutual Life Insurance Company. Maggie and 18-year-old Ancel did the driving, while Forrest served as documentarian on his second trip to the city in less than a year.

Their itinerary led them from Dallas to Oklahoma, through Kansas, Missouri, Illinois, Indiana, Ohio, and Michigan. At Detroit, they crossed the Detroit River to Windsor, Ontario, and followed the Canadian shore of Lake Erie, entering New York State at Niagara Falls. Forrest described it:

ANCEL IN PORT BRUCE, ONTARIO, 1929

Probably the most fascinating spectacle of all is the illumination at night, when colored lights are thrown onto the falls from powerful electric arc lamps, twenty-four in number, and a total capacity of 1,320,000,000 candle power. The wonders of this . . . unique spectacle of the night cataract reflected upon itself in . . . this . . . electrical achievement.

FAMILY AT NIAGARA FALLS –
ANCEL, MARGARET, MAGGIE, FORREST, HATTIE

Forrest kept a meticulous expense log. Total mileage from Dallas to New York was 2,160, averaging 200-300 miles per day. Their costs: oil, gas and grease $30.44, tire trouble and brake adjustment $2.25, groceries $15.52, tolls for bridges and ferries $3.10, and eight nights for "places of camp" $13.50, yielding a total of $64.81 for the entire trip.

G.O. lived at 133 W. 4th Street near Washington Square and NYU until the family arrived on June 16. As a group of six, including Maggie's cousin Hattie, they all moved across the Queensborough Bridge to Long Island City, where they rented a home for two months at 3939 47th Street in the Queens' Sunnyside neighborhood of two-story row houses. In the midst of an intense program of almost daily sightseeing, G.O. had to complete his written doctoral exams by July 31. Studying hard every weekday, he somehow managed to join the family for many of their evening and weekend adventures.

Exploring the five boroughs of Manhattan, Queens, Brooklyn, the Bronx, and Staten Island was of keen interest to the eager tourists. These 305 square miles of land had been consolidated into a single city in 1898 and linked by subway in 1904. In 1930 New York City's population registered 6.9 million, making it the most densely populated city in the United States. The Cloughs would make the most of the biggest, most impressive city they had ever seen. The excitement of actually living in New York City for two whole months was 20-year-old Forrest's dream come true.

They began their adventures to the five boroughs by heading frequently into Manhattan from their temporary Long Island home, both by auto and by subway, and took in important sites of the day: Grant's tomb, the Battery, the Metropolitan Museum of Art, the American Museum of Natural History, Wall Street, and Grand Central Station to name a few.

How did Forrest maneuver in that bustling metropolis when there were no ADA (Americans with Disabilities Act) accessibility requirements. Did Ancel carry him down the subway stairs or did he have to use his crutches? Today, 90 years later, only 36 of 147 Manhattan subways have elevators for folks in wheelchairs to use! There were no buses with doors that lowered to the ground or curb cuts for ease of rolling (or pushing) a wheelchair. Did someone lift him into a theater seat because there were no seating areas available for wheelchairs? Ancel was at work all day during the week, so for any daytime sightseeing his mother Maggie and cousin Hattie would have had to help him get about.

Chasing skyscrapers and other outstanding buildings in Manhattan was high on the Cloughs' list of must-do's. In 1929 with its 57 stories, the Woolworth Building at 233 Broadway reigned as the tallest building in the world. It remained so from the time of its opening dedication by President Woodrow Wilson in 1913 until it was overtaken by the Chrysler building in 1930. It is still one of the twenty tallest buildings in NYC.

At 3:20 we parked the car in front of Woolworth Building and just inside the door purchased our tickets for fifty cents each. We entered an elevator which carried us 54 floors without a single stop. On this floor we . . . entered a tiny elevator which carried us the remaining three floors to the observation gallery. About fifty people were on the gallery at this time . . . . I shall never forget the sight which met my eyes as I stepped out [using his crutches] on the observation gallery 57 stories above the ground.

Making a 360-degree sweep of the NYC skyline, Forrest's travelogue went on to enumerate landmarks in great detail.

These Texans had never seen such tall buildings. The Woolworth building was just the beginning of their effort to visit all the sites where rumored skyscrapers were to be built. They traveled down Lexington Avenue to see the Chrysler building under construction between 42nd and 43rd. Forrest had heard the building would be 68 stories high, 11 stories higher than the Woolworth. In fact, this Art Deco skyscraper topped out at 77 stories and 1,046 feet when it was completed in the spring of 1930.

Forrest also heard rumors of another skyscraper in the making:

Latest reports from New York say that on the corner of 5th Ave. and 34th Street there is to be erected an 85-story building known as the Empire State Building. There is to be a dirigible mast on the tower of this building for the mooring of zeppelins.

The Empire State Building, when completed in 1931, was actually 102-stories, overtaking the Chrysler Building and its brief reign as the tallest building in the world. Although zeppelins or dirigibles were at the height of their popularity in 1929, a mast was never erected to moor an airship atop this new skyscraper.

The Clough family visited other impressive buildings that did not warrant skyscraper status, such as the New York Public Library (NYPL) on 5th Avenue between 40th and 42nd. The NYPL, completed in 1911, was the third largest library in the world. The main public library building had "something like 65 miles [75 miles today] of book shelves...packed with books of all kinds."

Visiting Penn station at 8th Avenue and 31st Street, the Cloughs arrived just in time to see the first train inaugurating coast-to-coast air-rail passenger service leave the station.

By this system of airplane and train transportation, passengers can reach Los Angeles 48 hours after leaving New York City. They ride the trains at night time and the planes during the day.

Normally regular attendees at Methodist churches in Texas, Forrest mentioned visiting only two religious services during their two-month sojourn in New York. Both were Episcopalian. Forrest commented first on the Church of the Transfiguration located at E. 29th Street just off Fifth Avenue:

> It is . . . interesting . . . how the church got its name. In 1870, George Holland, a famous actor, died. A neighboring church declined to perform the funeral service, but suggested that the little church around the corner would perform the service. Since then this church has been affectionately known as 'The Little Church Around the Corner'. . . . [and is] popular with the theatrical people.

The following Sunday they attended services at the Cathedral of St. John the Divine on Amsterdam Avenue at West 112th Street, reportedly the fourth largest Christian church in the world.

> We can now say that we have been in the largest church in America . . . . The cathedral ranks favorably with those in the old world . . . . The cornerstone was laid in 1892 . . . . The service was very beautiful indeed.

Theatrical and musical events also ranked high on the to-do list, which included at least five movies, two live stage shows, and two concerts. The movies were always accompanied by the theater's orchestra and a featured entertainer prior to the showing of the film.

The first week in town they visited the Paramount Theater at Times Square to see *Innocents of Paris* starring French actor and vaudeville entertainer, Maurice Chevalier, in his first Hollywood film. The public show that accompanied the movie that night featured Paul Ash, popular stage bandleader in the 1920s and 1930s whose orchestra was engaged at the Paramount for the summer. Pianist Johnny Burke, a fine lyricist who won the Academy Award for best song ("Swinging on a Star") for Bing Crosby in 1944, was star of the Paramount show that night. Forrest described his first experience in the heart of New York's theater district:

> Broadway is truly 'A Great White Way.' Lights - Lights - Lights! Theaters — Theaters - and still more theaters! I'll tell the world it's worth it all to see Broadway at night. Whoopee!

Over the summer the family saw Eddie Cantor in Florenz Ziegfeld's live stage show *Whoopee!* Cantor had begun performing with the Ziegfeld Follies in 1917 and by 1923 had his own *Kid Boots*, a show that reportedly ran for 489 performances. *Whoopee!* would not be Forrest's only encounter with

Cantor, one of the most popular stars in show business in 1929.

The Cloughs saw Warner Baxter, a silent film star who had successfully transitioned to talkies, in *Behind That Curtain* at the Roxy Theater, said to be the largest (5,920 seats) and most beautiful theater in the world at the time. A 110-piece orchestra introduced the program. Ancel and Forrest ventured back to the Paramount Theater and Paul Ash's orchestra another evening to see *Dangerous Curves*, starring Clara Bow. She was 1929's top box office draw and the film star who personified the sexy flapper of the roaring twenties, this time playing a circus bareback rider in love with an emotionally distant trapeze artist.

I suspect that the family rode by car to some of these nighttime theater events. However, their next-to-last theater venture occurred to celebrate G.O.'s completion of his PhD written exams on July 31. According to Forrest, the "family piled onto an IRT subway" and headed to Times Square and the Paramount. *River of Romance* featured Charles "Buddy" Rogers and Mary Brian in a movie about Mississippi in the 1830s. Again, the stage show featured Paul Ash's Orchestra with comedian George Murphy to introduce the show. Murphy, who appeared in Broadway musicals before heading to the movies in California, was elected Republican senator there in 1964, paving the way for actors to become politicians.

Their last musical theater adventure on August 4 was to Ziegfeld's *The Show Girl* that featured Dorothy Stone, daughter of actor Fred Stone, who was a last-minute replacement four days before the Cloughs saw the live show. In a panic over his original dancer's illness, Florenz Ziegfeld tracked the young Dorothy down in California where she was on Will Rogers' ranch, which had no phones. So, Ziegfeld[52] apparently cajoled Dorothy's father into driving out to the ranch from Hollywood and putting her on a train to New York. Ziegfeld had shipped the script by airplane to Los Angeles but it arrived three hours after Dorothy left. Thereupon, Will Rogers quickly found an airplane, pursued the train to an outlying station, and dropped off the script for Miss Stone, who began memorizing lines and practicing tap steps in her drawing room on the train. Dorothy apparently filled in seamlessly, for Forrest made no mention of her July 31 substitution.

Earlier that summer, the Cloughs had enjoyed a free outdoor band concert:

Sunday, June the 23rd. We took a delightful drive over to Central Park . . . . About fifteen thousand people gathered about the Mall that night to hear a great band concert . . . by the Goldman Band under the direction of Edwin Franko Goldman. This was a sixty-piece band.

Edwin Goldman founded his band in 1911 and performed nightly during summers in New York, drawing over 30,000 people to its maiden 1923 concert in Central Park. Forrest naturally wanted to hear Goldman, who was a virtuoso cornetist with the Metropolitan Opera orchestra and had studied under Antón Dvorak.

The Cloughs' last musical experience in NYC occurred on August 13 just before they left for Dallas. Their landlord in Long Island City, who arranged music for the Eveready Hour at the National Broadcasting Company (NBC), secured the family's admission to NBC's Studio B at 711 5th Avenue. Along with twenty other spectators, they witnessed the hour-long nationwide broadcast of semi-classical and popular tunes by the Eveready Orchestra, a male quartet singing harmony, and a baritone soloist. This was likely Forrest's first visit to a recording studio.

Ocean liners were the primary means for crossing the Atlantic to Europe during the late twenties, and Forrest's family was eager to tour some of the passenger ships docked in Manhattan's harbor. The three largest liners in the world, all built by the Hamburg-America line before WWI and eventually turned over to the British as war reparations, were each docked at some point over the summer of 1929 in New York. In increasing order of size, they ranged from the RMS *Berengaria*, to the SS *Leviathan*, and finally the RMS *Majestic*, the last built.

Typically, these big liners allowed the public to come on board along with the passengers before they set sail around midnight. The Cloughs' first opportunity came in late June in the early evening when they drove south through Long Island to cross the Brooklyn Bridge into lower Manhattan. Proceeding up 11th Avenue, they noticed bustling activity at the Cunard pier—the RMS *Berengaria* was sailing for Cherbourg, France. "What an opportunity!" exclaimed Forrest. They parked the car and boarded the ship, looking around until 11 p.m.

It resembles a massive hotel . . . long hallways, lounging rooms, bed rooms, writing rooms, dining rooms and in fact all conveniences of a modern hotel. I particularly enjoyed the large promenade decks which afford the passengers an excellent

opportunity to enjoy the sea breezes . . . . A dance orchestra was engaged to play
. . . in the large dance hall. One can imagine the activity about the pier when . . .
some four thousand people sailed. Friends of those departing were down to bid
them a fond farewell.

At its commissioning in Hamburg in 1913, the SS *Imperator* was the
largest passenger ship in the world. Renamed the RMS *Berengaria* by the
British after WWI, it was reportedly the first ship to have a stock trading
office on board. In the summer of 1929, while the Cloughs were in New
York, the market was rising and people believed they were on a ride that
was never going to end. Everyone was buying on margin with only 10%
down. Pools of wealthy investors were secretly manipulating the market to
raise prices then sell off at big profits. The little man was caught up in the
frenzy too.

When the market crashed on October 29, 1929, and the bankers could
no longer stem the tide with credit infusions, the *Berengaria* was half way
across the Atlantic. Word spread through the ship. Investors came pouring
out of card games or the Turkish baths in their robes and headed to the
ship's trading office to try to sell their stocks. Many had left England wealthy
but arrived penniless upon docking in New York.

Living modestly on the salary of a college professor, the Cloughs were
not gamblers and had no money invested in the market. Although Forrest
and G.O. visited Wall Street and witnessed the frenetic activity, they were
mere observers of the pending crash. G.O. may have read a few frequent
warnings that summer of an already unfolding, inevitable upheaval, but he
had no worries about the possibility of losing everything.

A few days later, the family boarded the RMS *Carmania*, half the size of
the *Berengaria*, to say farewell to a friend from Dallas who was sailing for
Europe that same evening. Next came the RMS *Majestic,* the largest ship
afloat in 1929. The family picked up G.O. at NYU one evening and headed
to the pier at W. 18th and the Hudson River to board the ship, which was
sailing at 10 p.m.

There were thousands at the pier that night . . . . I got in a wheel-chair and one of
the dock men pushed me about a thousand feet to the gangplank where we got
aboard the ship . . . the Majestic is in every sense . . . . An Ocean-borne Palace.

This liner could cross from New York to Cherbourg and Southampton in under six days. A ship brochure described an elegance that preempted the grandeur of the RMS *Berengaria*. To these middle class Americans, the opulence and luxury were a sight hard to comprehend. After coming down the gangplank, the Cloughs passed through an oak-paneled entrance into the luxuriously furnished lounge. With a ceiling of carved wood and crystal overhead, it could easily be converted into the dance ballroom. Next came an elaborately furnished Palm Court restaurant, the reading and writing room, the library, a gymnasium, tennis courts, and its grandest feature—the Pompeian swimming pool surrounded by Roman columns. A second class lounge room, smoking room, dining salon, and staterooms, "all very attractive" were located on lower decks. How did Forrest get downstairs after being pushed on board in his wheelchair—via elevator, on his crutches, or was he carried down by a strapping deck hand?

An even bigger adventure on board an ocean liner came in late July, when Forrest, with family and friends, visited the SS *Leviathan*, or the *Levi*, as it was called. Forrest had spotted the *Levi* the previous fall on his trip up the Hudson to West Point.

I had always wanted to go aboard the mightiest of ocean liners and now my big chance had come.

The ship's head nurse, the sister of a friend of theirs from Tyler, Texas, facilitated their tour. The orchestra was playing "Indian Love Call" in the gallery while a banquet was underway in the dining salon to honor General Gouraud, French WW I veteran and VIP guest on board at the time. The Cloughs' group visited the typical luxury liner features, including the radio room, the Pompeiian pool, the engine room, the "immigrant quarters," and tourist cabins in the stern.

Most importantly, they negotiated their way into the luxurious suite of the French General and his entourage:

Sara [a friend in their party] *gave the attendant a million dollar smile and everything was rosy then. With mother's help she convinced the attendant of our great desire to see the suite of rooms. Presto! Like magic we were escorted in* [sic] *the Premier suite and began looking around with awe and deep satisfaction. It can best be described by comparing it with a swell suite of rooms in a fashionable hotel . . . . On a center table in the parlor were many unopened gifts for the General and his official escorts. In another room we saw the suitcases and trunks of the distinguished guests . . . we thanked the attendant, who . . . told us that Queen Marie of Roumania used the suite of rooms on her recent visit to America.*

After refurbishing in 1923, the *Leviathan* became the world's fastest ship, so its brochure claimed. Accommodating 3,397 passengers, the *Levi* reportedly made the crossing between the same three ports as the *Majestic* in only five days, six hours. Typically, the *Levi* and most of the other transatlantic liners, made two round-trip crossings each month.

These liners were always in competition with each other not only in speed and size, but also in popularity. However, the *Levi* and the *Majestic* were both "dry ships" during Prohibition, and the *Levi* often sailed with half its capacity, thus losing money. Consequently, the *Levi* was decommissioned in 1934 and sold for scrap to a British firm in 1938. The *Majestic* met a similar fate in 1943. What ignominious endings for such grand ships that had carried the movers and shakers of the Roaring Twenties before the market crash.

Beyond the five boroughs the family trooped in order to see more of New York. They spent July 4th at Port Washington on Long Island Sound and discovered that New Yorkers celebrated in much the same way they did in Texas: large national flags in front of homes, highways filled with autos, people and busses, swimming at the beach with motorboats, sloops, and schooners all around, as well as picnic suppers and fireworks displays.

Heading off in a different direction on a separate adventure, Forrest, his mother, and little Margaret motored to Roosevelt Field, a civilian airfield, about twenty miles further east of their Long Island home. Perhaps Forrest stayed in the car since Cousin Hattie was not along to help Maggie with her son. He noted:

There are some 18 or 20 hangars on the field, and, believe me, I saw every type and model of airplane made—practically. Charles A. Lindbergh took off from this field on his memorable flight to Paris in May 1927.

New Jersey was their next destination. Caravanning with some friends on a July Saturday, the family crossed into lower Manhattan and transited the Holland Tunnel for a fee of 50 cents. From Jersey City they drove to Thomas Edison's laboratories in West Orange, New Jersey, but discovered them closed that afternoon. All was not lost, however:

> We were permitted to go through Edison's private estate. Ancel and sister accompanied by some friends of ours went to see if he would pose for kodak pictures. He was resting and we were unable to see him. Mr. Edison would be glad to pose if he were not resting, the maid said. Edison gave permission for us to use his lawn and home as a background for some pictures . . . .

Sister Margaret, age six at the time, remembers waving to the elderly gentleman with his shock of white hair as he looked out a second story window—while Forrest waited in the car, probably sad to miss seeing the famous man. Taking photographs in the gardens of Edison's private estate was a rare privilege, hard to imagine today. The family returned home via Staten Island, the one borough they had not visited, and caught the ferry back to Manhattan.

One of their most memorable excursions came on an early-August Sunday when the family drove to Yale University in New Haven, Connecticut, about 80 miles northeast of New York City. G.O., as an

academic, was eager to see the famous university founded in 1701. After touring around the historic buildings with their rustic towers and the immense greens of the main campus, they drove out to the Yale football stadium, better known as "Yale Bowl."

FAMILY AT YALE UNIVERSITY

. . . . opened November 21, 1914, and . . . used for football only. The bowl is 950 feet long and 750 feet wide covering about 12.5 acres. It seats about 75,000 persons . . . . This huge structure cost $500,000 to build.

After visiting the stadium, the family spotted a grove of trees across the road where they enjoyed "a fine picnic dinner."

Dad expressed himself several times as having a great time. He was also very happy that we had come up to New Haven to see this historic and remarkable university . . . . It is beyond my words . . . . I would not have missed seeing . . . [it] for anything.

Returning from New Haven about 8:50 p.m., they crossed the Queensborough Bridge and looked down the East River

And to our surprise we saw the Graf Zeppelin, 'Germany's Leviathan of the Air,' as she majestically sailed over Manhattan . . . .Great searchlights were playing slim fingers of light on her . . . . New York's millions went wild with glee. Airplanes were skimming around in the now almost black sky bidding welcome to this great 'Bird of the Sky.' To tell the truth about the matter it looked like a 'Flying Whale.' Slowly it turned toward Lakehurst, New Jersey and with a burst of speed dashed into the night toward its mooring quarters.

We were all indeed glad that we had returned from Yale in time to see this great zep. Previous reports in the many newspapers in the metropolitan area had stated it would arrive at noon.

On their last weekend in New York the family had one more thing to do before leaving—climbing up inside the Statue of Liberty. After ferrying out to the statue in New York's harbor, Forrest went as far as the elevator would take him and waited while the others mounted the narrow stairs to the top. How many times during his life would Forrest have given anything to go wherever he wanted and see and do the things others were able to do so easily. From four points of observation, the climbers snapped skyline photos before making their way back down to Forrest's level and home through Manhattan's Chinatown.

The next day the Cloughs left Long Island about 9:45 a.m. with some friends, heading for Long Beach in Nassau County where they spent the day. They ate a picnic lunch within 20 feet of the Atlantic Ocean, relishing one last time the sandy beach and ocean breezes before heading back to landlocked Dallas.

The waves were plenty high. White caps on the breakers . . . . Out over the horizon steamers appeared . . . a sight which I for one would never tire of seeing . . . thousands of bathers . . . fancy colored . . . umbrellas . . . .

Regrettably, on August 16 the family bid farewell to the largest city in America to return to Texas following ". . . .this most enjoyable of summer trips. The time came for us to start south, into the land of sunshine, happiness, and prosperity."

Forrest's travelogue documented their trip home as well. The family visited Baltimore, the Naval Academy in Annapolis, Washington, DC, Mount Vernon, Virginia, and, in Kentucky, Mammoth Cave and Lincoln's birthplace cabin reconstructed near Hodgenville.

AT FRONT STEPS OF WHITE HOUSE, 1929

Their trip expenses for the 2,034 miles back to Dallas amounted to $81.42 for the 10 nights in motor camps along the way, with G.O. added as an additional mouth to feed. Again they averaged 200-300 miles per day, with overnights in seven states and three nights in Washington, DC, before arriving home. Remarkably, the use of his wheelchair on board an ocean liner was the only mention Forrest made of his disability in this travelogue. We can only imagine the effort made by others to help him enjoy this wonderful adventure.

This must have been the most exciting and memorable summer vacation the family ever spent together. It certainly whetted Forrest's appetite for more travel and also gave him new career options to consider. Just like everyone else, he was caught up in the excitement of the Roaring Twenties and probably had little inkling of what the next decade would bring.

EARLY YEARS AT SMU:
1929-1932

CHAPTER THREE

A SETBACK AND A LOST SEMESTER

Once home from the family's invigorating trip to the East Coast, it was time for Forrest to enter his third year of college at Southern Methodist University. It must have been difficult for him to return to Dallas and the routine of studies after such eye-opening experiences in New York City. Unknown to him at the time, the variety of career possibilities he encountered in New York would help expand his horizons during the next two rocky years.

Forrest was delighted when his brother Ancel joined him at SMU as a freshman that fall. Paying tribute to his brother, Forrest wrote:

> *He has always been very kind . . . and especially . . . helpful to me in carrying me about. It is a source of great satisfaction . . . to know that I have a brother who is so good to me.*

Ancel reportedly drove him to and from his private music lessons downtown. How many other places did Ancel hoist Forrest onto his back or transport him by car, especially in their younger years? Only 5'3" on his crutches, Forrest likely weighed about 125 pounds with his braces on when his brother and others were helping him get around. In a 2014 interview, Ancel's son Mike stated he never once heard his father say anything to indicate he was resentful of all the physical help and emotional support he gave Forrest over the years.

In addition to his brother, Forrest claimed all of his buddies at the university were always willing to help him whenever he needed it. He often wished he could repay them in some way for their support. When Forrest spoke of "their many kindnesses," he never specifically mentioned the type of help his brother and others gave him. He may have wanted to prevent his readers—primarily his sociology professor, Dr. R. D. Leberman, who gave him an "A" and commented his story was very interesting—from noting the tremendous effort required of others to assist him physically. Although a self-labeled cripple, Forrest wanted to be seen by all, including his professor, as a normal college student.

Floyd Patterson, a band colleague and good friend during college, described in 2001 how Forrest got around on all the many band trips: "In the big cities, someone would throw Forrest up on his back and hail a taxi." Someone else would scoop up the wheelchair or crutches and off they would go. Everywhere Forrest went he had to have help getting into his wheelchair, onto his crutches, through doors, up stairs, onto trains and buses, and into cars. Apparently, his agreeable personality made people, especially his male friends, willing to accommodate this talented trumpet player who had created an indispensable place for himself in the band and on the campus.

SUSAN AND FLOYD PATTERSON WITH SCRAPBOOK, 2001

SMU vs. Nebraska. Traversing long distances in the 1920s and 1930s was most commonly done by rail, thus giving passengers a wide variety of options among competing rail lines. The lines, eager to get their business, catered to groups such as football teams in a variety of ways.

The 1929 season's headliner trip sent the Mustangs to Lincoln, Nebraska, in early October by way of Chicago on the Missouri Pacific Railway Lines. Playing at that game brought the musicians some national attention. Forrest wrote:

> The grid battle was put on the air by the Columbia Broadcasting System of New York. Our band was indeed fortunate in having a special Columbia 'mike' sitting in front of it to pick up music at different intervals and broadcast it over the entire chain of stations. What an opportunity for us to have!

News clips touted 1929 as the biggest season opening game in the history of Nebraska with 20,000 fans in attendance, including the state's governor. The game ended in a scoreless tie, apparently a surprise for the confident Nebraska team.

Back at SMU, Forrest especially enjoyed his courses: religion, Spanish, political theory, geology, and sociology. The political theory course embodied all the "ancient and present theories in the science of politics and government." He began to make great plans for the spring and fall terms of 1930 when he would enter law school. Perhaps to impress his sociology professor, Forrest firmly believed that going to college meant gaining "enjoyment and satisfaction through true and constructive knowledge." Or it could have been unstated acknowledgement that academics was his primary goal because his college social life was dependent on others.

Forrest made no mention of the late-October 1929 stock market crash. It would be a couple of years before the subsequent economic depression hit the SMU campus. Thus, funds were available for the annual mid-winter band tour, to be Forrest's third such trip and one he would not forget.

Not Just a Simple Sore Throat. SMU performed much-appreciated community outreach with its February band tours. Although an often weather-challenged endeavor, the band members enjoyed the camaraderie of their colleagues and a break from classes. The itinerary for the 1930 tour took them to West Texas, including the towns of Ballinger, Big Spring, and

San Angelo. Helping spread the rising fame of the Mustang Band, these tours brought some culture to small rural ranch and oil towns and gave the boys an opportunity to engage with a less urban population.

Soon after the first concert at Weatherford, Forrest came down with what he thought was a "common old winter sore throat, but it kept getting worse and worse." He immediately started doctoring himself with throat lozenges, salt water gargle, and other home remedies, but they seemed to do no good.

> I played the concerts in Midland and Sweetwater when it seemed as though my throat would split. I'll never know how I managed to finish the concert tour, and how I played all the concerts. My throat was paining me terribly when we reached home. Little did I realize that my trouble was only beginning.

As it turned out, Forrest had a bad case of tonsillitis and required a tonsillectomy. The surgery was not performed until two weeks after his return from the band tour. Although Alexander Fleming discovered penicillin in September 1928, it was not until 1943 that scientists were able to produce enough of the antibiotic for clinical trials on humans. Until then, doctors could only hope their patients' immune systems would eventually fight off bacterial infection, which may have been one reason for the surgery's two-week delay.

Following the operation, Forrest hemorrhaged a great deal of blood. This must have scared his family as they awaited word from the surgeon about whether he was going to pull through. Get Well cards were numerous and included one dated March 11, 1930, that came with flowers, saying "With best regards from your 'buddies' in Mustang Band." The unexpected loss of blood slowed Forrest's recovery and left him too frail to attempt a return to school. He characterized this time as "just resting."

Despite his resolve to relax and build up strength during the remaining few months of the semester, Forest was clearly frustrated:

> My plans for the spring term and fall of 1930 were blown to the sky; it was a bitter dose but I had to swallow it!...A nose dive—a crack up—and half a year out of school as a result of a tonsil operation.

Two months later, Forrest was feeling better and continued in his autobiography:

Toward the first part of May I became strong enough to go to the University and sit around in my wheelchair for a few hours at a time. It was great to be back on the campus again, and a pleasure to greet my friends . . . after such a long absence.

YMCA Camp at Hollister, Missouri. Later in May several YMCA and Sunday School class friends on campus suggested Forrest join a group of young people planning to attend the annual YMCA and YWCA Conference retreat in Hollister, Missouri. Forrest agreed the trip would be good for him, one where he could "stay out-of-doors much of the time to build up strength and good health." No mention was made about funding for the trip, but presumably G.O. and Maggie felt it would be beneficial for Forrest and paid his way. Whether he traveled to southwestern Missouri by bus or as a passenger in some friend's car is unknown.

The conference was held at the YMCA camp three miles outside Hollister near the White River, which winds through the highland plateau of the Ozark Mountains. Tourism began to expand here in the 1880s and today hosts the Branson summer theatrical and musical productions. In early June 1930 thirty SMU students gathered for ten days

AT HOLLISTER, IN A CANOE, 1930

with 220 students from other southwestern colleges. Conferees attended educational and spiritual programs and enjoyed boating and swimming in the lake nearby. Forrest rode in a canoe with no life jacket, perhaps unavailable but also not wanting to advertise that he could not swim.

I received much good from this trip, the first of its kind I had been on. The fellowship with the students meant much to me. The communion with God and the wonderful lectures heard proved a great source of inspiration and thorough enjoyment. My health was improved . . . and I was . . . glad . . . my friends insisted on my going.

On June 28, 1930—Forrest's 21st birthday—he received a congratulatory letter written by G.O. from the Texas State Teachers Association meeting in Austin. At this important milestone, Forrest appeared very happy to be alive, thankful for his recovery from a serious illness and for his many good friends both at Hollister and in Dallas.

─╲╎╱─

A month before the opening of classes in his fourth year at SMU, Forrest composed a new school song he hoped to get adopted. His friend Eugene Slater, president of the Student Association, was "heartily in favor" of Forrest's song. Asked to present it at a Student Council meeting, Forrest played the two-stanza song as an instrumental solo and then read the words to the council members.

HAIL TO OUR COLLEGE

Hail to our col-lege, pride of ev'-ry heart!
Prais-es to thee, SMU,
U-nit-ed we stand, hold-ing true to the start,
Hon-or-ing the Red and Blue.
Friends of the cam-pus, how loy-al you've been,
All work to-geth-er for Var-si-ty,
Hail to our college, greater days are foreseen!
SMU, e-ter-nal-ly.

Here come our Mus-tangs, charg-ing on down the field!
Striv-ing for great vic-to-ry,
They come as staunch war-riors, to no one will they yield,
When they fight for dear Var-si-ty,
March, for-ward boys, we are with you, 'tis true,
Car-ry our col-ors on through the fray,
Win this game, Mus-tangs, for the Red and the Blue!
Fight for SMU, al-way.

An October 1, 1930, *Campus* headline read: "Council Adopts New Verse as Official SMU Song." Only Forrest's first verse, which would merely be added to the repertory of school songs, was adopted. "Varsity" would continue to be SMU's Alma Mater.

Although Forrest saved his original musical score written with 17 parts for "Hail to Our College," there is no indication he copyrighted the song. Nevertheless, Forrest was pleased with the song's reception and noted the band first rehearsed the entire score on October 20. He sent a copy to NBC in New York, the radio network that carried SMU Mustang football games nationwide. NBC's chief librarian informed Forrest by letter that the network had played his new song on a November Saturday in its after-game program.

Giving no captions or labels, Forrest pasted photos over two campus newspaper articles saved in *Scrapbook* about his song that were partially ripped out. Did the song receive a negative review? Although this song is listed in SMU publications for several years after this, SMU's two current band directors reported they had never heard of it. Presumably it was dropped after Forrest left campus and perhaps even before his father retired in 1948. "Varsity" along with "Peruna," the fight song, are long-time favorites still sung today.

Forrest tried his hand at other musical compositions over the years, copyrighting at least one of them. Of those pertaining to the college, he drafted an SMU March song and saved another one scored by Frank Rénard, a Dallas musician and SMU band colleague. Both pieces provided musical arrangements but no lyrics for each of the instruments in the band. Whether the band ever performed these scores is unknown.

SMU vs. Notre Dame. Knute Rockne, perhaps the most renowned coach in American college football history, emigrated from Norway to Chicago at age five with his parents in 1893. He put himself through pharmacy school while playing football at Notre Dame. Eventually becoming head coach of the Notre Dame Ramblers, he is credited with popularizing the forward pass and leading his "Rocknemen" to five national championships. His friendship with Doc Blackwell, SMU's athletic business manager, helped SMU schedule its historic 1928 Army game, which achieved national recognition for the team, and later games with Nebraska, Navy, Notre

Dame, and Indiana.[53]

Forrest, 39 other band members, and 350 fans accompanied the SMU football team to play Notre Dame in South Bend, Indiana. Leaving on October 2, 1930, the band entertained the crowds gathered at the Highland Park station send-off with alma mater favorites.

The MKT (Missouri, Kansas, and Texas) railway hosted the Mustangs on the Dallas-Chicago leg of the trip, honoring their passengers with a multi-course dinner choice of squab chicken burgundy or filet mignon and mushrooms. MKT's dinner menu, one of the many saved by Forrest, titled "Mustangs-Notre Dame Football Special," entreated "Let's beat Rockne!" Whatever it took to keep such lucrative business, all the railways accommodated.

Somewhere en route to South Bend the Mustang entourage transferred to the Chicago and Eastern Illinois (C and EI) Railway. As was usually the custom, it is doubtful they had to change trains, only signage, as they crossed into a new railway's territory, fortunately making it easier on Forrest and his handlers. After a noisy, rolling sleep on the train, the Mustangs luxuriated Friday night at the Auditorium Hotel on Michigan Avenue. The band toured a bit of the Windy City before the Michigan Central Railroad carried them to South Bend the following day.

ON MICHIGAN AVENUE
IN CHICAGO, 1930

News clips of the football match raved about the tough battle the team waged against Notre Dame in the Ramblers' new 55,000-seat stadium. The St. Louis Post-Dispatch's headline read: "Notre Dame Forced to Expose Trick Plays to Beat Methodists." Forrest too described the game:

It was a wow! We almost licked Knute Rockne and his Ramblin' Irishmen . . . . In the last four minutes of play, Notre Dame put over the winning touchdown and took the game to the tune of 20-14. A long pass in final minutes led to the Rockne victory. It was one of the most exciting games I've ever seen! Thrills galore and flying pigskins!

Returning via Chicago and Alton Railroad, the band spent Sunday sightseeing in St. Louis on a Gray Line bus tour, then traveled home on the Missouri Pacific Lines. Five months later, having saved a photo of Knute Rockne from the game folder, Forrest penned a tribute to the famous legend. Coach Rockne was killed March 31, 1931, in a TWA plane crash. He was en route to Los Angeles to participate in the production of the film *The Spirit of Notre Dame*. Writing for the *Campus* newspaper, Forrest said:

The greatest of all football mentors, Knute Rockne, was killed shortly after lunch today in an airplane crash at Bazaar, Kansas, near Emporia. There were no survivors... There was an explosion aboard the plane as it was fighting its way through a severe storm . . . . There will never be another Knute Rockne-coached football eleven. All of America is . . . greatly saddened by the loss of this wonderful character.

Soon after the band's return from Notre Dame, Forrest was asked to feature his new school song in chapel, playing the tune first as a trumpet solo, then accompanying the audience's singing rendition. The *Campus* proclaimed, "Students Like New School Song."

SMU vs. Navy in Annapolis. In mid-November 1930, more than 30 Pullman sleeping cars, six baggage cars, four diners, the team, and 400 fans made up the Baltimore and Ohio Railway's private Mustang special bound for Maryland. A $5,000 fund, started only a few days before the departure to defray the band's expenses, was not completed until just before the special pulled out with about 40 band members on board. As usual the band showed their appreciation and school spirit with jazzy renditions of school favorites for 30 minutes prior to departure. Passing through Harper's Ferry, West Virginia, the musicians serenaded curious station visitors.

Baltimore rolled out the red carpet for their southern guests, practically turning the city over to the Texans upon their Friday arrival. Local papers had displayed photographs of the "Methodist eleven" every day that week and not a single one of Navy's team. One unnamed newspaper recognized

SMU's musicians: "Snappy Band Leads Mustangs' Invasion."

De-training at Camden Station in downtown Baltimore, the band paraded the streets with a police escort, blaring brasses and booming drums, and stopping traffic as it marched six blocks to their headquarters at the Lord Baltimore Hotel. How Forrest maneuvered the streets is not mentioned.

Once in the lobby of the hotel, the red, blue, and grey-clad band members gave another concert. They startled observers with their popular, jazzy, and old-time minstrel music (including "She'll Be Coming 'Round the Mountain When She Comes") rather than the staid marches and military pieces these Easterners were used to.

Maryland's governor, the Assistant Secretary of the Navy, the superintendent of the Naval Academy, and SMU's president Selecman were on hand to witness the game. Nineteen hundred midshipmen made the trip up from Annapolis on a special train with their mascot, Ol' Bill, the time-honored Navy goat. Forrest wrote:

> Watching the U.S. Navy Band and the Corps of Midshipmen march onto the field with military precision was truly a scene . . . . After shouting words of welcome to the Dallasites and yelling in unison (1500 strong) for S.M.U. and the Navy, the 'Middies' filed in orderly double-breasted fashion to their reserved seats on the opposite side of the field from where the S.M.U. Band and the football team were to be located.

After the Middies left the field, the Mustang band, led by a nattily dressed, goose-stepping drum major, marched across the field playing "Peruna." While Forrest watched from the stands, the marchers serenaded the Navy supporters with "Anchors Aweigh" and "Honor Over All," the midshipmen's official songs. At half-time, several thousand fans clambered onto the field to witness a wonderful display by the Midshipmen of cardboard artistry in white, red, navy, and gold.

Dressed in new red jerseys and golden silk-like pants, the Mustangs used their forward-passing attack with effective rushing against Navy, winning the game 20-7 before a crowd of 20,000. One reporter said the Mustangs "converted another army of doubters to aerial football...that found the Sailors all but standing with their mouths open...." Forrest summarized with "The ...reception we had in Baltimore was perfect."

On Sunday following the game, the Mustangs boarded the Pennsylvania Railway cars and made a five-hour stopover in Washington, DC. A local Methodist minister coordinated a bus tour around the city for his fellow churchmen. Forrest encountered "slippery going and a rainy day," a rare admission about his handicap preventing him from seeing all he wanted to see. Presumably, he had left his wheelchair behind on the train, perhaps choosing his crutches to avoid asking someone to push him.

Leaving Washington, the Mustangs were offered Lake Superior whitefish for $1.25, a standard price on several of the train menus. In Harrisburg, Pennsylvania, their two SMU cars were connected to the "Spirit of St. Louis." In Missouri they picked up the Frisco Lines, which advertised its Fred Harvey dining car service. Joining the railroads during the Civil War, Harvey partnered with the Atchison, Topeka, and Santa Fe Railroad in Kansas in 1876 to establish restaurants at train stops every hundred miles and serve fine, low-cost meals in only 30 minutes. Eventually, his restaurant service expanded onto dining cars throughout the country, greatly benefiting the Mustang band on its cross-country travels during the 1920s and 1930s.

⁓⤙⤚⁓

Forrest's class-assigned autobiography ended in the fall of 1930 when he was just twenty-one years old. He was settled into his college routine, keeping up a grueling schedule of band trips and managing to do well with his grades. At this point Forrest's *Scrapbook* became the primary resource for revealing events and allowing me to guess at what he might have been feeling.

In the winter of 1931 the usual band tour to Texas towns did not occur because the international economic crisis had finally hit Dallas and SMU. Nor would it occur in 1932 for the same reason. Instead, Forrest saw Amos and Andy, a popular radio and (later) TV team who performed from 1928 into the 1950s, at the state fairgrounds. These two white actors developed a "Negro minstrel"-style repertoire that became the first syndicated radio program in America, giving 15-minute daily shows on 75 radio stations coast-to-coast at the height of their fame in 1930. Demeaning and reprehensible, using blackface and minstrelsy were commonly accepted entertainment in the days before civil rights activism and the 1960's legislation. In the 1930s racist slurs made their way into a few of the get well cards and in at least one letter Forrest received.

Forrest's travels and his interest in government led him to join the International Relations Club formed under sponsorship of the Carnegie Endowment for International Peace (CEIP). He also accompanied his Sunday School group on a spring outing to nearby Lake Worth. The group clambered into row boats and larger-capacity motor boats to tour this popular recreation area. Dressed in suit and tie, Forrest sat on the gunnels of a row boat, again with no life jacket. In early May Forrest played the only trumpet among 17 other orchestra members in a performance of the Light Opera Club of SMU. At a May 20 assembly honoring graduating seniors, Frank Rénard, Forrest's band collaborator on other compositions, arranged a mixed double quartet singing "Hail to Our College" before the band played some Victor Herbert favorites.

The 1930-31 school year was a rewarding one for Forrest, "the happiest and most enjoyable year of any I have yet experienced on the campus." After being so ill and losing a whole semester in spring 1930, Forrest wanted to return with a bang, which he did with his new song. As he prepared to enter law school in the fall of 1931, Forrest was flying high.

A "Cripple's" Philosophy of Life Sustains through Adversity.

Polios are notorious for forcing themselves to excel, often to the point of exhaustion, to be better than the best. This "drivenness" shows up in narratives of polios afflicted early in the century as well as in those who suffered the disease in the 1940s and 1950s. Despite the changing treatments from my father's era to the mid-century epidemic years, the psychological and emotional impact of the disease was the same. A disability that makes one different exerts tremendous pressure to conform, to fit in.

Two documents saved in *Scrapbook* attest to Forrest's determination to "keep on keeping on" despite any obstacles he encountered. The first appears to be from an M.K. & T. Railway newsletter dated June 21, 1931. An unknown author wrote *The Ten Demandments of How to Get Along with People*, probably something Forrest picked up on one of his trips. Under the heading "The Peanut Vendor," this list contains some sage advice that apparently inspired Forrest. Certainly, number four was the foremost persona he displayed to the world:

1. Keep skid chains on your tongue; always say less than you think. Cultivate a low, persuasive voice. How you say it often counts more than what you say.

2. Make promises sparingly and keep them faithfully, no matter what it costs you.

3. Never let an opportunity pass to say a kind and encouraging thing to or about somebody. Praise good work done, regardless of who did it. If criticism is needed, criticize helpfully, never spitefully.

4. Be cheerful. Keep the corners of your mouth turned up. Hide your pains, worries and disappointments under a smile. Laugh at good stories and learn to tell them.

5. Be interested in others; interested in their pursuits, their welfare, their homes and families. Make merry with those who rejoice, with those who weep, mourn. Let everyone you meet, however humble, feel that you regard him as one of importance.

6. Preserve an open mind on all debatable questions. Discuss, but don't argue. It is a mark of superior minds to disagree and yet be friendly.

7. Let your virtues, if you have any, speak for themselves, and refuse to talk of another's vices. Discourage gossip. Make it a rule to say nothing of another unless it is something good.

8. Be careful of another's feelings. Wit and humor at the other fellow's expense are rarely worth the effort and may hurt where least expected.

9. Pay no attention to ill-natured remarks about you. Simply live so that nobody will believe them. Disordered nerves and a bad digestion are a common cause of backbiting.

10. Don't be too anxious about getting your just dues. Do your work, be patient, and keep your disposition sweet, forget self, and you will be rewarded.

A poem written by Forrest in 1931 sums up his philosophy of life:

STRIVING

When you go about your work
Through the days in the week;
Always keep on striving ahead,
For it's knowledge that you seek
The road is long to real success;
It's a hard old climb to the top,
And when you feel you'd like to quit,
Just smile and say: "Never stop!"

Your friends will love you more and more
Of you they'll always say:
'There goes a pal of mine; 'tis true
Defeat never stands in his way!'

Achievement will be yours, my friend,
Rich life and happiness, too;
Just grit your teeth and work with vim,
It all depends on you.

Forrest Weldon Clough

As illustrated in the above two pieces, Forrest's philosophy served this extrovert quite well. He was not about to let the world see him when he was down, though he did carefully document each major illness and medical setback. Perhaps the medical references were unconscious efforts to show his determination to pick himself up and try again, as well as to explain why it took him so long to graduate from college.

CHAPTER FOUR

TWO MORE MEDICAL SETBACKS: 1931-1932

In June 1931 Forrest returned to Hollister, Missouri, and the YMCA camp where he had had such a grand time the previous summer. *Scrapbook's* 38 photos of the two-week encampment show the gang swimming in the lake and falling out of boats and off docks. They horsed around, made a trip to Branson three miles away, held a meeting to discuss camp problems, attended vespers, sang songs at twilight at the lodge, and drew their water from an antiquated pump. When they visited the Presbyterian Chautauqua-like camp above the Y camp (normally reached by a steep set of steps), someone must have escorted Forrest up "Presbyterian Hill" in a vehicle.

HOLLISTER MATES ON THE RUNNING BOARD,
WITH FORREST ON TRUMPET, 1931

Forrest, usually in a white shirt and tie, was always on his crutches in photos, never in his wheelchair. Obviously happy and feeling accepted, he helped organize a 12-person musical group called the "Damma Phi Data Boys," with him playing his trumpet. Forrest wrote the words and scored the music for a song about his experience:

HOLLISTER—HERE IS TO YOU!

Humming, whistling, singing a song of love.
Hoping, just hoping, it's heard by the heavens above.

Chorus: We are so happy, and very thankful to be back here once again,
Hollister's real life means something to us, Just as a true friend to friend.
Here with great pals from everywhere, Here where we're happy in all we do,
Gladness you bring us can we e'er repay? Hollister, here is to you!

Another student at the camp did the piano arrangement. Forrest kept a hand-written thank you letter from a woman at the Houston YWCA praising him for the "depth that your music had added to Hollister during . . . two summers . . . that wasn't there before."

Next came the Southwest Band Conservatory Summer Session, held at SMU for six weeks in July and August. Forrest was admitted to the advanced band, where top students and band directors from the Southwestern states focused on perfecting their solo performance as well as ensemble skills. Tuition was billed at $100 for the summer, but Forrest was charged only $12.50, perhaps receiving a scholarship.

Director of the advanced ensemble band was Joseph De Luca, an Italian trained at the Conservatory in Rome. He led bands all over Europe and on the east coast of the US before moving to the University of Arizona in Tucson. De Luca was a world-renowned composer and soloist who played the trombone and the euphonium (a valved brass instrument resembling a small tuba). He performed as guest conductor of John Philip Sousa's organization for eight seasons.

This Advanced Ensemble All-Southwestern Concert Band gave several performances in Dallas, in surrounding communities, and a radio show on

KRLD. The band ended the summer session with a recital of nine pieces at SMU's McFarlin Auditorium, where De Luca did a solo on his euphonium and handed out certificates. In an August letter the Southwestern Band Conservatory's president thanked Forrest for how well he held down the solo chair in the cornet section. Although invited, Forrest did not return the following summer to complete the Bandmaster Diploma.

Forrest had mentors for both his personal and musical development. He was especially inspired by great band leaders and their orchestras, composers, and musicians. He squeezed into his schedule and out of his pocketbook every Big Band performance in Dallas and in New York City that he possibly could.

Forrest found time to send off fan letters to those he admired. Upon hearing an international broadcast from Grosvenor House, he corresponded with Jack Harris, director of London's Embassy Orchestra. One photo of a 12-piece band is signed, "Sincerely, Bernie Cummins," a jazz drummer and dance bandleader from 1919 through the early fifties. Receiving a postcard, Forrest likely caught Oregon-born George Olsen's orchestra in Eddie Cantor's Broadway hit *Whoopee!* and/or listened to him on NBC radio. Vincent Lopez, in white tie and black tux, who was a pianist and one of America's most popular bandleaders through the forties, sent Forrest a photo.

"Del Staigers, World Famous Cornetist," offered words of advice for young musicians. Born in 1899, Staigers became perhaps the greatest cornet soloist in history during a century-long period when such cornet musicians were the pop stars of the day. Radio and recording artist Staigers performed as soloist with the bands of John Philip Sousa and Edwin Franko Goldman. His most touching moment came when he was selected from among many talented cornet soloists to play "Taps" at John Philip Sousa's gravesite in March 1932. Forrest likely took Staigers' pointed advice to heart:

   1.   Practice to accomplish one thing at a time. This requires thought . . . all the time . . . . When you practice correctly you form correct habits.

2. If you cannot believe what your teacher tells you, give him up.

3. Procure the best instrument possible . . . .

4. Do not be jealous of the fellow who sits ahead of you in your section. Practice until you are capable for his chair and eventually it will be yours. By practice, I . . . mean ensemble practice . . . .

5. Listen to your leader even if he is wrong. It is still his band, and he is boss.

6. Study transposition. If possible . . . the Italian system of transposition by clefs . . . the method employed by all successful symphony and opera players . . . . Some day transposition will be an absolute necessity . . . If you are prepared, you get the job. If not, you will remember my words.

7. Do not talk about the ability of your colleagues unless you have something good to say about them. All the world despises a knocker.

8. When a veteran in the business gives you advice, listen carefully...Do not argue with him. When you are alone, try out his advice. The chances are a hundred to one that he is right. If he is wrong, you do not have to accept it. Remember: He meant well.

9. Most great performers are playing the same mouthpiece they started with.

Another mentor was John Philip Sousa, a composer and conductor known especially for military and patriotic marches. His most famous compositions were "The Washington Post," "Semper Fidelis" (official march song of the US Marine Corps), and "The Stars and Stripes Forever" (national march of the United States). Sousa served as Director of the US Marine Corps Band from 1880 until 1892 when he formed his own band. He led the "President's Own" band under five American presidents, played at two inaugural balls, and represented the United States at the Paris Exposition in 1900. Having become known as the most famous musical act in the world, his band performed at 15,623 concerts between 1892 and 1931.

In later years, Forrest often listened to his phonograph collection of recordings from the Big Band and jazz eras. Al Hirt was a favorite. In the late 1950s on our first visit to New Orleans, he and I shared a special connection when I wheeled him down Bourbon Street to hear the jazz musicians at Preservation Hall. I can still see him tapping his hand on his knee keeping beat to the music in the small, dimly lit, smoke-filled room. He was once again living his dream.

No Band Trips but Other Musical Opportunities. At the beginning of the 1931-32 school year, Forrest's fifth at SMU, *Scrapbook* newspaper clips mention only two football games that season, both held out of state. The band likely performed at all of SMU's home games, but the Great Depression sidelined funds for the band to accompany the football team to "away" games. Traveling to Annapolis in November to play Navy again, the team was apparently treated like royalty. SMU won 13-6.

With the deepening economic crisis no benefactors surfaced to finance a band trip to San Francisco with the team to play top-ranked St. Mary's Gaels in Kezar Stadium. The *Campus* reported that Band members threatened to turn in their uniforms if they did not go amidst rumors until the last week that they might. Some members requested a guarantee of a big trip the following year or there would be no band. Forrest took a more conciliatory stance when quoted in a news article entitled "Band Boys Sad Over Losing Trip to West Coast:"

> We'll just have to listen to the game over the radio Saturday . . . . No united effort for disbandment exists among the band members. I am disappointed that we cannot make the trip because . . . [the band leader] has worked hard with us and because it would be best to carry the band on our first West Coast game. But we don't have the money.

In San Francisco in early December, the football team suffered its only defeat of the season, perhaps because their loyal tooters could not cheer them on. They won the 1931 Southwest Conference championship anyway.

Forrest served as organizer/director of the Highland Park Methodist Church's Young People's Department orchestra. An 18-piece ensemble conducted by band colleague Floyd Patterson, the group presented a concert in November with works by Austrian composers Mozart and von Suppe, a harmonica piece by Forrest's friend Stuart Sewell, and a vocal solo. Forrest devoted several *Scrapbook* pages over the years to the class and its leader, Dr. H. K. Taylor—a testament to how much both meant to him.

Usually receiving accolades for his appearances at churches, Forrest performed two programs at Dallas' First Methodist Church in December. In one he played "Song of the Volga Boatmen," and welcomed a thank-you letter stating: "No part of the program was better done, or more thoroughly appreciated than yours. The whole occasion was 'toned up' by your music." At the Greater Young People's Banquet he was listed in the program as "An Ace on the Trumpet." After playing a cornet solo for a Yuletide Musical at M.E. Church South, the Ennis, Texas, paper called him a "cornet soloist of wide reputation" and "truly an artist in his line."

Sometime during the school year 1931-32, the Pony Quartette was organized. The musical group consisted of Forrest and band colleagues Floyd Patterson, Ben Fulghum, and Rolland Storey. However, Rolland, Forrest, and Floyd were billed as "the original trumpet trio," who began performing together a year before the quartette was organized. There was no mention of where this group performed. Once again Forrest's extra-curricular activities dominated *Scrapbook* rather than his college course work.

THE PONY TRIO, 1931
L TO R: ROLLAND, FORREST, FLOYD

KRLD Radio Broadcasts. In the midst of an already jam-packed fall semester schedule, Forrest added new excitement to his musical repertoire: performing 15-minute broadcasts over KRLD Radio. Having played trumpet solos at this Dallas radio station five times previously, he began a new series of recitals on November 17, 1931, called Studio Musicale broadcast every Tuesday from 9:45 p.m. to 10 p.m. Each show generally featured five pieces, including "Taps," which he played to end each broadcast. Forrest was accompanied by one of three volunteer pianists.

Several Western Union telegrams and letters arrived in care of the station from friends and strangers who heard his broadcasts. Studio Musicale's featured artist, Forrest wrote and typed the "continuity" (script in radio lingo) sheets announcers used for his broadcasts. Forrest noted the adrenaline rush this recognition gave him:

> Telegrams and cards such as these make radio artists feel great . . . . Fan mail is a blessing! . . . . My programs have been heard from Coast to Coast—from San Bernardino, California, to Atlanta, Georgia.

When asked to add the weekly broadcasts, Forrest simply could not say no. Broadcasting his own show boosted his ego and fed his soul. These extra-curricular activities required great effort on his part and that of unknown others who transported him to and from the radio station at night. No mention was made of his disability, leaving the casual radio listener to assume Forrest was mobile.

Medical End to a "Good Thing." Apparently well-received, these radio broadcasts might have lasted indefinitely. However, they came to a sudden halt two months later. Forrest's last written entry in *Scrapbook I* revealed why he had to quit:

> The series of radio recitals was suddenly cut short due to a nervous breakdown I suffered around January 15th. The last broadcast was on the night of Jan. 19th— I got out of the bed to make my engagement. Due to health reverses I've been forced to temporarily give up radio work, which I enjoy so much.

Forrest pencils into the beginning of *Scrapbook II*:

> 1931-32 Another crack-up—as a result of a nervous breakdown—a forced withdrawal from Law School and another half year lost, which in reality means no credit for whole year—I got sick before mid-term finals . . .Better luck next time!!!

The Courier Times, Tyler's newspaper, dated January 25, 1932, reported that "Forrest Clough Is Near Nervous Collapse." The article states:

> The many friends of Forrest Clough will regret to hear that after making such a brilliant record at S.M.U. for the last three years, he was forced to

drop the last week of the past semester, his first in the School of Law, because of a near nervous collapse. With his physical handicap and weakened condition, brought on by studying too hard and the nerve strain of a too rigid course, it seems that he will not be able to continue with law school work . . . .

Some might conclude from reading *Scrapbook* that it was the voluminous extra-curricular activities that interfered with his legal studies rather than the difficulty of the law course!

A doctor's handwritten medical prescription from the Dallas Medical and Surgical Clinic on January 29 ordered what Forrest needed in order to heal:

1. Eat regularly—a balanced diet daily.
2. Turn out light at 10 p.m. and take two tablets—every other night—Do not repeat.
3. After 1 wk. (or 3 medicine nights) take only one tablet—one or two wks.
4. Nujol or Emulserol at p.m. or a.m. & p.m.
5. Stay awake during day and keep busy.

The prescription gives us a glimpse of how the "nervous breakdown" may have manifested: stomach upsets, acid reflux, constipation, insomnia. No name was given for the two pills he took every other night, but presumably they were some kind of sedative. Nujol is mineral oil for constipation. Although his constantly pushing himself was what brought on his breakdown, it is interesting that the doctor told him to "keep busy." This prescription was a common home remedy for depression in the days before Prozac and prior to bringing mental health counseling out of the closet.

Being forced to abandon his dream of a legal career must been quite a blow to Forrest, who may have felt like a failure. He never discussed his interest in the law with me. Following his death, my mother revealed his wish to become a lawyer, but the law school classes were on the second floor and prevented him access, as there were no elevators. Perhaps he openly blamed this lack of access as his reason for dropping out of law school. But, there were other motivators: his nervous breakdown and loss of physical stamina, the difficulty of his law classes, and, not least, his unwillingness to give up the band and other activities in order to focus on his law studies.

Following his exposure to the entertainment world and broadcasting in New York City, he may have simply lost interest in the tedium of law school in favor of a more immediate way to express his talents. He received get well cards and letters empathizing with his decision to drop out of law school and the need to take care of himself. Forrest felt close to his cousin, J.D. King, Jr., who lived in Ennis and responded to Forrest's letter regarding his decision:

> I am . . . glad . . . you feel satisfied . . . it would be a very dull life for anyone
> . . . if he were concentrating his entire efforts on some vocation that was
> not within his interests . . . you have the brains to be a good lawyer or
> anything else . . . the man who really succeeds is the one who is following
> the vocation he feels most interested in . . . . I am very glad . . . you are in a
> position to change to some course more desirable to you. You have the
> brain, ambition, and nerve to be a very successful man . . . .

Did Forrest really tell J.D. he was no longer interested in law? Did he mention his other budding career interests? Or did he simply want to save face in the midst of another medical setback? No one knows. However, it is clear from his enthusiasm about his KRLD radio shows that broadcasting was something he really enjoyed. It must have been on his mind as one way to escape the rigors of law school and combine his love for music with making public presentations.

A letter of encouragement signed "Your 2nd Mother" probably came from Mrs. Lewis Newton. Dr. Newton was a colleague of G.O.'s who taught at North Texas State University (NTSU) in Denton. The Newtons were good friends of the Cloughs from their earlier Tyler days. Josephine Newton, a daughter close in age to Forrest, sent him her sonnet that appeared in a publication of unknown origin called "The Avesta:"

SONNET
by Josephine Newton

I wanted all of life to be a song
Like golden rainbow colors in the wind;

I wanted souls to be gigantic, strong,
That little passions could not break nor bend;
I wanted all of love to be ideal,
Outlasting death, or time, or distance far,
Lending power to those who lack the will
To build their lives to touch the highest star.

But now I know that life is but a name
For puppet motions in the claws of fate,
And love burns out; it is a short-lived flame
That leaps toward sudden joy and turns to hate.
Dear God! I wanted all of life ideal,
But now I only ask for something real.

Josephine likely wrote the sonnet while recovering from a failed romance. She sent it with an inscription to her old friend Forrest: "It's too bad both our sentiments are like this at such an age, isn't it? But just remember me when I was much more optimistic and had my illusions. I'll remember you the same way—and all the grand times we've had all our life. After all, I think we have the same ideas about things—so we understand each other. I'll always love my pal, Forrest. Josephine." (Apparently, Josephine's troubles did not last long for Forrest saved her wedding announcement from August 1933.) Josephine's allusion to Forrest's similar mood presumably reflected his recent health crisis and the decision to drop out of law school—or could he have been suffering from a thwarted romance as well? Recuperating at home left Forrest with too much "alone" time for someone who lived on adrenaline and needed his friends around.

Wasting no time in seeking a new career direction, Forrest queried a Hollister friend working at the YMCA regional headquarters in Atlanta. Claud Nelson discouraged him from taking on the responsibility of running the YMCA student association at SMU and from going into YMCA work full-time. He felt Forrest could make a "wonderful contribution" with his "contagious spirit" and his "musical ability" as a volunteer or part-time worker sharing the responsibility with two or three other workers. Nelson probably felt the physical demands of the Y job would be too much for Forrest to handle on his own.

Another Hollister friend, under the impression that Forrest had had a bad case of the flu, spoke of Forrest's need to build up his physical reserve.

Perhaps Forrest had failed to mention his nervous collapse to his friends outside the Dallas and Tyler communities because his Southern values considered anything akin to a mental breakdown to be a weakness, a taboo subject.

—✦—

During his convalescence in the winter and spring of 1932, Forrest glued himself to the radio. If he could not do his own broadcasts, he could certainly enjoy being a listener. He noted a "memorable radio broadcast" honoring the bicentennial birthday of George Washington given by President Herbert Hoover before a joint session of Congress. In addition to a chorus of 12,000 school children singing "America," John Phillip Sousa, just before his death, directed the combined army, navy and marine bands in playing his own "George Washington Bicentennial March" and "Hail to the Chief."

Forrest also heard a humorous radio sketch by Eddie Cantor, D.D. (Depression Doctor), who was treating Uncle Sam for terrible stresses he had been under in recent years. After reminding Uncle Sam of previous, far worse sicknesses in his life, such as 1776 and the internal trouble of 1865 that nearly upset the whole system, Dr. Eddie said:

> You haven't even got a bad cold now. Your blood pressure is a little too low and your temperature is below normal but everything will go up soon; the worst is over . . . . The time you were really sick was late in 1928 and during '29. That's when you . . . were running really high fever . . . suffering from enlargement of the spendiorum, speculationitis, and inflationary rheumatism. And you didn't even know it . . . you spent 1929 under the influence of intoxicating ideas. You got a drink of that Wall Street cocktail . . . one drink and you get a seat on the curb with your feet in the gutter . . . but you didn't get a headache until 1931. . . .
>
> In 1929 you went on a spree, in 1930 you had to be put to bed and 1931 was the morning after the year before. But now, do what I tell you. Keep cheerful . . . . If you think you are in the soup, get acquainted with the people who could thank God if they could get a bowl of soup . . . . You've got plenty of assets, Uncle Sam . . . the place I want you to visit especially is the Grand Canyon . . . the biggest, deepest, widest place to drop all your troubles and start off fresh for 1932.

Forrest may have seen Cantor's radio sketch about the trauma of Americans as a metaphor for what he was experiencing. One of his favorite radio personalities suggested that he simply pick himself up and make a fresh start.

Forrest saved several news pieces about SMU's success and growth in the seventeen years since it had opened its doors in 1915. By 1932 the SMU College of Arts and Sciences, in which Forrest was enrolled, had 1,532 students, over two times more than at its beginning. Full-time teaching staff had increased from 18 to 73 and had published 30 books and innumerable articles. In its short history, SMU had already produced three Rhodes Scholars. Nearly half of the full-time faculty possessed doctoral degrees, at last including G.O. Over half were Democrats and Methodists. The rest were mostly Protestants. There were no Catholics.

However, the national economic turmoil was finally having its effect on SMU, its students, and its staff. Financial resources to sustain the school's growth had not kept pace, and the university had to spend scarce endowment funds on infrastructure and maintenance rather than program expansion. With the increasing depression, SMU's enrollment began to decline, which brought with it staff lay-offs, heavier teaching loads, and a 20% salary cut for all employees that lasted through 1934. It was so dire in mid-1934 that salaries were cut to 50% for three months. In 1935, after cuts, G.O.'s salary would have been approximately $2,500-$3,000, depending on his rank. Finally, in the 1936-37 academic year, salaries were restored to 84% and by the early forties to their full 1932 level.[54] No wonder things were tight at home.

Forrest wrote an editorial for SMU's student newspaper, the *Campus*, that showed his concern about the decline in convocation attendance and thus spiritual interest, student indifference to religion, and their need for scientific proof of God. Forrest asserted that "faith or hope in a profound Providence is the only sustaining spirit in life." Dr. Selecman, as university president and a Methodist minister, shared his publication *Christ or Chaos* with Forrest and likely conversed with him about spiritual disinterest during hard times.

Although still recuperating and not enrolled in classes, Forrest jumped into campaigning that spring for brother Ancel's student council race. He wheeled around campus handing out flyers and cards. Ancel won one of the five seats on the council with 374 votes, "something unusual in the political history of the school" because he was a "non-fraternity man," according to a news clip. Apparently, Greek society members were the campus leaders and lived very separate lives from the majority of SMU students.

Another Hospitalization.

Only four months after Forrest's nervous collapse, he was hospitalized again, this time with an unrecorded ailment. According to family legend, Forrest received a black widow spider bite on his lip while drinking a glass of milk during a visit with relatives in Ennis. His sister Margaret, then only nine years old, remembers the swelling being so bad and ugly that her parents would not let her see him. In the middle of the night someone drove Forrest the 35 miles from Ennis to Dallas to the hospital.

On May 14, 1932, a doctor's prescription from the Dallas Medical and Surgical Clinic supports the spider bite idea:

1. Diet as desired—force fluids.
2. Citrocarbonate two (2) teaspoonfuls at 8-12-4 & 8.
3. Hot applications—salt one teaspoonful for pint of water—for 1 hr. during day at 8-12-4- & 8.
4. Movol Tab 1 at bedtime.
   Repeat if quite restless.

Forrest's determination and encouragement from family and friends kept him going. He had encountered in little more than two years a tonsillectomy with major loss of blood, a nervous breakdown, and a poisonous spider bite, all of which challenged his career goals.

The summer of 1932 offered Forrest continued opportunity to recuperate. He did not go to either Hollister or the band conservatory, perhaps due to lack of funds, but did play a trumpet solo in late August at the First Methodist Church South in Dallas. One in-state family vacation took them to Junction, Texas, near Austin, to visit an academic colleague of G.O.'s. Dr. Wisseman's farm, located next to the South Llano river, flooded with a 30-foot rise while the Cloughs were visiting. Margaret remembers the flooding and the fact that they all had to move quickly into a different, smaller cabin on higher ground. Since Ancel was away working in the Louisiana oil fields, some other strong individual had to move Forrest in a hurry.

In August the family motored to the Panhandle of Texas to visit Forrest's Grandmother Mary's twin sister Marina Deason and her family. Holding their skirts at knee length, the two sisters went wading in a stream at Palo Duro Canyon, 25 miles southeast of Amarillo. Their husbands Dan and Samuel (Granddad Popee), Margaret and others went swimming while Forrest donned a hunter's pith helmet and "waded" in the water on the back of a strapping male. Returning to Amarillo where his aunt lived, Forrest performed trumpet solos, including "Old Rugged Cross," at two Sunday services for the Polk Street Methodist Church.

The lengthy nine-month recuperation from two medical setbacks gave Forrest renewed energy to change career directions and start over again in the fall of 1932. The big national campaign for President was under way following FDR's nomination on

FORREST'S "NAUTICAL MELODY"
IN THE COOL STREAM, 1932

the Democratic ticket to challenge President Hoover. Forrest would cast his vote for FDR, a fellow polio survivor. He could not have known then how FDR's election would bring national awareness to the crippling disease.

President Roosevelt's Bout with Polio. Several biographies document Franklin Roosevelt's polio in August 1921 and efforts to overcome its paralyzing consequences. His case illustrates the limited knowledge doctors had at that time about treating those paralytic polios who did not die from the disease. FDR, exhausted from a stressful lawyer's workload, traveled to Campobello, the family's vacation home off the coast of New Brunswick, Canada. He went to bed feeling quite ill one night soon after arriving, lost the ability to walk over the next couple of days, and was misdiagnosed for ten days. The family summoned a doctor vacationing nearby who ordered deep massage. This turned out to be a harmful and painful torture as it reportedly hastened and worsened paralysis, causing him to lose the use of most muscles.

Eventually, Dr. Robert Lovett was called in from Boston and diagnosed polio. Dr. Lovett's book on the care of the paralyzed patient had been published in 1916 and laid the groundwork for treating patients in the 1920s, FDR being one of them. He divided the disease into three stages: the acute, the convalescent, and the chronic. The acute lasted until muscle tenderness disappeared. In the convalescent stage it was determined how best to restore muscle function. In the chronic stage surgical procedures were introduced to improve muscular function, often transplanting nerves and tendons. For FDR, Lovett prescribed hot baths and no massage. FDR was paralyzed from the waist down, his arms were weak, thumbs, bowels and bladder were unable to function, and he could not sit up or turn over. Eleanor and his assistant Louis Howe nursed him. He was dependent on Eleanor to help him with all his basic bodily needs.

After a month at Campobello, he was taken to a hospital in New York City where he stayed for six weeks before being taken in late October to their home on E. 65th Street. During his convalescence FDR was confined to bed because his doctors knew little about helpful treatment. This caused his muscles to atrophy, and the sinews behind his knees tightened up. So his legs were put into plaster casts with wedges behind the knees that were expanded daily, forcing the legs to straighten out a little more, an extremely painful procedure. [55] Over the winter of 1922, FDR regained use of his bodily functions and strength in his upper body and lower back. Because his paralyzed leg and hip muscles did not improve, he was fitted with crutches and braces and, with a pelvic band, he was finally able to stand up erect.

For three years he worked hard at physical therapy, various kinds of exercises and treatments, and walking in his braces every day—trying to regain strength, hoping to overcome his paralysis. Eventually, in 1924 he found some relief in the warm waters of a rundown spa in Bullocksville, Georgia. There FDR could walk in the water for two hours without excessive fatigue or dehydration. He felt he had received such relief and improvement at the resort that he bought the place, renamed the town and the spa Warm Springs, and opened his popular treatment center for those afflicted with infantile paralysis. Polios were treated there for well over twenty years, many on scholarships.

Denial of any disability by polios and their families was the primary coping mechanism of polio survivors as they encountered the fears expressed by much of society. FDR was a prime example. So fearful his disability would ruin his chances in politics, he did everything possible to hide his affliction from the public. The press was never allowed to question him about his disability, nor were they permitted to photograph him getting into or out of vehicles, onto stages, or sitting in a wheelchair, except for one photo with a young girl that is publicly available. He never discussed his affliction or his painful treatments, portraying his condition to the public as a non-event. During the seven years of his rehabilitation, prior to running for governor of New York, he had complete confidence that he would walk again and practiced walking with his crutches and braces every day. Simply walking, supported by one of his sons as he always was in public, was extremely painful for him.[56] He refused to acknowledge unpleasant falls, insisted on good cheer at all times, and never complained regardless of the pain. All polios in the early-and-mid-century era adhered more or less to a similar persona they displayed to the world.

ILLNESSES FORCE A CHANGE IN DIRECTION: 1932-1935

CHAPTER FIVE

TOWARD A B.A. IN GOVERNMENT: 1932-34

Having lost a full year and a half of college credit, Forrest had to adjust his vocational goals since law school was no longer an option. Traveling across country with the band and his 1929 summer experiences in New York City with the family certainly broadened his career horizons. He already had a large number of credits in government acquired for his law degree to graduate with a BA in that field. The short-lived broadcasts of his musical programs on KRLD-radio the previous year had whetted his appetite for more on-the-air adventures. He hoped a degree in government, and perhaps journalism afterward, would give him a good background for news broadcasting. Once again, Forrest managed to set aside the disappointment of abandoning his original goal for one more practical.

At the beginning of the 1932-33 academic year, an SMU Mother's Club booklet listed Mrs. G.O. Clough as head of the club's year book and member of the executive committee, thus allowing her to experience the campus life that so consumed her husband and two sons. The annual M Book publication confirmed Ancel M. Clough as one of five representatives on the Student Council from the College of Arts and Sciences. Another page spelled out SMU songs with complete lyrics, beginning with Forrest's "Hail to our College." The Clough family, both parents and sons, were quite visible on campus.

The fall football season found the band traveling with the team to Texas Tech in Lubbock and hosting Rice in Dallas (at the new Fair Park Stadium that became known as the Cotton Bowl in 1936), and Texas A&M in Ownby Stadium on the SMU campus. Once again, lack of funds kept the Mustang band in Texas and forced Forrest to focus on other things.

Following the upcoming Presidential elections with great interest, Forrest felt the country needed a change in the midst of the Great Depression and saved an 11-page monograph by Francis P. Garvin titled "Fair Play for Him that Overcometh." Many people opposed FDR's candidacy and used his paralysis to promote the idea he was not up to the job. Garvin noted many prominent doctors who had examined FDR and certified that "his health and powers of endurance are such as to allow him to meet any demand of private and of public life." Indeed, numerous life insurance companies joined together to insure FDR's life for $500,000 in October 1930, naming the Georgia Warm Springs Foundation for the Study and Cure of Infantile Paralysis as the beneficiary.

Garvin cited several famous people who had overcome major health obstacles and gone on to greatness. President Andrew Jackson, plagued throughout his life with tuberculosis, endured hemorrhage after hemorrhage through two terms as President. Louie Pasteur had paralyzed limbs, Thomas Edison was a diabetic, and the list went on. He stated: "Vote for or against him on any other grounds, if you will, but he has demonstrated in his fight that . . . you cannot . . . base your vote on lack of health, lack of courage, or lack of character."

An election campaign poem sung to the tune of "Frankie and Johnnie" promoted FDR (Frankie) and John Nance Garner (Johnnie) to run our Ship of State. The November 1932 elections voted in a new President who, although he would not be sworn in till March 1933, gave Americans hope he could solve the economic crisis and joblessness brought on by the Depression.

A Surprising Medical Problem. A few days after the election, on November 11, 1932, a news article in a local paper announced: "Band Soloist Has Serious Illness" and "Forrest Clough Undergoes Major Oper-ation; Is Now Recovering." Operated on for acute appendicitis, Forrest was hospitalized in room 203 at Dallas Medical and Surgical Center. Brother

Ancel was quoted as saying he was improving and getting along as well as could be expected.

So much was made over his hospitalization this time because it was his second appendectomy! Everyone, especially his parents, thought Forrest had had his appendix removed eight years earlier and were shocked at this latest episode. Apparently, when his appendix ruptured at age 14, doctors had simply sewn him up and never removed it, figuring he was going to die anyway. They did not tell his parents. In retrospect, how else could one explain the excruciating pain he suffered following the first operation before the dedicated Tyler osteopath saved his life?

At some point Forrest was moved to Room 215, spending over a month in the hospital and experiencing a painful convalescence. Perhaps Forrest got an infection. Why would a routine appendectomy require such a long hospitalization? During this illness, Forrest received many cards and flowers, the majority of them from female friends. One attested to his remarkably cheery spirit and brought him up to date on the little dog named Pep that followed the midget pony Peruna around campus. (Peruna was gifted to the student body to be the Mustang mascot in 1932.) The Cheerful Cherub wrote him two short poems with hand-drawn pictures of a patient in a hospital bed.

Although he had withdrawn from law school, Forrest received an invitation to the Law Students Association banquet in mid-December 1932. Having been released from the hospital on December 10, he surely did not attend a banquet that might have been a bittersweet reminder of his vanished career dream. Nor was there any indication whether he was able to complete the semester's schoolwork.

Forrest used the December holiday season to begin a recuperation that would last through the winter. A Christmas telegram arrived in Dallas from his Mother and Dad, indicating that Forrest did not spend Christmas with them in Ennis. Perhaps Ancel stayed home with him.

Maggie, Forrest, and Popee celebrated Maggie's and her father's joint birthday on January 19, 1933, as they had done and would continue to do until 1941 when Popee died at age 91. Hearty old soul, he stepped on a nail climbing on the roof of his chicken coop. According to Margaret, the foot became infected, gangrene set in, and his foot was amputated before he succumbed.

WITH MAGGIE AND POPEE
ON THEIR JOINT BIRTHDAY, 1933

On March 30 Eddie Cantor and George Jessel packed the Palace Theater's 5,000 seats in Dallas, twice performing their collaboration of *Pals*. A local paper proclaimed Cantor a national institution, the second most important citizen next to President Roosevelt. He eclipsed Al Jolson and Will Rogers as the "biggest hit of radio, stage and screen" and took his public persona seriously. He frequently put in a good word for his colleague in Washington, who was "working a jigsaw puzzle" and needed only the audience's "confidence" and "cooperation."

At age 41, Cantor was called "the great commoner" for getting out and talking with people about their lives, their children, their gas bills and telephone service, and trying to get his audience out of their blue funk over the national situation. Forrest went backstage and met Cantor in his dressing room after the show, obtaining his autograph on the playbill. He penned the comment: "A great chap!!"

In the campus elections of spring 1933 Forrest campaigned for band and journalism buddy, Stuart Sewell, who ran for Associate Editor of *The Semi-Weekly Campus* and later would become his roommate. By early May Forrest was apparently recovered enough from his appendectomy to resume a full schedule, although he likely had lost at least a semester of college credit. He played in the orchestra at Farsity, a Men's Pan-Hellenic program that portrayed life on an American university campus, tempered with local color from SMU. Later that month the Arden Club of SMU did a presentation of *Macbeth*, with the program listing Forrest and Floyd Patterson as the musicians.

Forrest missed the yearly YMCA retreat in Hollister, probably due to lack of resources, but received many notes from friends who did attend. Male and female alike, they all missed him and his horn, which they could still hear echoing from the hills. Meanwhile, he joined his friend Robbie D and her beau Bill on an outing to White Rock Lake in Dallas. A local newspaper featured a photo of Margaret with her kitty Little Babe.

Four summer wedding invitations arrived along with a letter from Senorita Haydee Avecedo G, daughter of a Lt. General in the Ecuadorian Army and a medical student at Guayaquil University. Forrest corresponded in English and she wrote back in Spanish, sending along an 8x10" glamour photo of herself. How they became pen pals is not known. Forrest admired many women from afar and surely harbored mixed feelings as he watched family and friends walk down the aisle that summer.

During the 1933-1934 academic year—24-year-old Forrest's seventh at SMU—he and other band members practiced three days a week. They did a series of programs every Friday afternoon over WFAA Radio in conjunction with athletic forecasts given by various Southwest Conference coaches.

The 1933 M Book again listed the lyrics to "Hail to Our College." Full pages dedicated to the YMCA and YWCA student campus associations, invited students to join. Fraternities and sororities were merely mentioned by name. These Y organizations, including their summer camp retreats, served as popular alternatives for those like Forrest who did not pledge Greek social societies.

In mid-October Forrest joined his bandmates in presenting a variety show of two Chautauqua programs in Navasota, Texas, en route to the SMU-Rice game in Houston, the first "away game." The following day they played a sacred concert at First Methodist in Houston. The *Houston Post* reported: "Rarely, if ever, has a college band been known to remain after a football game to offer a sacred concert." It also described the band's versatility and the national reputation it had gained.

The Big Trip to San Francisco.
The Big Trip to San Francisco. The band desperately wanted to accompany the team to San Francisco in December to play St. Mary's Gaels

in Kezar Stadium. As a fundraiser to support their hoped-for trip to California, the boys held their first ever Pigskin Revue in early November in McFarlin Auditorium, which introduced a tradition that continues today. A local newspaper stated the program was a "loosely connected series of skits, music, songs, and oddities." Besides the band's music, Tom Johnson, a.k.a. Minnard the Magician, performed along with ex-SMU football stars from 1923-1933 and the band's first ever sweetheart leading other co-eds in song.

But more money was needed to pay the band's expenses to San Francisco. The manager of the Melba Theater, a benefactor, offered the band a percentage of two show receipts. The band, including Forrest, gave two preview performances in front of the theater at 11:30 before Friday and Saturday midnight showings of *The Sweetheart of Sigma Chi*. In mid-November the band accompanied the team and 1,500 students to Shreveport, Louisiana, for the SMU-Centenary grid clash. The boys took charge of concession sales in an effort to increase their coffers. The band's fund-raising efforts paid off. When one enthusiastic supporter was asked how the band boys managed to make the trip, he replied:

> They used everything but a Texas six gun to get the money. On trips during the regular season, they peddled sandwiches and soft drinks; they had dances in the baggage car and . . . . If you bought a ham sandwich you were lucky to get any ham and it was certain . . . you got no change.

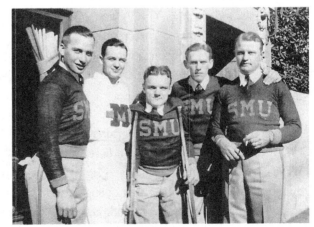

AT UCLA, 1933
L TO R: ROLLAND STOREY, BLAIR MERCER, FORREST, CHARLES MEEKER AND BOB GOODRICH

Reportedly, this was the longest trip made by any school band in the US that year. On Forrest's first trip to the West Coast, the band members left Dallas on the

T&P Railway December 5th for San Francisco. The boys announced their 6:30 a.m. arrival in El Paso with a concert in the terminal that echoed off the nearby Davis Mountains. After the T&P engine and diner were switched in El Paso to the Southern Pacific line, they stopped in Tucson, where they performed a surprise musical rally in front of the Pioneer Hotel. A local taxicab company carried them gratis out to the University of Arizona campus to entertain during the team's practice session. At five that afternoon Forrest cabbed from the hotel to the university's music school to visit his summer conservatory bandmaster Joseph De Luca, who was rehearsing for an upcoming concert. This would be Forrest's last meeting with his mentor, who died in 1935 at age 40.

Back on the Sunset Limited, a.k.a. the Gold Coast Special, the group rolled on to Los Angeles (L.A.). The alias may have referred to the $240,000 in gold bullion destined for the California mint the train carried under armed guard. In L.A. they paraded up Fifth Street by Pershing Square to the Hilton Hotel for breakfast and an overnight stop. That afternoon the band made a surprise appearance at the University of Southern California (USC) while the Mustangs practiced.

USC's *Daily Trojan* exclaimed how Director Bob Goodrich led the band members from a stately marching tune into a modern jazz number with a flip of his baton and labeled the band "one of the most versatile groups of musicians ever to appear on the campus...playing alma maters

AT UNIVERSITY OF ARIZONA WITH BOB GOODRICH (FRONT LEFT) AND TOM JOHNSON (MIDDLE), 1933

and selections like 'Tiger Rag' and 'Sweet Sue' as well as 'I Shall Not Be Moved' without a bit of music…" Before heading on to San Francisco, the band gave a 10-minute broadcast over KFAC.

After a night in San Francisco at the William Taylor Hotel, a 28-story Art Deco building now used by Cal Berkeley's Hastings School of Law, the musicians paraded down Market Street. They were invited for lunch aboard the S.S. *President Polk*, a passenger ship that was shortly due to depart San Francisco on its 31st circumnavigation of the globe. Forrest appeared on his crutches in photos, although his wheelchair must have been with him. A busy few days for Forrest, but he and his two handlers were keeping up the schedule.

A pep rally led by the band in front of their hotel initiated game-day events on the 9th. Afterwards, Forrest met up with old friends from Hollister before accompanying the band on visits to the Presidio and Mission Dolores, en route to Kezar Stadium in Golden Gate Park. Being first trumpet chair, Forrest joined his bandmates in the bleachers when they performed their game-long repertoire. Remaining in the bleachers, he documented with his Kodak camera the band marching on the field during half-time. After the game, which SMU lost 18-6, friends of his Dallas friend Robert Gengnagal invited Forrest out to dinner and a nighttime tour of the city.

Back to Los Angeles on Sunday along the scenic coast route, the Mustangs overnighted again at the Hilton before touring Fox Studios in Santa Monica the next morning. At the Grauman's Chinese Theater, Forrest spotted Eddie Cantor's signature. However, he knew little at that time about Cantor's ties to FDR and nothing of the March of Dimes campaign yet to unfold.

En route back to Dallas, Forrest enjoyed for awhile the scenery from a chair someone set up for him on the open-air observation platform at the rear of the train. He said it was his favorite spot.

The trip to San Francisco cemented the reputation of the Mustang musicians as probably the hottest college band in the country. They had now traveled coast to coast spreading their music far and wide and over the air waves as well. The *San Francisco Chronicle* commented that the Mustangs were a band of 38 soloists, each of whom could hold his own, and two [male] cheerleaders who came together with jazzy, fast-moving, diverse music "different from any college band in the country. They start playing at the kickoff and…never stop until the final gun."

Instead of simply playing between halves like other college bands, the band performed during the whole contest, setting the game to music. They played soft music while the team captain barked signals on the field and increased the pitch louder and louder as the play took shape and spread throughout the field. The drummer played the key role, going into a rolling crescendo with the start of the play and finishing it off with a vigorous hacking of the bass drum. When Southern Methodist was winning their trumpets exulted, when the team was losing their instruments moaned, sobbed, and pleaded. When the enemy was repulsed the band boys poured scorn through their clarinets, and when one of their boys got off on a long run, they gave him a terrific ride. Thus, Forrest was able to toot his horn the entire game, only missing the half-time marching performance.

A sports writer for the *San Francisco Examiner* asserted, "The band caught the fancy of the crowd, the first time any band has done any such thing since football began in these parts." The band set several endurance records that year, often playing through all four game quarters without a substitution or a time-out. Ed Hughes, sports reporter for the *San Francisco Chronicle,* claimed "that Southern Methodist band . . . kept playing all the time and . . . had the feet of the customers tapping. Boy, how they did play 'There'll Be a Hot Time in the Old Town Tonight,' the national anthem during the Spanish American war."

Friends and family were key elements in Forrest's life. During the holidays he accepted an invitation to an Alpha Delta Pi sorority formal to which he was to come "stag." He saved a news clip about the death of his beloved church youth group leader, Professor H.K. Taylor, age 75. And, he grieved with ten-year-old Margaret the death of her dwarf Russian wolfhound Babe. A local newspaper featured a photo of Margaret and her Persian cat Kitty Babe, who was keeping a vigil over the wolfhound's grave in the Cloughs' backyard. The cat refused to leave the grave for the first two days after its friend was buried. It would not eat much or drink warm milk when taken into the house, plaintively crying at the back door until she was let out to resume vigil over the grave.

Father G.O. addressed the Texas State Teachers Association in early December on "Basic Problems of Education in a Period of National Economic Recovery." FDR had been in office for a year and people were beginning to use the word "recovery" to replace "the great depression."

Forrest must have been saddened by Ancel's December 1933 departure to work for IBM in St. Louis, Missouri. With Ancel gone, Stuart Sewell moved into the Asbury home to help Forrest in exchange for room, board and transportation to his roommate's various activities. The two colleagues remained lifelong friends. Stuart spent many years as editor of the *Asheville Sun-Times* in North Carolina (today the *Citizen-Times*).

L TO R: STUART SEWELL, BLAIR MERCER (YELL LEADER), FORREST IN SAN FRANCISCO, 1933

Always interested in finding a cure for polio, Forrest saved an *Associated Press* article dated January 4, 1934: "Negro Scientist Discovers Mineral Oil in Peanuts Aids Infantile Paralysis Victims." Dr. George W. Carver, head researcher at Tuskegee Institute, said he had not found a cure yet but was hopeful. He had treated 250 patients by rubbing peanut oil on affected limbs and claimed the treatment never failed. Muscles increased in size by actual measurements. After nine applications of massaging oil into the skin, one of his patients "who had been walking with crutches was able to walk with the use of only a cane." Although Carver's assertions may have intrigued Forrest, research revealed that home remedies of hot olive oil, salad oil, or cocoa butter massages, though soothing, were ineffective.[57]

FDR's Birthday Balls. On January 30, 1934, cities all over the country hosted birthday dances to celebrate President Franklin Roosevelt's 52nd birthday. One news clip claimed the President's Birthday Balls were an opportunity to pay tribute to a much-loved first citizen and to the

. . . . valiant battle which he fought to overcome the physical handicap of a mysterious malady. It will celebrate the victory which he has achieved . . . . And, best of all, it will open the way for a further intensive study of the strange disease which in recent years has stricken so many American homes.

The theme for the event was "Dance so that others might walk." Proceeds were meant to recruit "the best of the nation's scientists in the field of medicine to fight the war against this scourge, seeking out its cause, contributing to the restoration of its victims. The facilities of the Georgia resort will be extended." FDR had found that "bathing in the medicinal waters of that resort, performing the exercises which his specialists prescribed, brought strength to his helpless limbs." He wanted to give other polios a similar opportunity.

The first year 4,376 communities joined in 6,000 separate birthday dances held all over the country. A Dallas news clip reported that somewhere between 6,000 and 10,000 persons were expected to attend five balls to be held at three downtown hotels, at the Dallas Athletic Club, and at the Fair Park Automobile building. Five local orchestras played from 8:30-12:30 with a one-hour intermission at 10:15 in order to hear a nationwide broadcast from the Washington, DC, ball (at the Shoreham Hotel to be attended by the First Lady) and a message from FDR speaking at the White House.

The news clip also announced that "Negroes in Dallas" would hold two dances of their own, one at the Pythian Temple and the other at Elks' Rest. Segregation was so entrenched in the thirties and forties, one can easily understand why Eleanor Roosevelt's stand against the DAR (Daughters of the American Revolution) on behalf of Marian Anderson was such a revolutionary statement. When the DAR's Constitution Hall refused Anderson's performance, Mrs. Roosevelt urged Secretary of the Interior Harold Ickes to have her sing before thousands at the Lincoln Memorial in April 1939. Her moving presentation occurred almost 25 years before Martin Luther King's "I Have a Dream" speech in the same location and passage of the 1964 Civil Rights Act ten months later—over 100 years after President Lincoln emancipated the slaves.

Tickets for the balls were priced differently in cities around the country. For each ticket sold, one dollar was destined for the Foundation. The birthday balls were so successful they continued for over ten years, ending with FDR's death in April 1945. On average, the balls raised about $1 million per year. Proceeds from the events were divided between the permanent endowment fund of the Georgia Warm Springs Foundation for Infantile Paralysis and local communities where the balls were held to fund treatment for their victims. One editorial noted it was rare to honor a living person with the pomp equal to an inaugural ball but that FDR deserved it because "the nation is already returning to prosperity." Whether Forrest attended one of the balls is not known, but he saved news articles from all the local papers.

Another Mid-Winter Band Tour. After three years away, Forrest again joined the 1934 mid-winter tour made to nine east Texas towns. The band used the same Pigskin Revue program that had filled their coffers for their 1933 trip to California. A journalism class assignment had Forrest writing up the story for the *Campus*. Filed from Texarkana, TX on February 6, 1934, he penned:

> The nationally famous Mustang band and Varsity entertainers presented the Pigskin Revue of 1934 before a capacity house in the high school auditorium . . . . People in the "Four States" city cheered the . . . group in a two hour program as they desired a show triple its length.
>
> Minnard, the mystifying magician, with his sensational tricks including the escape from the coffin, "Cheating Death," continues to draw the acclaim of the audiences wherever he performs.
>
> . . . . the bandsters . . . including a quartet of beautiful co-eds . . . have played to packed houses every night . . . .
>
> The sacred concerts Sunday afternoon in Commerce and that night in Paris drew capacity crowds . . . . Quite unusual was the fact that Forrest Clough, trumpet soloist, received such hearty applause in his number, "Drink to Me Only with Thine Eyes," that an encore was necessary.
>
> While traveling . . . the trailer in which the band's mascot, Peruna, was riding turned over and proved a near catastrophe for the diminutive mascot, who was not hurt in the least and seemed to enjoy the thrill. Peruna, after having gone through the top of the trailer, was found standing nearby trying to determine the extent of damage . . . .

Forrest did not mind tooting his own horn in the news report, since the acclaim was true. The Shreveport paper described the band's concert at Centenary College and gave similar accolades:

Perhaps the act nearest perfection . . . was that of Forrest Clough, trumpeter, who played exquisitely two trumpet solo numbers. Mr. Clough, who has the use of neither of his legs, was presented by the master of ceremonies as the most widely traveled member of the SMU band.

The band members once again stayed with local citizens. A telegram from H.W. Stilwell sent to Forrest Clough, SMU Band, Clarksville, Tex., stated "We are expecting you to stay with us while in Texarkana." The ten-day winter band trip was grueling by anyone's estimation. Once back in Dallas, a *Campus* news clip read:

> One morning last week, Forrest Clough, trumpetist in the SMU band, met Duvall Williams, bass-clarinetist . . . in the rotunda of Dallas hall.
>   Both boys, tired from their extensive 10-day tour with the band, looked at each other sleepily and grinned.
>   'How do you feel, Dovey?' Clough asked anxiously, seeing that Williams looked as tho he could go no farther.
>   'Well, Clugg, it's like this,' mumbled the sleepy-eyed Williams, 'I'm so tired I've slept 52 hours out of the last 48.'

Soon after returning from the tour, Forrest received a poem titled "The Cripple" by Karle Wilson Baker (1878-1960), a Texas Woman of Letters whose collection of poems barely lost out to Robert Frost for the 1931 Pulitzer Prize. (See flyleaf.) Forrest's female friend "D.N.R." sent it and ended with a personal comment: "To those of us who know you—your personality and your marvelous acceptance of your place in this life—it seems that your 'wings' are so much stronger than ours that the rest doesn't really matter at all!"

While the SMU Board of Trustees elected G.O. the new director of extension and Ancel spent the spring at IBM school in New York City, Forrest pursued his plans for a second bachelor's in journalism. In late March he was chosen to pledge the national professional journalism fraternity Sigma Delta Chi along with several other students. A letter from the national president (and later editor of *The Fort Worth Press*), Walter R. Humphrey, listed requirements for official membership. Forrest was initiated as Sigma Delta Chi pledge at a fraternity dinner in early May 1934.

His roommate Stuart Sewell was elected president and Forrest the treasurer of the organization.

The first half of May was also spent getting out *The Semi-Weekly Campus*, with Sigma Delta Chi pledges and members putting it together on their own. Forrest wrote twelve articles for this edition, including the first-page lead story with his byline. The Unwanted Want Ads of that edition included: "LOST—One pair of false teeth uppers; last seen in my glasses case; case is missing also. Liberal reward if returned to Dr. G.O. Clough, 3482 Asbury." Some journalist's good-humored tribute to Forrest's absent-minded father.

CAMPAIGNING FOR WILBUR CUNNINGHAM

Forrest followed the campus's political campaigns, actively supporting one candidate. A *Dallas Times-Herald* article titled "Cripple's Chair is Used as Billboard in Student Campaign" reads:

Boasts that he will do anything to help his friends were proven by Forrest Clough, SMU student who attended all his classes in a wheelchair because he once suffered infantile paralysis, when he became an active participant in one of the campus political contests.

That Clough's wheelchair that trundles back and forth through all the corridors of the class buildings would make a fine billboard for campaign advertising had never occurred to any candidates before Wilbur Cunningham, close friend of the professor's son, entered the race for associate editor of *The Semi-Weekly Campus*.

Wednesday morning though, Clough's habitual invalid's chair blossomed out in the corridors of Dallas Hall bearing bright red and blue signs furthering Cunningham's editorship race.

'Cooperation with Capable Cunningham' read the words on the signs plastered all over the wheelchair.

For someone who had had several illnesses in recent years, Forrest showed no signs of slowing down. He was initiated into Pi Sigma Alpha, the national honorary political science fraternity, and was elected its on-campus President for 1934-35. Along with seven other reporters on the *Campus*, he received one of the 43 Gold "M" Awards for service to the student body, recognized for quality of work produced, dependability, accuracy, and interest in the work.

Forrest's graduation activities were plentiful and began in April 1934. First came Piker's Day, an annual event in which the seniors, dressed in costumes, put on a comedic show for the student body. Forrest wore his street attire, perhaps unable to change clothes on campus for another event scheduled soon after. Who would help him? On Senior Recognition Day Class President Rolland Storey turned over the baton to Junior Class President Layton Bailey, Jr. Both leaders were Forrest's musician buddies at a time when band membership was at least as popular as being an athletic star. From late April to early May, Forrest attended a student comic operetta, his senior banquet, a senior luncheon, an open house for the band at First Methodist Church in Fort Worth, an engineering open house on campus, "Farsity 1934," as well as the Men's Panhellenic play, an opera written by Bob Goodrich and Charles Meeker in a musical satire that suggested Gilbert and Sullivan. Someone was busy getting Forrest to and fro.

On May 4, 1934, Forrest purchased his last trumpet—C. G. Conn, Ltd. (Elkhart, Indiana, USA), Cornet #290108. It is the instrument he used in the SMU Pigskin Revue in 1961 and the one he loaned to family friend Wayne Arrowood to use in the 1950s and '60s. His great nephew Shaun used it in the 1990s, and his grandson Nathan is the current owner of this family heirloom.

Putting his new horn to the test, in mid-May Forrest traveled to Corsicana with President Selecman, Coach Morrison, his dad and others to the first meeting of the newly formed SMU ex-students club. The new alumni group hosted a dinner honoring the senior class of Corsicana High. Forrest, Rolland Storey and Bob Goodrich provided musical numbers.

Later in May there were even more end-of-the-season parties to fill Forrest's calendar. Receiving several invitations to spring sorority formals, he wore a white sailor costume to a Phi Delta Theta event at Dallas

Country Club. He escorted a Miss Katherine Waldrep to the band's banquet on May 20. Prior to the beginning of final exams on May 25th there were a few senior class exercises; two senior music recitals of female friends; the Saner oratorical contest; an Arden club play, Shakespeare's "The Two Gentlemen of Verona;" and finally a university convocation and baccalaureate program. He paid a $10 fee to graduate with the group of 223 classmates from eight SMU schools. It is a wonder Forrest obtained two A's and 2 B's in his final college term in spite of his busy extracurricular schedule and recent health challenges.

Forrest received cards and gifts from family and friends. A touching letter from his Grandmother Mary Johnson stood out:

> I am writing you this letter on this, the most momentous day of your life, to try to tell you how great is our love for you, and how we rejoice with you in your graduation. To have achieved such an honor in the face of almost insurmountable obstacles, obstacles before which a less resolute character would have faltered, is to have won the admiration of all who know you, we sincerely congratulate you . . . .
>
> . . . . How nobly you have fulfilled every ambition and surpassed our fondest hopes for you; we look confidently toward the future for still greater achievements; there is no stopping a man of your character and ability.

At last—A B.A. degree, 1934

Remember always dear Forrest to whom you owe your heritage of excellence and strength; your wonderful parents whose untiring devotion has brought you to your present position; give to them always your best.

May our Heavenly Father have you always 'in His blessed keeping.'

Lovingly, Popee and Grandmother

A female friend from Tyler ended her letter to Forrest with the comment: "I don't suppose anybody that ever graduated from SMU has had more friends than you have. And I'm happy to be one of them." Someone else wrote: "What will your alma mater do without that famous 'million-dollar smile' of yours!" These and other tributes must have made Forrest's head swell. Despite the two-and-a-half years of illness, his "Keep On Keeping On" philosophy had paid off.

Warm Springs Efforts. The *Dallas News* ran Forrest's photo along with an article on June 20, 1934:

> Efforts to enlist the aid of the great specialists on infantile paralysis at Warm Springs, Ga., on behalf of Forrest Clough of Dallas, were begun Tuesday when S.D. Flanz of Dallas brought the case to the attention of the directors of the fund raised by the President's Ball . . . . Although confined to a wheel chair, young Clough has mastered the courses leading to a degree [in government] . . . at Southern Methodist completing the work this month. By his persistence despite the handicap he has attracted the interest of a number of Dallas persons who hope that he might be benefited at Warm Springs to the extent, at least, of getting around on crutches. He is the son of Prof. G.O. Clough of the School of Extension.

G.O. received a letter dated June 29, 1934, from the Georgia Warm Springs Foundation that told how the Birthday Balls had generated many applications from among the 200,000 known cases of infantile paralysis in the country at that time. The balls had raised funds for full- and partial-pay Warm Springs charity cases, but there was a 2-year waiting list for those slots. Robert Mack, Service Secretary of the Foundation, urged G.O. to provide a medical report from an orthopedic surgeon, and if approved, send his son as a full-pay client. He further stated:

> With this material . . . we will be in a position to deal intelligently . . . after Dr. Flanz returns to Dallas.
> From Dr. Flanz's conversation he apparently sees a way . . . the financial hurdle can be cleared from your end. It is a sheer physical impossibility to render direct aid to even a fraction of the thousands of worthy cases brought to our attention and it is with the purpose of ultimately doing the greatest good for the greatest number that a portion of the funds contributed during the Birthday Ball parties has been allocated for . . .

attempting to coordinate the orthopedic centers of the country in this common cause . . . .

Apparently, Dr. Flanz made a trip to Warm Springs to promote Forrest's case and later sent medical records. However, nothing more is known about this generous effort by Dallasites interested in the talented young man's welfare. Perhaps the Warm Springs staff did review his medical records but did not believe they could improve Forrest's mobility. More likely, the funds required to send Forrest to Warm Springs as a paying patient simply could not be found. Forrest would have relished camaraderie with fellow polios, whom he had never had the opportunity to meet, and perhaps the chance to encounter FDR himself on retreat to his Warm Springs White House.

Instead of receiving hydrotherapy, Forrest spent most of the summer of 1934 in Dallas, traveling vicariously through letters and postcards sent by friends from such places as Yellowstone, New York, and Clovis, New Mexico, where five band members were playing gigs. Letters came from another band buddy who was cycling around Europe and attending Shakespeare plays in England. He heard from old Hollister friends and received wedding invitations, including that of his cousin Oma, who had lived with the Cloughs for a year prior to her marriage at G.O. and Maggie's home on Asbury Street. Forrest appeared in his bathing costume floating in an inner tube on a lake near Dallas with two male friends. Next to this photo is evidence of one that had been ripped out and the inscription of "R . . . . and Forrest" scratched out. A girlfriend or love interest gone awry?

Ancel had been working at IBM in St. Louis and New York but returned to Dallas in late June. His fiancée Adele Coombs' parents hosted a dinner dance engagement party for the couple on the Peacock Terrace at the Baker Hotel. Forrest collected autographs that evening from Jan Garber's orchestra and jazz band performing a "sweet" style of music similar to that of Paul Whiteman and Guy Lombardo.

The family vacationed in August at Mount Sequoyah, a Methodist retreat center established in 1922 that overlooked Fayetteville, Arkansas. From there they traveled to Springfield, Missouri, where Ancel, on leave from IBM, joined them at a motor court for a couple of days. Finally, they visited Forrest's beloved Hollister, Missouri, and the Y camp at the foot of Presbyterian Hill. Stuart Sewell, who did not graduate until August 1934, held the fort down in Dallas while the Cloughs traveled. His letter complained of the heat, told Margaret he was taking good care of Kitty Babe, and that the key the Cloughs left him did not fit the keyhole—he had to come and go through a window!

Probably disappointed about not going to Warm Springs that summer, Forrest at least rested up for the push to collect his journalism degree the following spring.

CHAPTER SIX

WRITING HIS WAY TO A B.A. IN JOURNALISM: 1933-1935

Perhaps you could say that Forrest backed into his coursework in journalism, having discovered broadcast journalism in the fall of 1932 with his weekly trumpet programs on KRLD radio. He had always loved to write, as evidenced by his many detailed accounts of family travels and news articles for the *Campus*. He enjoyed debating, was interested in world affairs, and had a BA in government to replace the law degree he thought he had wanted.

Forrest was also a performer and performers need an audience. He could get an audience for his trumpet music, but the likelihood of that highly competitive field offering him a paying career was not great given his disability. So, why not journalism? He could write for a newspaper, compose scripts for radio programs, or, better yet, sit behind a microphone. So off he had gone in the fall of 1933 to pursue a second BA degree, fortunate to have family support for this endeavor.

Forrest's tattered journalism notebook contained 121 news articles or clips written for SMU's *Semi-Weekly Campus* newspaper. Crafted during the 1933-34 academic year for his professor, Mr. Henning, Forrest contributed to 42 of the 55 issues. His beat as a cub reporter included the Schools of Government and Education, Mustang Band, Sigma Delta Chi and Theta Sigma Phi (journalism fraternity and sorority). He also tried his hand at several feature articles as well as 27 editorials. These writings demonstrate Forrest's interests, opinions, and concerns during this year and give us a flavor of various issues confronting the US and Europe, e.g., the build-up of National Socialism in Germany as well as the social mores of the times.

Forrest longed for international peace and feared various European trends that pointed to another war. He opposed a narrow brand of economic nationalism that would impose tariffs on imports. A loyal American citizen on national issues, Forrest was also a loyal Mustang who cheered locally his state, college, its teams and students. He took popular stands, not ones to cause controversy or folks to dislike him.

Several editorials reveal Forrest's staunch support for FDR and sympathies for the Democratic Party. In one effusive testament written in March 1934 titled "Roosevelt's First Year," Forrest stated:

> The restorative works of this valiant leader emerge in a blaze of glory, hailed as the greatest measures for restoring prosperity [that] America or any other country has ever known . . . .
>
> Benefits have come to Southern Methodist University in the form of CWA [Civil Works Administration] funds to beautify the campus . . . and . . . enable ambitious, though financially handicapped, students to pursue their studies . . . [130 students received $15 a month for 5 months as federal aid] . . . .
>
> . . . . Franklin Delano Roosevelt can and will restore America to normalcy. For the good of all, let's back the President!

Forrest also lauded President Roosevelt in his January 1934 editorial entitled "An Ace from the Deck?" with regard to the ratification of the Twentieth Amendment to the Constitution ending lame-duck sessions:

> . . . . that the session of Congress . . . will always be remembered as the first regular congressional session ever to meet in January instead of December . . . . For the first time in fifteen years the opening session of Congress was addressed by the President, in person.
>
> . . . . Learning of unprecedented aids-toward-prosperity . . . coast to coast through the N.R.A. [National Recovery Administration] and the New Deal, we are even more assured that with the never-say-die cooperation of each American citizen, Roosevelt and his administrative forces can and will restore our country to 'Happy Days are Here Again!'

Poll taxes were legislated in Texas in 1902, paralleling the actions of several mostly southern states seeking to keep African Americans and other minorities away from the election polls. The taxes worked as well against women and poor whites who could not pay the hefty $1.50-$1.75 fee during the Depression. However, Forrest's "Drive for Taxes" editorial in January 1934 mimicked the sympathies of other Texans who did not question the legislation or its intent:

> The "Pay Your Poll Tax Drive" sponsored by the Young Democratic club of S.M.U. is deserving of careful attention from all young Texans of voting age . . . .
>
> Thursday and Friday, there will be a tax collector at the University to receive payments for poll tax . . . it is the duty of each student of age to secure his poll tax receipt at once, and be ready for the 1934 elections of national and state consequences.
>
> The Campus commends the Young Democratic club for its efforts in this all-important matter.

For his glowing editorials of FDR's recovery program to be published, presumably Mr. Henning, faculty advisor for the Campus, had to be in agreement with this cub reporter's opinions. Stuart Sewell as associate editor and Frederika Wilbur, SMU's first female editor, reported the Democratic Party's views of the majority of SMU faculty and students.

Forrest also kept an eye on international events and wrote with caution about issues surfacing in Europe in the early 1930s. He dedicated one editorial to Premier Benito Mussolini's plans to create a new Italian state that, "though socialistic in part, will retain the principles of capitalism." Citing Mussolini's chief purpose as an attempt "to free the modern industrial system from antiquated feudalistic and individualistic policies based on an 18th century governmental system," Forrest ends his editorial with a wait-and-see attitude about this new style of "governmental machine, of 20th century design . . . . because Mussolini believes his fascism will eventually out-rank all other governmental systems."

Following the break that occurred with the 1917 Bolshevik victory, the US re-established diplomatic relations with Russia by signing the Roosevelt-Litvinov Agreement in November 1933. The Soviets agreed to settle debts incurred by previous Soviet governments owed to the US, to not interfere in America's domestic affairs, and to honor the legal rights of Americans living in the Soviet Union. Forrest's editorial reflects a common belief of the time that the Russians would be a welcome counterbalance to the emerging power of Germany's National Socialist party. Avoiding war was of primary concern, not the existence of two totalitarian dictatorships in Europe. Forrest wrote that:

> President Roosevelt acted wisely in negotiating for recognition of this country of 160,000,000...Russia is a strong advocate for peace, and a friend of the worker.
> .... With the United States and Russia in joint agreement, the international world will feel easier, and more confident that peace of a lasting quality is nearer at hand than ever before.

France was also in Forrest's periscope in the winter of 1934. He expressed his support for Premier Doumergue, called from retirement to quell civil disorder in Paris with "a council of four to have dictatorial powers in case of need." Thirty thousand troops and an enlarged police force would also be available to lend their aid in restoring order throughout the French Republic. Forrest agreed with Sir Philip Gibbs' assertion that "French stability and strength are the chief guarantees of European peace...." Quoting Gibbs in his editorial: "'If these are seriously weakened or overthrown there are hostile powers, with Germany as their leader, who would make terrible use of the situation.'"

Forrest favored FDR's efforts to ensure the American dollar could compete in international trade with the rest of the world. He supported the President's April 19, 1934, executive decree:

> .... forbidding the export of gold, gold bullion or gold certificates from the United States, [which] sent the dollar away from par value. The president's desire to protect the gold reserves of the country against any risk, pending return to the gold standard, and his belief that a lower dollar in terms of foreign exchange would stimulate the consumer's demand, the purchase of commodities, and the recovery of business furnished impetus for such proclamation.
> .... Great praise is due Mr. Roosevelt for his courageous stand against countries, particularly European, trying to make the American dollar fit their own nationalistic desires.

With tensions in Europe mounting over the slow demise of Germany's Weimar Republic, pacifists on campus drew fire from patriots who were supported by the consolidated local American legion units. Forrest had pacifist sympathies and avidly supported Woodrow Wilson's Fourteen-Point plan ratified in 1919 by European allies that established the League of

Nations. However, Wilson could not convince the US Senate or the American public to join the League, and Congress prevented him from attending the 1918 disarmament conference at Versailles. Wilson, in absentia, was unable to prevent the Allies from placing punitive reparations on Germany. Forrest saved a poem by Casper Butler noting that "a stable world has now relapsed, since reparations have collapsed." Germany's war reparations to Allied countries assigned by the Treaty of Versailles were suspended in 1931 by the Hoover Moratorium in an effort to stave off Europe's economic downturn and help the Weimar Republic with its banking crisis.

On the fifteenth anniversary of the conference Forrest scripted a November editorial titled "Is Armistice Permanent?" He stated the world is just as disillusioned as ever with regard to the promise of peace by international understanding.

> That the League of Nations . . . has failed is evidenced by Japan's abrupt adventure in Manchuria and the present German episode in Europe. The League has not failed as an organization, but rather as a body sufficiently strong enough to cope with the nationalistic ambitions of the various nations.
>
> . . . . the Disarmament Conference turned into a free-for-all for advocates of various nationalistic programs . . . . Europe is again swinging to that old system of balance of power so prevalent before America's entrance in the world war. She is on the brink of another armed conflict . . . . The National Socialists, under the leadership of Adolf Hitler, are planning a German state to dominate the continent . . . .
>
> Had the nations of the earth, including the United States, sacrificed their nationalistic desires following the tragic conflict of 1914-18 the course of international peace would be farther down the road toward success.

Forrest pressed for international debates between colleges to be seen as "international literary events likened to present-day international athletic contests." At that time in the fall of 1933, Tulane University was hosting the University of Cambridge, England, whose debaters were on a tour of southern and mid-western colleges.

> World athletic contests, originating with the Olympiad in 756 B.C., have stood the test of time . . . . Such events have brought about friendly competitive relations between the nations represented and have developed a spirit of unity among participants. . . .

In like manner, international literary events would make for a better relationship between nations . . . .

Ideals of international cooperation on many fronts held by Forrest and thousands of others were eventually upended and cleverly used as a ruse by Adolf Hitler when Germany hosted the 1936 Olympics. In 1933 Forrest's concern focused on Hitler's aggression against neighbors in Europe with no inkling of the horrors the world would face over the next twelve years.

Turning to local campus activities, Forrest paid tribute to the Mustang band and its three-day tour to present concerts in the Houston area (Did Forrest go?); to the college's decision to reduce chapel programs to once-a-week to help unify the student body; to the YMCA and YWCA for offering a free skating party on a Saturday night that was attended by 600 students; to SMU's junior debate team's second-place win at the Southwestern Debate Tournament in Durant, Oklahoma; and to the faculty for its decision to move finals up by four days so students would know whether they were going to graduate. He also noted that fall 1933 football attendance was up nationwide for the first time in four years, indicating that "better times, better schedules, and lower prices" were a result of the national economic recovery.

One issue Forrest focused on was that of fraternity versus non-fraternity students at SMU. Apparently student council representatives were fraternity members and non-fraternity folks simply did not participate in the annual class elections. In spring 1934, Forrest wrote an editorial urging all students, both frat and non-frat, to attend the class meeting and exercise their right to vote. He chastised the non-frats:

Fraternity folk have always been on hand at such gatherings, but the non-fraternity group have made themselves conspicuous by their absence. Such a lack of interest manifests itself disastrously to the class group as a whole.

A week later his editorial, entitled "Landslide Conclusion," praised the outcome:

The Better Government party with the help of non-frat members walked away with all major positions tucked under their arms . . . .

Results of this landslide election show quite conclusively that Southern Methodist students value the man . . . rather than the party which backs him . . . . Despite the fact that the fraternities and sororities making up the New Combine party segregated themselves with the boast that they could defeat any person the opposition would run, results speak much louder than fanciful boasts.

Likely, Forrest, as a non-frat man at that time, felt somewhat boastful himself, perhaps believing that his challenging editorial had made a difference in the turnout.

Always a supporter of good manners and institutional rules and not one to defy authority, Forrest claimed the moral upper hand and blasted out at 50-75 unruly freshman as "poor sports." Their "lowly and unruly conduct" "disastrously marred" the annual Pikers' Day celebration, a day of "dress-up festivities on the part of the seniors....It is unbelievable that students attending a university of such high standing would stoop to such tactics."

Forrest wrote one local editorial focused outside the campus in celebration of the 98th anniversary of Texas Independence from Mexico in March 1934. He remembered the Alamo and the sacrifices made there in 1836, which led to large enlistments for General Sam Houston's army that defeated Santa Ana's forces only a month later.

Far more examples of Forrest's straight news reporting, as opposed to his editorials, surfaced in his journalism notebook. We can glean some of his interests but less of his opinions from these samples. He wrote stories about people he admired or were his friends when they engaged in a newsworthy activity, such as the exploits of Charles Gill Morgan, Forrest's band colleague from 1927-1928.

Charles Morgan's Trip to Antarctica. For Sigma Delta Chi's edition of the *Campus* in May 1934, Forrest's front-page lead story was titled: "SMU Student At Pole with Byrd." Dr. Charles Morgan, an SMU alum, was chief geologist and geophysicist of the second Byrd expedition to Antarctica. After finishing SMU, he did graduate work at Harvard, then returned to SMU as a geology instructor until he left for the expedition. Forrest wrote several articles about Morgan's expedition experiences for local papers and the *Campus* over approximately a year and a half.

Forrest had seen photos of the first Byrd expedition in New York in 1929 and wanted to follow the second Antarctic adventure. SMU students had been so intrigued by Morgan's participation in the expedition they made an 8x16" pennant in SMU's colors and sent it to New Zealand where it intercepted the expedition en route to the South Pole.

Two ships in the second Antarctic expedition, *Bear of Oakland* and *Jacob Rupert,* left Boston on September 25 and October 11, 1933, respectively. They headed through the Panama Canal, then to New Zealand before arriving at Admiral Byrd's base camp Little America II in January 1934. Among the 56 participants in the 1934 wintering party, Morgan was one of fifteen research scientists on the expedition.

The Antarctic base was well-equipped according to the *Little America Times,* which gleaned its information from radiograms and actual radio broadcasts. According to Forrest's article, the base had:

> . . . . *light and power, a radio broadcasting and communication plant, tractors, airplanes, dog teams, repair shops, a maternity ward for dogs and emergency hospital and medical office, a meteorological station, a library and science hall, a dairy consisting of three cows and a young bull, microscopes and lathes, a mess hall, seating for 28 men that can be converted into a motion picture theater seating the whole camp, a wind-driven electric generator, and two Manx kittens.*

In November 1934 Forrest interviewed Morgan's mother Frances in Dallas for another story. According to her, the crew at Little America was able to make weekly Saturday night broadcasts through the facilities of the Columbia Broadcasting System (CBS) and its own radio station FKZ. She had also shipped a Christmas trunk on a 10,000 mile journey to her son, first by train to San Francisco, then by steamship to Dunedin, New Zealand, where the two expedition ships were collecting new cargo to re-supply Little America.

The trunk traveled aboard the *Jacob Ruppert* to the base camp to await Morgan's return in late January (1935) from his three-month expedition by dog sled and plane to the South Pole "plateau." He and his scientific team had left base camp on October 16, 1934, carrying with them a range of geophysical instruments to compute the thickness of the Ross Ice Shelf and polar plateau or ice cap. They wanted to discover what lies below the ice crust. Morgan returned to the States in late February or March before the pitch black Antarctic winter of 1935 set in.

Finally, on May 5, 1935, the *Dallas News* featured an article written by Forrest about Charles Morgan, whom he interviewed following Morgan's return to the States. Planning to attend SMU's May 9-13 twentieth anniversary celebrations, Morgan was eager to return the SMU pennant he had carried to the South Pole. One of Morgan's most thrilling incidents during the trip was hearing his mother's voice from 10,000 miles away via WFAA, the *Dallas News* and the *Dallas Journal* station, and a short wave station at Schenectady, NY. As a result of the expedition's scientific findings, international backers funded ten weather stations with the goal of making more accurate weather forecasts the world over.

Morgan told Forrest the expedition found fossilized vegetation in rock, evidence that Antarctica at one time had a normal climate. They also found tremendous coal beds, enormous mountain ranges as high as 16-17,000 feet, as well as active volcanoes. Interestingly, when Dr. Morgan measured the thickness of the ice caps near the South Pole, he came to believe the "huge ice barriers of the Antarctic . . . is [sic] gradually receding. This change will result in higher sea levels all over the world . . . and a possible change to a normal climate for the barren continent . . . approximately the size of the United States and Mexico . . . . This change, of course, may take 50,000 years." At the time of his trip, Morgan calculated the glacial ice cap to be 1,000 to 2,000 feet thick.

Forrest would have liked to be around to test Morgan's theory in 2019. Antarctic sea ice is increasing while Arctic sea ice is receding by 2.64% per decade relative to the 1981-2010 average [58] and three times faster than Antarctic sea ice gain.[59] Global warming, while largely responsible for these sea ice changes, is occurring far faster than Morgan estimated in 1935. Scientists maintain that changes in the strength and directions of the wind over the last few decades as well as the opening of the hole in the ozone layer each year over Antarctica have caused large parts of the Eastern Antarctic, in particular, to have cooler temperatures and hence more ice. On the other hand, the Antarctic peninsula positioned near South America is losing ice each year in the warming Southern ocean.

SMU vs. Fordham in New York City.

During the 1934-35 academic year, his eighth at SMU, Forrest left fewer writing samples for the *Campus* and local newspapers due to other activities but completed requirements for his journalism degree. In September Forrest pledged a social fraternity— Pi Kappa Alpha (Pi KA). Likely, as one of twenty new pledges, he had secretly wanted to join a social fraternity but had never been asked. Finally, after seven years—four-and-a-half of which he was very active on campus— the frat boys saw the wisdom of including such a prominent and well-liked classmate. He probably felt proud and perhaps relief that he had finally been socially accepted by the fraternity guys even though sorority girls had often sent him invitations to their events.

Forrest pulled out his trumpet for yet another busy season with the Mustang band. The only out-of-state football game mentioned was scheduled against Fordham University in New York City. It would be his third trip to the Big Apple (a moniker popularized in the 1920s). The band staged a giant pep rally at 3 p.m. on October 24 at the Highland Park rail station just prior to leaving Dallas on the MKT railway. The team special, including half-pint Peruna making his second New York trip, changed trains in St. Louis. They stopped in Indianapolis for the ball team's three-hour workout at Butler University while the band paraded through the downtown area.

Arriving at Grand Central Station in Manhattan on the 26th, the band burst forth with an impromptu concert before marching next door to a standing-room-only crowd in the lobby of the Commodore Hotel where they each resided for $1.50 per night. That afternoon the spirited group met at City Hall with Mayor Fiorello LaGuardia, who made a special request that the musicians play "Tiger Rag" after their planned program for the mayor. Just as he had pranced through the Commodore Hotel lobby, little Peruna accompanied the group to meet the mayor. The *New York Evening Journal* claimed LaGuardia must have been mighty impressed with the Mustangs' reputation to make time to meet with them, because not a one of them could vote in New York and were all Democrats anyway.

The New York Times, The New York Herald Tribune, The New York Sun, New York American Sports, and the *Daily News* all featured lengthy articles about the Mustangs' visit. The *Journal* stated the Mustangs moved from town to town in a special train, just like a circus, and that Coach Morrison's aerial display was the "greatest football show on earth." Forrest filed a Western Union telegram for the *Campus* to Editor Stuart Sewell describing the band's

NEW YORK'S *DAILY NEWS* SHOWS MAYOR LAGUARDIA (DARK SUIT)
WITH BAND, OCTOBER 27, 1934

arrival and the several performances they did in the city prior to the game.

SMU won 26-14, using a "crushing, smashing, running game" instead of their expected "celebrated aerial attack," a switch that caught the Fordham Rams completely off guard. The 25,000 fans, including 200 rooters from Texas, witnessed Fordham's most devastating defeat in its five-year reign as an Eastern football power. One news account reported a near-riot after the game as New Yorkers tore down the goal posts, selling pieces as souvenirs, and bought up all the Mustang pennants and lapel buttons. One spectator tried to get astride Peruna but was pushed off by the pony's student caretaker. The band would have been mobbed if it had not been for 25 New York policemen encircling them as they made their way off the field to their bus, something that may have been a bit scary for Forrest. That evening the band was invited to broadcast for a half hour over Columbia Broadcasting System (CBS)'s national network. The Texans had truly taken the city by storm.

Just before their return trip to Texas, Forrest and a band colleague visited the National Broadcasting Company (NBC) at the new Rockefeller

Center, not yet open to tourists in 1929 when Forrest had last been there. The special train arrived back in Dallas early Tuesday to a crowd of well-wishers, and the band put on an hour-long pep rally as it marched back to campus. All eight o'clock classes had been cancelled to celebrate their team's success in New York.

Only a few hours after the Mustangs (a.k.a. as the Ponies) returned from New York, the campus was jolted by the sudden death of beloved mascot Peruna. The 38-inch high,[60] 150-pound Shetland was struck and killed by a hit-and-run motorist about midnight not far from Ownby Stadium. He had apparently escaped from his tether to one of the goal posts through an unsecured gate. Famous from coast to coast, Peruna was eulogized by *The Washington Post* on November 1 in a news clip titled "Famous Mascot Is Slain:"

> Today 500 members of the university faculty, student body, and . . . football team marched in a funeral procession. The little pony . . . was borne to his grave [near Ownby Stadium] in a casket, draped in red and blue—the school colors. Plans were launched immediately to erect a monument.

AT PERUNA'S GRAVE, 1934

The band played "Peruna" in the form of a dirge before finishing the ceremony with SMU's alma mater "Varsity." The Mustangs refused the offer of several replacement ponies, including Peruna's only son. Grieving students wanted to wait until the football season was over to name a successor.

Within a few days after Peruna was laid to rest, the Mustangs played Texas in Austin to a 7-7 tie, the band put on a revised version of its popular Pigskin Revue of 1934, and Forrest was initiated into Pi Kappa Alpha. During homecoming weekend on November 10 the team played Texas A&M. There was no mention of the score, unlike the previous year when the Ponies were so mad they whipped A&M 19-0 because some spirited Aggies cut off Peruna's tail.

Over 20,000 Miles with the Mustang Band. The anointing of Forrest as SMU's most traveled band member had occurred with his 1933 trip to San Francisco. Titled "An Orchid to You, Forrest," the commentary read:

> Seldom is it the policy of *The Semi-Weekly Campus* to congratulate individual students in the editorial columns of the paper, but in this instance we are making an exception. Our congratulations to Forrest W. Clough, who has the distinction of being the only SMU student who has traveled from coast to coast with the nationally famous Mustang band . . . he has the honor of being one of the oldest band members, having played first cornet for . . . seven years.
>
> Forrest went to the Atlantic coast five years ago when the Mustangs played the Army. And he is one of the . . . Peruna players who has just returned from the Pacific coast, where SMU played St. Mary's . . . Forrest's lengthy stay in school has been caused by two and a half years' illness . . . . Congratulations to you, Forrest.

At the same time, *The Dallas Dispatch* titled its news article "And He Puffed His Way from Coast to Coast."

A year later, shortly after the Mustangs' return from New York in October 1934, Forrest was featured in a *Dallas Journal* article titled "Crutches Fail to Hobble Trumpet Player in SMU Band, Who Has Traveled 20,000 miles with the Ponies." Quoting Forrest in the article:

Yes, I suppose it is some kind of a record to have traveled almost 20,000 miles tooting a trumpet with a college band . . . .Of course, I'm not a ten-second man, as my crutches, which I have to use because of an attack of infantile paralysis, hamper me some, but anyone who travels from coast to coast in eleven months is doing his share of getting around.

At the time of the interview, Forrest was wearing a bandage on his head and was accused of jumping off the Empire State Building to set another record. Denying the accusation, Forrest stated he had slipped and fallen on Broadway—another rare admission that using his crutches was sometimes hazardous. Besides listing his many trips, the article went on to say Forrest was due to get a second BA in Journalism in June 1935 and noted he was a

. . . . member of Pi Kappa Alpha, a social fraternity; treasurer of Sigma Delta Chi, the honorary journalism fraternity; president of Pi Sigma Alpha, honorary political science fraternity; holder of the coveted gold 'M,' awarded for his journalistic ability; and student reporter of SMU news for *The Dallas News.*

He has three hobbies: writing to university students in foreign countries, listening to short wave radio programs from every part of the world and trying to blow as mean a note on his trumpet as does Frank Masters, the world's best trumpeter, according to Paul Whiteman's rating.

With the 1935 summer NBC artists' tour and the following football season still ahead of him, Forrest would travel over 25,000 out-of-state miles with the band before he finished SMU in 1936. This does not account for the many miles he clocked for in-state games and the mid-winter band tours.

As *Scrapbook III* closes, it is January 1935. The SMU Mustangs were surprised to learn their acclaimed Ray Morrison, head football coach for 13 years, had accepted a five-year contract at his old alma mater, Vanderbilt, where he had been a football star. In early March SMU hosted a farewell banquet for the famed coach and also welcomed new head coach Matty Bell, who had been recruited from Texas A&M to replace Morrison.

More Musical Events. Next came the annual mid-winter band tour, which presented an updated Pigskin Revue to west Texas towns. Packing audiences into their performances, the Paramount theater in Abilene had to offer three shows in one day to accommodate the demand. As usual when traveling with the famous band, Forrest received mail addressed to him in care of "The Mustang Band, General Delivery" followed by name of town and state. Even in rural parts of Texas, everyone knew about the Mustang band.

Forrest returned to a Ziegfeld Follies show in Dallas on February 11, sponsored by Mrs. Florenz Ziegfeld (Billie Burke), who did not want the Follies to end when her husband died in 1933, only four years after Forrest had seen *Whoopee!* in New York. Eventually dropping the Follies, Billie Burke went on to become a popular screen artist best known for her role as Glenda the Good Witch in *The Wizard of Oz*.

Later, Forrest picked up Ted Lewis, leader of the second most popular jazz band in the country behind Paul Whiteman, during his orchestra's one-week engagement at the Majestic in Dallas. Maestro of the well-known song "Me and My Shadow," Lewis had opened the door for African American entertainers to perform as his shadow and mimic him on stage. Lewis's band, including clarinetists Jimmy Dorsey and Benny Goodman, got its start in the 'teens and played for stage shows, television, and the movies through the 1960s.

Joining Floyd Patterson and Joe Rucker, both interviewed for this book, in mid-March Forrest played trumpet with a small orchestra for the Panhellenic musical comedy *Plato's Daughter*. A well-autographed playbill gives credit to four students and band director Bob Goodrich, who brought together "their second authentic, original and astonishing musical comedy."

Politics and Journalism. Tossing his hat into college politics, Forrest ran apparently unopposed for graduate representative on the student council in the spring 1935 elections. Most likely, he realized he would not find a job in journalism upon graduation and was hedging his bets. By lining up something different and interesting for the following school year, he would begin a master's degree program, this time as a "frat man."

G.O. was in the news too. A humorous clip in the *Dallas Dispatch*, a daily metro paper, likely provided by Forrest, tells a story about Professor G.O. Clough. He boarded a train for Greenville, Texas, on a Monday afternoon in March to address the County Teacher's Association. When he arrived at the school house, he found it dark with no janitor in sight. He tried to telephone the school superintendent, but learned he was out of town. Bewildered, Dr. Clough caught a train back home to Dallas and re-read his invitation to speak. He was scheduled for Tuesday, not Monday, evening.

Forrest was initiated into Kappa Tau Alpha, national honorary scholastic journalism fraternity while Editor W. Stuart Sewell was making changes to the college newspaper. In particular, Stuart had joined the trend at other colleges to run news articles about the outside world and to use illustrated news pictures to brighten up the pages of the school newspaper. Stuart was the first non-fraternity man ever to be elected to the office by vote of the student body. Under Stuart's leadership Wilbur Cunningham was promoted to Associate Editor and Forrest moved up to Editorial Editor of the *Campus*.

The entire April 13 edition of *The Semi-Weekly Campus* was pasted into *Scrapbook*. Its headline read "20th Anniversary to Draw Thousands." In a relatively short time, the college had anchored itself in the Southwest as a respected higher educational institution whose band and football team had achieved national prominence. According to the front-page editorial, presumably Forrest's, "Never in the history of the Southwest has such an array of oratory, music and dramatic entertainment, departmental programs, athletic events . . . been assembled." Over 44 colleges and universities, including Brown and Duke, and the Texas Governor's office were expected to send representatives to the May 9-13 celebration.

This special edition announced Stuart Sewell's sudden resignation as editor of the *Campus* to assume the Managing Editor position of the newly founded *Tyler Daily News*. Although Stuart graduated in August 1934, he stayed on as *Campus* editor while applying for jobs.

Undoubtedly, Forrest was sad to see his close friend leave Dallas. The edition's masthead listed Forrest's promotion to Associate Editor and Wilbur Cunningham as Editor.

It is unknown who, if anyone, took Stuart's place as Forrest's roommate and helper. Margaret remembers him getting rides with Layton Bailey and Rolland Story among others but is not aware of anyone else who lived with the family to assist Forrest.

Published only four days later, the annual Sigma Delta Chi Edition of the *Campus* also saved in its entirety, provides the only mention found in *Scrapbook* of the dust storms, the greatest environmental disaster in

America's history. The storms were currently wreaking havoc only a few hundred miles north of Dallas in Oklahoma and the central plains states. Dr. J. D. Boon, physics professor at the North Texas Biological Society, declared that man was to blame for the dust storms and that "restoration of native grasses and taking much of the land out of grazing and cultivation are the ultimate requisites." Although the Cloughs suffered economically along with the rest of the country, they were removed from this ecological disaster not only by miles but also by lack of impact on their personal lives.

Contributing to this special edition, Forrest wrote a blistering editorial titled "Dictatorship." In it he chastised the student council for letting an unnamed president of the council dictate their actions, including apparently rigging the election.

> Never has there been such evidence of dictatorship on the campus. Council members . . . have . . . again . . . bowed to the will of their all-too-aggressive dictator....Needless to say, innumerable students will be glad when the term of office for the would-be-dictator expires. Dictators have no place in a democratic country. F.W.C.

For one usually bent over backwards to be diplomatic, this editorial is the most outspoken of Forrest's writings. Going to bat for maligned but deserving individuals was much more typical of this young man. Presumably, after seven full years on campus, and as a graduate student and a fraternity member, he at last had the confidence to speak out.

Another Bachelor's and Then What? The usual frenzy of graduation activities kept Forrest on a treadmill that spring of 1935. On May 6 he joined a large group of band boys at Texas Women's College in Denton and snapped several photos with one "D. Lee Taylor, the object of our affection," likely the band's sweetheart. Next, Forrest participated in several events of the 20th anniversary celebration, including a big barbecue the afternoon of May 11. That evening he attended the Pi Kappa Alpha dinner dance held at Hotel Adolphus where Forrest's friend Phil Harris and his orchestra were playing. He added several sorority parties and weddings to his agenda that spring as well.

With graduation and his journalism degree behind him, Forrest anticipated an exciting NBC Artists' Tour that summer, but then what? He had spent some effort to no avail looking for job opportunities, as reflected in the draft of one letter written in March 1935. Using his hunt and peck method of typing with his left hand, he wrote to a Pi KA fraternity contact, the assistant general manager of Hearst Newspapers, in New York:

> Dear Brother Gortatowsky:
> I note with particular pleasure the interesting story of your recent promotion in the Hearst Corporation in the latest issue of Shield and Diamond, Pi Kappa Alpha magazine . . . .
> Particularly am I inspired by your success for I, too, am a journalist . . . who will receive a B.S. degree in Journalism from Southern Methodist University in June. This school year I have been university correspondent for the Dallas Morning News, and have worked on The Semi-Weekly Campus, student publication, in the capacity of editorial editor. I'm a member of Sigma Delta Chi . . . and was recently elected to membership in Kappa Tau Alpha, scholastic journalism fraternity.
> Having received a B.A. degree in government last June, I am indeed very interested in governmental reporting . . . . On the Dallas News staff this year, I have also done dramatic and musical criticism work for John R. Rosenfield, Jr., dramatic editor.

Here his hand-written notes in the margins of the draft interject the need to mention his band experience, traveling from coast to coast and being in New York last October for the SMU-Fordham game. Forrest continues:

> I have a problem . . . that causes me some dissatisfaction—that of being crippled and having to get about with crutches and braces. Much to the surprise of my friends, however, I have carried on successfully my reportorial duties with the Dallas News this year. With a car at hand and some one to help me, there's no story I can't bring in. . . .
> My problem now is to secure permanent work after graduation in June. What advice could you offer me on entering the New York journalistic field? . . . . Do you know of any managing editor who might be able to use a person of my type? If so, I would greatly appreciate hearing from you. . . .

Gortatowsky's quick reply contained sage comments:

> Dear Brother Clough,
> . . . . I do not know how to advise you concerning your ambition to come to New York, except to say that I should think you would prefer to get more experience in journalistic work in smaller cities before trying to

locate here. I think you should try to make connections with some of the good newspapers in Texas. There are two excellent newspapers in Dallas, and the *Star-Telegram* in Fort Worth would be a splendid place for you if you could find an opening there. Why not write a letter to the Managing Editor of the last named paper, or drop in to see him some time—his name is Jimmie North, and he is a splendid chap.

I have a cousin suffering with an affliction somewhat similar to yours, who has become a newspaper man, and who also has an ambition to come to New York. At present he is on the Macon, Georgia, *News* . . . .

I shall be glad to hear from you at any time and to render such assistance as it is possible for me to give from this great distance..

Fraternally yours . . . .

Perhaps it would take the upcoming grueling summer on the road for Forrest to accept the wisdom in Gortatowsky's letter and set his sights on finding a job locally.

MUSTANG BAND THRILLS: 1935-36

CHAPTER SEVEN

MUSTANG BAND HITS THE BIG TIME

Appearing at the New York Polo Grounds in October 1934 for the Fordham-SMU game, the Mustang Band had created a sensation with syncopated jazz numbers like "Sweet Sue" and "Wabash Blues." "Easterners had never heard a college band which mixed sedate marches and current popular music with such abandon as did the SMU boys," and they wanted more.[61] Reportedly well-known band leaders Fred Waring, Paul Whiteman, and Guy Lombardo came to visit them after the game with Fordham. The *Chicago Daily News* on July 3, 1935, claimed what caught the New Yorkers' attention was that the band is

> . . . . essentially, a jazz and syncopation outfit, including in its instrumentation such non-band instruments as a bass fiddle and a guitar. The boys not only play music, they sing in tricky harmonies; they clown and frolic; one of them is a magician of ability.

Following the Fordham game, Band Director Bob Goodrich was invited to New York in December 1934 to discuss terms with several bookers and entertainers for bringing the band back in the summer of 1935. The band was so broke that members chipped in $3 each to pay for Goodrich's plane ticket to New York and again in April to continue the negotiations. Finally the telegram arrived in late May stating that a contract with the NBC Artists Bureau, which had been given exclusive rights to handle the bookings for the band, was finalized. The message stated the band was scheduled in Chicago for two weeks and in Detroit for one week with other places to be filled in during the June 20-September 3 tour.

The NBC Artists Tour to the Midwest and East Coast. During this tour the Mustang Band would be trading its traditional football stadium enthusiasm for "big time" vaudeville venues. Popular in the US and Canada from the 1880s into the 1930s, vaudeville was a type of theatrical entertainment of several individual acts pulled together under a common billing into a single production. Vaudeville was likely shadowed by the Great Depression and finally eclipsed by World War II.

Forrest was one of the 38 band members selected to make the tour—despite his disability, the intense performance schedule, and anticipated rigors of the trip. From all appearances, the NBC artists' tour was the crowning reward for Forrest's hard trumpet work the previous fifteen years. The summer's engagements would allow him to see just what a career as a performing musician really entailed.

Typically, theaters in large cities throughout the country featured vaudeville acts between each showing of the main movie. Two major circuits, Loew's and Keith-Albee, later known as RKO, competed for the best talent to attract audiences. Vaudeville structure included an opening or "dumb act" with no dialogue, often a juggler or a performing dog, and occurred while some of the audience was still arriving. The second act was a tap dancer, magician or comedian, and the third act, the headliner, generally a well-known vocalist, musician, or movie star—in this case, the Mustang Band.

The Mustangs had a ready-made headliner act created from their Pigskin Revue of 1935 that had been wildly popular in Texas. Under Bob Goodrich's direction, featured numbers in the Mustang show were the Co-Eds, three pretty SMU freshman singers; baritone/bass singer Buster Raborn, famous Mustang football center; Minnard the Magician a.k.a. band member Tom Johnson; the Glee Club; the 8-man Trombone Choir; three trumpeters, including Forrest playing his solo piece "Drink to Me Only with Thine Eyes."

Oklahoma, Arkansas, and Tennessee. Beginning their two-and-a-half-month tour in Oklahoma City, the band played 16 shows in four days at the Criterion Theater, with its Art Deco facade atop the corner marquis, and overnighted at the Huckins Hotel. The band headlined for a Betty Grable movie, a slapstick murder mystery called *The Nitwits*. One Yankee transplant reviewer criticized one portion of the band's use of a spiritual medley that included the words "It's me, it's me, oh Lord! Standing in the need of prayer." He felt uncouth Yankees might not appreciate this Methodist sentimentality.

Performing 16 shows in four days generally required doing two matinees and two evening performances, according to Joe Rucker, who offered me some insight into their summer of 1935. At some theaters it was one performance in the morning, two in the afternoon, and another in the evening, but occasionally only three performances total. Forrest put on his band uniform in the morning and usually stayed backstage between shows, there being no easy way for him to maneuver in and out of the theater. Other band members would bring him food and help him get to a theater restroom.

Joe commented that Forrest had been spoiled by caregivers all his life but was treated just like everyone else when the band traveled. The band director's only concession was to assign two bandsmen to help Forrest get from place to place. Whereas the other band members could go outside the theater between shows and try to cool off, Forrest sweated backstage in his full band regalia in the days before air conditioning was common. Doorman Jimmie Turner at the Criterion Theater probably kept him company between shows while his bandmates were exploring the town. Jimmie

mailed a letter to Forrest in Chicago, lamenting the heat and humidity. Apparently the weather did not dampen Forrest's enthusiasm for this big adventure, for he never once mentioned the heat.

Next they performed one day at the Joie Theater in Fort Smith, Arkansas, with four concerts that

IN LITTLE ROCK, 1935

accompanied the movie *Hooray for Love*, starring Ann Southern and Gene Raymond. Welcomed with a noontime parade by the local high school band, the Mustangs stayed at the Goldman Hotel overnight before traveling on to Little Rock for six performances over two days at the Arkansas Theater. Shows that cost 25 to 40 cents each featured the movie *Charlie Chan in Egypt*. The band stayed at the Capital Hotel, first opened in 1877. Today its old-world style is considered "the front porch of Little Rock."

On June 28 in Pine Bluff the band played three shows at the Saenger Theater and Forrest celebrated his 26th birthday. Joe Rucker with three band members gave him a flashlight, and Forrest received telegrams and birthday cards from others. The price for admission listed in the Pine Bluff newspaper ad read: "Adults 40c, Children 10c, and Colored 10-20c" with "passes suspended."

In Memphis, Tennessee, the boys stayed at the Hotel Chisca and performed eight shows over two days at the Orpheum Theater where Richard Dix was starring in *The Arizonian*. Whether they traveled by train or bus from Dallas through Arkansas to Memphis is not mentioned. Forrest did take an automobile tour around Memphis and down to the Mississippi River with a friend named "Cram."

From Memphis to Chicago, the band hopped on the train, making the July 1st inaugural trip of the new "streamlined steam train" called The Abraham Lincoln from St. Louis to Chicago. Said to be the first railroad in the world to air-condition its trains, the Baltimore and Ohio claimed this new train was the "world's most modern train." The air-conditioning was surely relief for the boys.

Playing Chicago. Arriving on July 2 in the Windy City, the band resided at the Hotel LaSalle, two blocks from the RKO (Radio-Keith-Orpheum) New Palace Theater, with opulence that had the look and feel of the palaces of Fontainebleau and Versailles in France. Opening in 1926, the theater was converted to a movie palace in 1931 due to the decline of vaudeville and just in time for the Mustangs. Today called the Cadillac Palace, it is a prime venue for pre-Broadway shows.

The band participated in the Palace's gala on July 4, playing 33 shows to capacity holiday crowds for eight days. Here they headlined with other acts, including comedian Cookie Bowers, who did his 12-minute shows seven days a week traveling the vaudeville circuit, typically in New York, Philadelphia, Washington, Boston, Chicago and Detroit. Sometimes in smaller towns Bowers would be the headliner act. Although a grueling life, the money was great for him, as much as $200-500 a week versus the $35-40 a week the average worker made. A second act prior to the band's was the Bryant, Rains, and Young dance trio, who performed throughout the twenties and thirties, before Bryant went off to WWII.

NBC TOUR, ON STAGE IN CHICAGO, 1935
FORREST, FIRST ROW, 2ND FROM RIGHT

Chicago was their first exposure to big city vaudeville reviewers, including one unnamed reviewer who picked up their show on July 6:

That Texas Mustangs . . . booking was oke [sic], perhaps, from a price angle, but it is an unknown . . . and really not a redhot b.o. draw. Plenty of college hurrah and background, though, with band and specialties giving satisfaction. They...have a long distance to go before being considered anywhere close to the Fred Waring standard.

. . . . Breaking up the musical numbers are solos by Buster Raborn, lusty-voiced football center, who has pleasing and well-handled baritone pipes; Three Freshman Girls, in modernistic tri-voiced harmony; Minnard, doing some really nifty bits of 'now you see it and now you don't' with his egg trick his standout; and Forrest Clough, trumpet, who shows unmistable [sic] talent.

Palace performance, as a whole, A1, considering that the band pace today is hotter than other . . . flesh entertainment.

Reviewer Lloyd Lewis in the *Chicago Daily News* of July 8, 1935, was more complimentary about their first big city debut:

Their brasses blare the most heated and strenuous of modern tunes, while various commediens [sic] in the youthful ensemble jump about, whang each other on the head with rolled newspapers or dump large receptacles of water upon rival hornsmen.

These Texas youths are easily the most interesting collegians to come to the big time since that day, some twelve years ago, when Waring's Pennsylvanians came out of the east to prove themselves a riot at the Chicago theater.

They are unaffectedly collegian, but not so bored as Yale and Harvard boys and much more vital and untamed . . . .

. . . . the most amusing of the group is a solemn young magician who makes a clarinet disappear before your eyes.

On the stage the boys have no opportunity to perform the feat which brought them celebrity—the complete cueing of a football contest.

Detroit and Milwaukee. At the Fox Theater in Detroit, the company's largest original surviving movie palace that opened in 1928, the band boys found multiple features of Asian decor and over 5,000 seats. They stayed at the Wolverine Hotel and headlined 28 shows over seven days from July 19-25. That's four a day—imagine the pressure and energy required. Trained in opera and called the screen's loveliest voice, Grace Moore was star of the feature film *Love Me Forever*.

In one news article, the usual highlighted programs were mentioned. Forrest was listed as trumpeter, one of at least six traveling that summer. As the band continued on its tour, certain acts and artists emerged as more popular with audiences and were picked up in local news clips, Forrest being one of them.

PI K A BAND MEMBERS, MILWAUKEE
BACK ROW (L TO R): ED GREEN, JOE RUCKER, ROLLAND STOREY
FRONT ROW: WESLEY GREEN, WINTON MOORE, FORREST CLOUGH

While the band was in Detroit, Ford dealers provided twelve vehicles to ferry them out to Sylvan Lake to give a surprise performance for young children at the Free Press Fresh-Air Camp. At the lake, Forrest, still in band attire, went out in a rowboat while comrades in bathing costumes took a dip. On several outings around Detroit that included the Ford plant and taking a ferry into Canada, Forrest toured with Layton Bailey, who had taken his car on the two-month adventure.

Saving his signed booklet titled "Stretching for Health," Forrest picked up a performance of Clarence E. Willard (1882-1962), "the man who grows" in Detroit's Lee Plaza Hotel. Reportedly, Clarence gained anatomical information in the dissecting room of a hospital and eventually became known the world over as a person who could grow his body in height by almost seven inches. At age 50 he claimed to be in perfect health. Numerous medical researchers, though baffled, attested to his growth right before their eyes.[62] Forrest must have been impressed, perhaps envious, of Willard's control over his own body.

Next stop was Milwaukee for a week's engagement at the Fox Wisconsin Theater, where they played 28 shows in seven days, headlining the comedy *Lady Tubbs*, and housed themselves at the Tower Hotel. Again, Forrest's trumpet solo was given special mention by critic Don Reel in the *Wisconsin News*.

Although it is difficult to imagine where they found free time in their tight schedule, Layton Bailey once again hauled him to a beach in South Shore Park on Lake Michigan, where Forrest watched his friends from the shore as they enjoyed a swim. From Milwaukee, the band headed to Madison for a one-day engagement of four shows at the Orpheum Theater before returning to Chicago via Greyhound bus. They again stayed at the LaSalle Hotel for a much-deserved weekend off.

Pittsburgh and Philadelphia. On Monday morning the boys climbed onto a Greyhound bus and arrived in Pittsburgh, their first truly East Coast city, on Tuesday August 6. Those bus overnights required at least a day's rest upon arrival in each new place. Before beginning their grueling 26-show engagement they had two and a half days to recuperate at the 24-story Pittsburgher Hotel that today houses Pittsburgh's most prestigious law firms. The band played to capacity audiences at the Stanley Theater, built in 1928 as a 3,800-seat movie palace that featured first-run Warner Brothers films. Here the Mustangs added a tap dancer from New York and a torch singer from Chicago to their stage show.

Despite the hype and glowing advance publicity in Pittsburgh, the Mustang show attracted at least one spoiler. *Variety House Reviews* for August 14 featured a critic named Cohen, who attended the band's first performance and essentially panned it.

> Collection of youngsters from Southern Methodist University at Dallas, Tex., might be hot stuff for the campus, but they have plenty to learn and absorb for the professional stage.
>
> No doubt presentation [offers] possibilities for a properly fashioned show of the rah-rah-rah type, but as it now stands, pros have it all over the amateurs so far in resurrecting the Alma Mammy stuff . . . brassy blare they give off is more suited to the striped gridiron than it is to the stage. It's a monotonous routine and relieved none by any smart showmanship.

Scrapbook revealed several other negative reviews about the Mustang show that summer. When staged with a lackluster film, the band was often the big draw. At other times it was the film or "flicker" accompanying it that drew the crowds. One Pittsburgh reviewer stated:

> Widely-heralded collegiate musical outfit from Southern Methodist U a disappointment on stage, but flicker has plenty of sock appeal and looks headed for sizzling $18,000. Cagney dynamite around here.

Another reviewer in the *Pittsburgh Post-Gazette* on August 10, 1935, said:

> The Mustangs capture the old campus spirit if little else . . . they indulge in a series of fraternity house jam sessions, occasionally coming up with something different but most of the time revealing nothing out of the ordinary. Perhaps it isn't fair to subject these undergraduates to a comparison with their professional elders.

Kaspar Monahan, a *Pittsburgh Press* reviewer on August 10 was more impressed:

> Yesterday's audiences . . . enthusiastic when the 'Mustangs Band' from Southern Methodist University unleashed their ear-smashing rhythms . . . .
> This is their first big-city engagement I'm told. I'll venture to say it won't be their last. The kids are good.

On to Philadelphia, the band stayed at the Hotel Sylvania and performed 24 shows at the Earle Theater, which opened in 1924. Built in lavish neoclassical style, it was one of the leading theatrical showcases for the most popular vaudeville and big band era stars in the second quarter of the 20th century. It was demolished in 1953 after TV surpassed live show entertainment. Two reviewers picked up separate shows at the Earle. One named Murdock offered positive comments:

> A good house considering the steady onslaught on [sic] hot weather. Good part of the billing went to the Texas Mustangs, unknown here, but registering very nicely with a good array of talent . . . . A young chap plays Drink to Me Only with Thine Eyes, trombone [sic] solo, in beautiful style . . . . Minnard steps out of the band to do some sleight-of-hand, going over in a big way and ending up by having eggs pop out of the mouths of the entire group. Good work here . . . there is a constant supply of pantomime for laughs, mischief maker, etc. Seems like a bit of the old Waring spirit, but

it's off the campus and good entertainment. Rated a real reception and got it.

A second reviewer named Hobe was less laudatory:

Three Queens, vaudeville tappers open show . . . . Two brunettes and [a] blonde . . . All are oke [sic] on looks . . . .

Mustangs act opens with Bob Goodrich batoning band in 'Coming Round the Mountain.' . . . they then do 'Bugle Call Rag.' Boys make up in freshness and good-humored informality for lack of smoothness and professional presentation . . . . Fault . . . is amateurishness . . . .

Another specialty, this time trumpet solo, 'Drink to Me Only with Thine Eyes' by Forrest Cloth [sic] gets big hand, lad's clear tone being obvious . . . .

As whole, bill is little better than fair, not up to Earle's average.

The Three Queens were a vaudeville dancing act of Edy, Peggy, and Ann, who were billed with the Mustangs in Philadelphia. Numerous photos indicate Forrest was particularly enamored with Peggy Little. In her letter to Forrest she acknowledged receiving a "very sweet and kind letter" from him, especially the "thought behind it." Giving him her home phone number in Washington, DC, she urged him to call her mother when the band arrived in DC and tell her "'hello' for me." Many of these stage beauties must have plucked Forrest's heartstrings, people he could admire from afar but only file away in his romantic fantasies.

On Friday August 16, while the band was still in Philadelphia, the world received the sad news that Will Rogers—cowboy, vaudeville and movie actor, humorist, columnist—had been killed in a plane crash in Alaska along with his pilot Wiley Post. Among several newspaper articles was a *Dallas News* editorial about the famous humorist accompanied by a cartoon by the *News'* internationally known cartoonist John F. Knott. Titled "Well, Folks, My Time's Up," Knott posted a sketch of Rogers in front of a microphone with an alarm clock ringing loudly beside him.

Washington, DC, and Baltimore. The Mustangs' next venue was another Earle Theater, this one built by Warner in 1924 and located on Pennsylvania Avenue, in Washington, DC. Although sleeping at the Annapolis Hotel, they spent most of their time at the Earle, the last of the great movie palaces in Washington, where the band performed 28 shows.

WITH KAY PICTURE
IN WASHINGTON, DC

This engagement offered no down time between Philadelphia and Washington. Show times for the Mustangs between flicker features were at 12:40, 3:30, 6:15 and 9:05 p.m., with each show lasting 50 minutes before the movie came on. Forrest had almost two hours back stage between performances to recuperate. The flick for their DC engagement was *Annapolis Farewell*, touted as the grandest Navy picture ever filmed and starring Sir Guy Standing, an ex-actor noted for his naval prowess in the Great War. This movie premiered in 1935 as rumblings about war were building in Europe.

Despite this rigorous schedule, Forrest found time to photograph various sites, including "old friend Thomas Rawlings" at 1616 16th St. NW. Unlike in 1929, he had to photograph the White House through the iron-barred fence right in front of 1600 Pennsylvania Avenue.

A Swiss juggler, a dance trio of three brothers, and a talented tap dancer named Kay Picture joined the show. Forrest called her a "wonderful little lady!!" Later, sending Forrest an 8x10" glossy, Kay penned "To Forrest—sweet of you to write to me and I'm happy to have your friendship too." How lonely these vaudeville actors must have been, going from town to town, being added to a show for a few days, then moving on.

Annapolis Farewell had premiered to a VIP audience at DC's Metropolitan Theater on Thursday night prior to opening at the Earle on Friday night. Mabelle Jennings, drama critic for the *Washington Herald* on August 24, 1935, reported:

Headlining the stage show . . . the Texas Mustangs . . . . As a band, they're a horse of the same familiar color going through medleys and horseplay by the boys when the leader isn't looking . . . . From the wings emerged their vocalist, an SMU football player. Planting his hulk before the 'mike' he stolidly headed for the last round-up off key.

On the other hand, the *Washington Times* reviewer, who picked up the first Earle performance, was more complimentary of the band. Then an unnamed reporter for the *Washington Herald*, on the 26th, wrote an article about mustangs being corralled at the Earle, the most supportive review of their work while in DC. He actually acknowledged that the band loomed as a rival for Fred Waring's famous Pennsylvanians.

They're collegiate, yes, but . . . a complete show in themselves, with a magician, glee club, comedy act, dancers, a girl trio, and soloists.

They have a swing to their music that approaches that of Cab Callaway and Duke Ellington. They are 'blue,' 'hot,' or 'smooth' as the number demands, and their basses are a treat. They even have a trombone octet and saxophone and trumpet sextets.

The band members surely had some "off" performances that reviewers caught and were not as sophisticated as some on the east coast had seen. Among *Scrapbook*'s reviews, it is easy to see that each writer was highly subjective in assessing the Mustang Band and its accompanying vaudeville acts. Also, there were no women band members, only female singers, dancers, or a sweetheart. Comments about women or women performers in these reviews and in several *Scrapbook* articles would today be considered sexist. However, they illustrate the accepted role of women in all walks of society in the 1920's and 1930's.

Apparently, the NBC Artists Service was happy enough with the band's hour-long performances that they asked them to continue touring into the fall. On August 28 in the *Dallas Times Herald*, writer Jimmy Lovell lamented that the football team supporters would miss their band should they be tempted "to stay on the road and forget about education temporarily." He stated that band members were disappointed at not receiving one telegram or letter from school officials congratulating them on their success. They wanted to be thanked for all the "publicity given SMU by their tour."

From DC the band traveled to Baltimore where they headlined for Katherine Hepburn in *Alice Adams* at the Hippodrome Theater for eight shows on August 30 and 31. Sadly and unexpectedly, it was time to go home.

Back to Dallas—No Roxy in New York. On August 27, the *Dallas Times-Herald* published a wire sent by Bob Goodrich to the paper stating:

> . . . . all plans for Eastern bookings have been cancelled . . . . This meant turning down offer from Roxy Theater in New York and other attractive propositions . . . . I hope university will appreciate sacrifice made by some of the boys and provide them with some sort of scholarships . . . . I leave Sunday for New York for conference with NBC concerning future plans . . . There possibly will be some sort of continuing organization formed.

Writer Jimmy Lovell supported Goodrich's suggestion about scholarships for the boys "in view of the fact that the band has given the school publicity this summer that it would have been unable to buy."

Finally, on September 1 a *Dallas News* article reported that

> The Mustang Band . . . will leave Sunday for Dallas . . . . Following the last Hippodrome Theater performance Saturday, the band had its annual supper at the Emerson Hotel at Baltimore, with Bob Goodrich, as toastmaster. With this supper the band celebrated its successful adventure into big-time vaudeville. Goodrich turned the director's baton over to Tom Johnson, who will direct next year.

The band boarded a Greyhound bus in Baltimore, arriving in Dallas Tuesday evening September 3, 56 hours later. They stopped at the Nashville, Tennessee, bus station long enough to have a group photo taken with their old coach Ray Morrison. Forrest wore a three-piece suit and tie while most of the others dressed informally for the bus trip.

Two nights on a bus returning to Dallas must have been a downer for a group who had anticipated ending their big adventure at the Roxy Theater in New York City, where Forrest and the family had seen movies in 1929. News reports claimed the sudden change of plans was the band's need to get back to Dallas for the university's opening. Probably a larger factor was the lack of intervening bookings to pay their expenses between Baltimore and New York, three weeks later.

Several of the boys jumped ship during the following school year and joined professional dance bands. For example, Fred Stulce, Jr., lead clarinet and arranger of "Limehouse Blues," "Sugar Blues," and others for the band's summer tour and the Decca recordings, was snatched up by Tommy Dorsey, who had heard him in Detroit. Fred dropped out his senior year to earn enough money to pay his tuition and expenses upon returning to SMU to finish his degree. "Stulce makes Good!!" exclaimed Forrest in *Scrapbook*, probably secretly envying him the thrill of being in a big-time dance band.

For Forrest, the summer had been exciting, if grueling physically. He played 216 shows and spent many days backstage between performances, likely sweating and uncomfortable, and dependent upon others for his basic needs. Doing backstage stairs on crutches could not have been easy. And even if he had had a wheelchair, there were no publicly accessible ramps in those days. Forrest learned that physically, and perhaps emotionally, the life of a theatrical performer was not a possibility for him without an assistant to help him get around. The life that appeared so glamorous on the surface could also be a lonely one.

Back to his real world after a glitzy summer, Forrest enrolled for his ninth year on campus, this time in pursuit of a master's degree in government. Music called him back to the band under its new leader, Tom Johnson. Signed "Minnard," Tom's letter urged Forrest to make it to the first rehearsal on Sunday September 15. He was counting on him, as one of the old guard, to help make the season better than the previous year.

The Mustangs received a gift of Peruna II, the son of their beloved mascot killed the previous fall. Tom Jones, Dallas horse fancier, had presented the first midget to SMU in 1932 and also purchased Peruna II. He gave the pony to the school in time for the SMU-Rice game where the Shetland made his debut wearing "his daddy's red and blue blanket," according to a *Dallas News* photo.

The big event of the fall football season was the Mustang Band's third annual Pigskin Revue held the night before SMU's homecoming game with the Texas Longhorns. Touted as the best ever, the Revue packed in more than 2,000 at McFarlin Auditorium. The owner of a local drugstore chain purchased 200 tickets for his employees and donated 3% of the proceeds from store sales to support the band's hoped-for trip to UCLA in December. The *Dallas News* showed Garner Clarke, the feature attraction of the Revue, as a one-man band who played ten different instruments. Mentioned in the *Campus* for the "widespread notice" he received "during the summer for a similar act," Forrest presented a solo titled "A Tone Poem." And, according to Forrest, Joe Rucker "staged this time with superb scenic and lighting effects, which added greatly to the colorful spectacle."

Charles Meeker, then a columnist for the *Dallas Times Herald* and a former SMU band member, claimed the Revue was "undoubtedly 'tops' for all time." The eleven-week summer tour was "well in evidence as the fifty-odd performers discarded amateur bashfulness and turned in a performance that was easily equal to many professional units . . . high spot of the evening was furnished by the closing number" when the band and the SMU Glee and Choral Clubs "presented Tchaikovsky's 'Overture of 1812.' Under the careful direction of Tom Johnson the entrance into the field of classical music left little to be desired and was certainly more than expected."

Forrest's name does not appear on the masthead of the *Campus* in the fall of 1935, probably because he needed to focus on his graduate studies and still wanted to be a part of the band. However, Forrest did continue to write. *The Shield and Diamond* (October 1935) published his article titled "Pi KA Mustangs Tour U.S." with a photo of the six "Pikes" on the NBC tour.

Two full copies of the student newspaper gave big coverage to the homecoming weekend and highlighted other events that spoke to the times. Seeing the repeal of prohibition as a revolution supported by many college students, the pastor of a Methodist church in Kansas lectured at chapel on balance and moderation when it comes to personal liberties. Overturning prohibition does not "give us a right to do and act as we please." The pastor also cited the higher death and accident statistics for those who drink. Forrest's mother Maggie, active in the Temperance movement, would have applauded this sermon, though not necessarily Forrest.

Articles on the last page of Scrapbook IV hinted at an exciting holiday period ahead for the Mustangs. The upcoming events promised to be headier for Forest than the summer tour had been.

CHAPTER EIGHT

MUSTANGS STORM THE WEST COAST

Following their successful East Coast tour in the summer of 1935, it was time for the SMU Band to look toward the Pacific. Although the Mustangs had made two previous jaunts to Kezar Stadium in San Francisco to play St. Mary's, with the band accompanying them in 1933, this would be the first opportunity to appear in Los Angeles. If the players proved themselves against University of California at Los Angeles (UCLA) and won the Southwest Conference championship, they would be invited, along with the band, to the Rose Bowl for the 1936 New Year's Day game in Pasadena.

SMU vs. UCLA in Los Angeles: November 1935. Financing the weeklong trip to California for the UCLA game was Band Director Tom Johnson's major concern. Eager to hold on to the past summer's glory and connections made, he had mentioned a possible solution to funding troubles in his September letter to Forrest, asserting:

> Besides the Conference games, there is the California trip to Los Angeles to look forward to, and I feel safe in saying that we will make it. McCaffrey at NBC showed me a letter the other day written to Fanchon-Marco, trying to get us a week there when we go out for the game ($3,000) . . . . I am going to talk with Dr. Selecman . . . to see what can be done in the way of scholarships. Know that I will do my best to get something for the band.

The band hoped to obtain a week's gig at Paramount Theater to earn expenses for their longed-for Rose Bowl trip. Eventually they got the gig but not before the UCLA game occurred. While they held a number of fundraisers and fans donated monies, it is not clear where they found all the money needed for the UCLA trip.

Over 800 students and fans jammed Dallas' railroad station on November 7 to give the Mustangs their most enthusiastic send-off since their trips to Notre Dame and Army. The 35-person band was be-decked in classy new uniforms of blue-with-white-striped pants, red jackets with gold braid, and white cross-straps on back and chest, all provided by the Dallas Chamber of Commerce and local businessmen. The band joined the 31 ball players, coaches Matty Bell and Vic Hunt, three yell leaders, Peruna II, and about 100 fans.

Southern Pacific's special train stopped in Tucson for four hours the next afternoon so the team could work out while the band gave a concert at the Pioneer Hotel. They also paraded through Tucson's main streets and serenaded fans outside the University of Arizona stadium where practice was in session. A news clip reports that Forrest was met at the Tucson station by someone who remembered him from the St. Mary's trip the year before. The Arizonans had followed the saga of the late, lamented Peruna and were eager to meet Peruna II, who had created a stir at the Lordsburg, New Mexico, stopover, bolting out of his crate in the baggage car.

Arriving in Los Angeles, the band settled into their rooms at the Hayward Hotel, built in 1906 as one of L.A.'s first high rises and later converted to rental apartments. They made a guest appearance at Saturday's Stanford-USC (University of Southern California) football game in Olympic Stadium, and the next morning they performed at the Trinity Methodist Church, playing a symphonic version of "Evolution of Peruna" and "St. Louis Blues." Forrest, Rolland Storey, Eugene Key, and Garner Clarke also offered sacred and classical pieces. Forrest spent the afternoon with his older cousin Winnie and her fiancé at Santa Monica beach.

On Veterans Day over 250,000 people viewed the most impressive and colorful military parade the city had seen since the boys came back from the trenches, according to the Los Angeles Evening Herald Express. Stationed by the parade committee at Broadway and 7th Streets, Forrest played "Taps" at 11 a.m. along with the other buglers posted at key points along the five-mile route.

Peruna II got plenty of news coverage too, having been pictured in the Los Angeles Examiner with band sweetheart Betty Bailey. The news clip claimed that Peruna at 25 inches high and weighing 60 pounds, much smaller than his father, was one of the tiniest horses in the United States. Not only was Peruna housed in a stable on the rooftop of the Hayward Hotel, he also traveled to the ball game that day in a taxi cab, like his father had done in big cities.

In front of approximately 45,000 fans, SMU won handily, 21-0. At half-time Forrest snapped photos of his bandmates marching on the field. So enthralled with the band's jazzy tunes, UCLA fans kept them playing encores for 30 minutes after the game was over. Several reporters were betting (and hoping) the Mustangs, would be back for the Rose Bowl.

The *Herald Express*'s final edition reported on the game and gave details of L.A.'s 17th annual Armistice Day parade. Other stories in that edition provided glimpses of current history: Two US Army captains soared into the stratosphere in a patched balloon, to a height of 74,187 ft. (14.5 miles), higher than any man had ever gone before. After eight hours the balloon landed in South Dakota, 240 miles southeast of its take-off point. President Roosevelt, speaking at Arlington National Cemetery's tomb of the Unknown Soldier, cited trade restrictions as a cause for discord among nations and pledged the US to peace in a world plagued by threats of war. And, Italy protested to the League of Nations the arms and munitions embargo placed on them by its members. The embargo came at the same time Italy's forces penetrated 250 miles across the southern border of Ethiopia where Haile Selassie's army was trying to defend its territory.

After the game the exhilarated Mustangs climbed back on the train. Their victory over UCLA moved them to the number-one spot—at least briefly—as top team in the nation. Reaching El Paso by Tuesday night, they all made a quick trip to Juarez between trains, presumably with Forrest along too. SMU's special train roared into Dallas on Wednesday afternoon to the cheers of thousands, including students dismissed from their classes. At city hall the Chamber of Commerce turned the town over to the Mustangs, naming them "ambassadors," and declared it officially "Mustang Day." According to the *Dallas Morning News*, it was the "most enthusiastic greeting ever given the Mustang team."

Although SMU was leading the race, Matty Bell spoke sober reminders that SMU still had to beat Texas Christian University (TCU), third-ranked in the nation, and others before they might get invited to the Rose Bowl. After winning at Arkansas and Baylor, they went to Fort Worth set to take TCU and cinch the Southwest Conference title and crown the Rose Bowl choice.

SMU had beaten TCU only once since 1927—the previous year in 1934 when it won 19-0. Accounts vary, but 36,000 to 40,000 spectators jammed TCU's unfinished stadium, the second biggest crowd in Texas football annals. The score was tied in the 4th quarter. SMU was on TCU's 37-yard line, with 4th down and four yards to go. Grabbing a long pass from Bob Finley on the four-yard line, Bobby Wilson stumbled but evaded the defense, and crossed the goal line to snatch a 20-14 victory for the Mustangs.

Nationally-known sports writer Grantland Rice in the *Dallas Morning News* on December 2 declared Southwest football gives you 60 minutes of "actual play" that the other conferences (East, Midwest and Pacific Coast) have never seen. The players "gamble to the limit in the type of game the players and crowds demand."

Texas Governor Allred had made an appeal at half-time for donations to the Will Rogers Memorial Fund, established in 1935 to support research on lung disorders like tuberculosis. He passed collection buckets throughout the stadium, as was being done in movie theaters all over the country. Later, unable to find his ride among the crowds after the game, Allred unexpectedly boarded the band's bus for a lift to his hotel, telling the boys he had been thrilled to speak over a national radio hookup.

Although record numbers attended the game, a *Fort Worth Star-Telegram* article the next day revealed that many Texans were still hurting financially. Workers and their labor leaders in a Works Progress Administration (WPA) project met in San Antonio to demand that workers' hours be reduced by half so that twice as many people could be employed. Some Americans were not as financially squeezed as others during the Depression. Certainly, SMU supporters that day were oblivious to the major ills threatening the country.

Shortly after SMU's victory over TCU, the Stanford Indians extended the most sought-after honor in college football: an invitation to the Mustangs to play them in the Rose Bowl on January 1, 1936. No other team was considered. Undefeated and untied, the Mustangs emerged triumphant in the biggest "upset year" in the history of college football. It would be the first time a team west of the Mississippi had ever represented the East in Rose Bowl competition. On the heels of this announcement, SMU beat Texas A&M in College Station 24-0 on December 7, and the Mustang Band was offered its eagerly-sought gig at the Paramount that would pay its way to the Rose Bowl. Additionally, proceeds from the Rose Bowl game—whether win or lose—would help SMU retire its debt that was due on Ownby Stadium.

Excitement about the upcoming bowl game filled December. Bedlam and controversy reigned over the 4,000 tickets SMU was given to sell. A crowd of 84,000 was expected and 200,000 wanted tickets. While Dallasites fought over tickets, Forrest performed with the Student Symphony Orchestra on December 15, jumping briefly into his classical repertoire.

Several receptions in California were scheduled for the Mustangs. A huge Texas pep rally was set for Saturday the 28th, the day the team was expected to arrive. The Texas State Society of California was slated to sponsor a New Year's Eve banquet at the Biltmore Hotel for SMU students and followers. Dancer and movie star Ginger Rogers, a resident of Dallas, was scheduled to appear. To no one's surprise, *Collier's* magazine announced Bobby Wilson, halfback, and Truman Spain, tackle, as members of the all-American football team. And at the request of the Dallas Police Chief, enthusiastic supporters collected enough donations to outfit the football team in new uniforms for the trip west. The Mustangs were rolling!

Christmas Week at the Paramount Theater.

The band was making its own preparations. Forrest was one of the 30 lucky fellows contracted by NBC Artists Service and Fanchon and Marco (F&M), Paramount producers, for the one-week engagement. The Paramount Theater, the largest movie palace ever built in L.A., opened in 1923 as the Grauman's Metropolitan Theater. Acquired by Paramount Pictures in 1929, it was used through the 1950s before being demolished in 1961. Famous for creating the Fanchonettes (a chorus of up to 48 females performing remarkable dancing feats), the F&M producers insured that a ticket bought you a news reel, a cartoon, a short subject, a feature film plus the live stage show—the Mustang Band, which would be opening on Christmas Day and closing on New Year's Eve.

The band piled onto Texas and Pacific railcars on December 21, transferred to the Southern Pacific in El Paso, and made their second trip to the West Coast in less than two months. A *Los Angeles Evening Post-Record* photo of the band arriving in L.A. shows Forrest standing next to movie actress Eleanore Whitney, reputedly the fastest tap dancer in the world at that time. A short *Los Angeles Examiner* article dated December 23 stated: ".... the SMU gang brings along Betty Bailey; Forrest Clough, champion trumpeter; Clyde Holloman, eccentric comedian; Garner Clarke, one-man band; and a midget horse mascot." The *Los Angeles Evening Herald Express* congratulated F&M for having bagged the Mustang band which would headline for the movie *Mary Burns, Fugitive*. The comedy billing slot went to the Three Stooges in a movie called *Hoi Polloi*.

Forrest's four-page handwritten document titled "Highlights of Xmas Trip to California" describes a schedule that only able-bodied college students could muster. Here are a few excerpts.

Dec. 23 - *Arrived 7:30 a.m. in Los Angeles . . . and went to Hotel Hayward for morning rehearsal. Afternoon, played for newspaper people at Ritz Theatre . . . . Arrived at 3:15 p.m. at Fanchon and Marco studios . . . for rehearsal—24 Fanchonettes, Paramount house precision chorus, stepped through the numbers.*

Dec. 24 - *9:00 a.m. rehearsal again at Fanchon and Marco's, leaving about 11:00 a.m. for a bus ride to see movie stars homes and on to Santa Monica . . . for lunch. Returned to Hotel Hayward at 2:40 p.m., and left immediately for Herald-Express bldg., for radio program over KFAC at 3:15 p.m.[where they stood in the lobby and played around the Christmas tree.]*

The band began Christmas week with five of 32 rigorous shows at the Paramount. Forrest's hand-written page titled "Routine for Theatre Show" read:

Opening (symphonic, 'Out of the Blue')
'Peruna' (no announcement) - 3 choruses, singing the second, and screaming the
     3rd
'Limehouse Blues' - arranged by Freddie Stulce
College Medley (Yale's 'Boola Boola,' 'Fight On' for USC, Army's 'Army Mule,'
     UCLA's 'California Rambled,' 'Eyes of Texas,' 'Stanford Forever,' and 'Peruna')
Trumpet solo - 'Drink to Me Only with Thine Eyes' - Forrest W. Clough
'Sugar Blues' - featuring Garner Clark, trumpeter
Introduction of Band Sweetheart, Betty Bailey
'Tiger Rag' - Betty Bailey directing
Minnard's Magic - with Duvall Williams, stooge
'Truckin' - with Clyde Holleman, trucker
'I Found a Dream' - Jerry King singing, featuring Fanchonettes, 24-girl dancing
     ensemble, Spanish costumes, big red hats. Pit orchestra accompanying.

'Overture 1812' - Mustang Band - with stage effects
Football dance by Fanchonettes, Betty Bailey, the referee. Accompanied by pit
*   orchestra, Mustang Band in Finale.*

The band's jam-packed schedule on the first two days of Christmas week showed the boys living on adrenaline and little sleep, which they did for 12 nights running.

Dec. 25 - *9 a.m. rehearsal, with Fanchonettes, on stage of Paramount Theatre, Los Angeles—5 shows that day, with first scheduled for 1:13 p.m. After last show band piled into bus and headed for Riverside Breakfast Club where members were guests for turkey dinner and Xmas party, at which bandsters exchanged silly presents. Returned to hotel about 2:30 a.m.*

Dec. 26 - *4 shows that day. Following last one, band taken by bus to Times bldg. [to their roof garden auditorium] for appearance over KHJ's Times Sports Edition of the Air at 10:30 p.m. Back to theatre, then to hotel with Dick Fuller in his car. He went along to broadcast.*

In the meantime spectators were coming from far and near for the New Year's Day events. The bowl game and Rose Parade brought more tourists to L.A. than had been seen there since 1929. Reportedly, a parade of cars from Texas through New Mexico and Arizona choked highways. Extra trains and planes were added to the regular schedules, with trains alone coming from all directions and unloading 5,000 visitors. Hotels had to turn people away. Texas movie actor John Arledge reportedly hosted his Crockett neighbors and University of Texas pals in his Hollywood home, using it as a base of operations for the big event. The team arrived to a jam-packed schedule of entertainment as well:

Dec. 28 - *Up at 5:30 a.m. to leave for Alhambra, Calif. at 6:30 to meet SMU football team, scheduled to arrive at 7:05 a.m. Back at hotel 7:45-8:45 to eat, then out to NBC, Hollywood, to rehearse for Shell Chateau broadcast that evening. [Forrest failed to mention the band did three shows prior to going to the Shell program.]*
    Shell program - *Wallace Beery, master of ceremonies [doing his last show before turning the mike over to Al Jolson]. Jackie Cooper movie star there too. Victor Young's orchestra playing. SMU band played 'Tiger Rag,' 'Peruna,' and 'Limehouse Blues.' Matty Bell, SMU coach, interviewed by Wallace Beery. Left at 7 p.m. for Paramount and 4th show. Played 4th show and left immediately for Olympic Coliseum for Texas Pep Rally [attended by 2,000*

Texans]. *Then back for 5th show. (We got to Shell program 7.5 min. before we hit the air; and got back to theatre 7.5 minutes before the 5th show).*

Forrest somehow managed to keep up with his band colleagues, although he turned in one night an hour earlier than they did:

Dec. 31 - *4 shows, plus Mid-Nite New Year's Eve Frolic. After 2nd show, Mary Barth, Fanchonette, and I had dinner together, as we did on several other occasions. After 3rd show, back to NBC, Hollywood, for sports program coast to coast on air at 7:30 p.m. (We arrived just 2.5 minutes before we took the air; NBC friends had doors flung wide, and we made dash for studio) . . . . Back to Paramount stage for 4th show. Rest-up for mid-nite frolic. Dorothy and Lonnie came to see me back stage. Mid-nite show house sold out. Monte Blue, movie star, m.c. Fanchonettes, 3 Stooges [in person], Mustang Band, and 17 other acts. Gala show. Monte Blue helped me in wheel chair after show over. Harry Zimmer, friend of doorman, Henry Gussman, pushed me to Hotel. To bed at 3 a.m. Band went back to Breakfast Club for awhile; they hit bed at 4 a.m.*

During the best Yule Week since 1929, the SMU Band with its movie was a big draw, bringing in $20,000. A critic named Hane for *Variety House Reviews* did not belittle the group for lack of professionalism as had critics on the East Coast. Attending the second show on December 25, he stated the house was three-fourths full as well as:

Swingology with a lot of capital letters—that's the stuff bleated out by the . . . Mustang Band . . . appears right at home before a theater audience and gives out plenty. Gang has youth, enthusiasm, and the old rah-rah spirit which makes for a great show.

The Parade of Roses and Rose Bowl Game.

On New Year's Day, with many dignitaries on hand, Governor James Allred of Texas was crowned grand marshal of the Rose Parade. Allred, in his ten-gallon hat, rode downtown with California's Governor Frank Merriam to the Biltmore Hotel in an old stagecoach with mounted escort. Los Angeles Mayor Frank Shaw then presented the two with the keys to the city.

With only three hours of sleep at most, Forrest congregated with the band in chairs set up in front of the Governor's reviewing stand at the parade. All were decked out in their new uniforms. Forrest remained with former band director Bob Goodrich, who had come out for the event, when his colleagues marched. At the game during half-time he sat on the sidelines in a folding chair while the band was on the field but apparently sat in the stands for most of the game.

Stanford defeated SMU by a score of 7 to 0. Team captain Harry Shuford blamed himself for a fumble on Stanford's five-yard line that prevented an SMU touchdown. Here are Forrest's brief notes for the day:

Jan. I - *Left hotel at 7:45 a.m. for Pasadena and Tournament of Roses parade. Saw it from Governor's reviewing stand at Tournament park. Left for game at I p.m. with police escort . . . .* "CLUGG" AT ROSE PARADE *Game, colorful affair; wrong side won. The night out with Dorothy and Lonnie to their home in Torrance, Cal. then down to San Pedro to see the fleet at night. Back to hotel by I a.m.*

The hot topic of conversation on January 2 was the special 24-page New Year's Day edition the *Dallas Morning News* had put out at the plant of the *Los Angeles Times*. Sold as game souvenirs for Texans and other visitors, the publication was a feat of cooperation between the two newspapers and the Associated Press, along with the magic of both wirephoto and the airplane. The upcoming $25,000,000 Texas Centennial in Dallas in the summer of 1936 was announced in the paper. Texans wanted to recruit Californians to attend their celebration.

In addition to coverage of the Rose Parade, the *Times* reported other news, including the British media's hounding of Charles Lindbergh and family who had arrived in England for a six-month private visit to "escape kidnappings and crime in the United States." Also, veterans organizations, following their 1932 campout on the Washington mall, reached a compromise with President Roosevelt on a proposed bill for payment of the soldiers' bonus. It had been sought for 17 years by veterans of the Great War in the face of presidential vetoes and congressional intransigence. Many Americans were still too distressed to think about football games and parades.

PERUNA II AT THE ROSE PARADE,
JANUARY 1, 1936

With a little more sleep that night, the band was focused on other things more directly important to them the next day.

Jan. 2 - 11 a.m. to 3:30 p.m. made . . . recordings for Decca Recording Co. at their studios in Hollywood: Peruna, College Medley, Tiger Rag, Eeny Meenie Minnie Mo, Sugar Blues, St. Louis Blues, Limehouse Blues. Back to hotel by 4 p.m. Over to theatre at 4:30 p.m. to say good-bye to Fanchonettes, and give Henry money for band pictures which the boys wanted. Short chat with Mary Barth and back to hotel by 5:30 p.m. Sent wheel chair back to company where I got it. Up to room to finish packing. Eating at Pig n' Whistle at 6:15 p.m. Left hotel in bus for terminal at 7 p.m. On to Dallas, much to my regret at 8:15 p.m.

Arrived Dallas at 3:30 p.m. Saturday January 4, Grandest trip I ever experienced.   [Signed] *Forrest W. Clough*

The fact that the Mustangs had lost the Rose Bowl game made no difference to the 25,000 fans who greeted them at Union Terminal on the team's return to Dallas. Coach Matty Bell was overwhelmed with emotion at the unexpected reception and proudly stated how well the team fought to hold Stanford to only one touchdown after so many SMU injuries in the first half. A veteran gateman at the station declared the enthusiastic welcome was a much larger turnout than appeared when a United States President last visited Dallas. The band also received accolades from the *Campus*: 32 shows at the Paramount, two nationwide radio broadcasts, two local radio hook-ups, seven recordings at Decca (the largest such company in the world), performing with the Fanchonettes, and an invitation for a week's engagement in San Francisco from January 2-9, which they declined. Dallas could not have been prouder.

Forrest's trip account mentions in a couple of places how he handled his need for a wheelchair at times when crutches, his most-photographed mode of transport, would not do. He rented one to use in Los Angeles, since he was residing at a centralized location. Playing a trick on Forrest, band members placed his rented wheelchair on his bed one night and covered it with sheets to create a ghost-like effect. As usual, Forrest was a good sport about the razzing his friends were known to give him.

Whether he took his own wheelchair, rented one, and/or only used crutches at each stop on the 1935 East Coast trip is unknown. Herbert Everest, paralyzed from a mining accident, and his friend Harry Jennings, both mechanical engineers, patented the first lightweight, steel, collapsible wheelchair in 1933. Seeing the business potential and designing their "X-brace" still in use today, they became the first mass manufacturers of wheelchairs. *Scrapbook* includes college photos of Forrest sitting in a manually propelled, rigid wooden chair that was probably not collapsible or portable enough for travel. Maybe the Everest-Jennings chairs were available in 1935-36.

Why did Forrest think this was the grandest trip he had ever made? The balmy weather and the 11-day glitz of Hollywood with its hype and celebrities surpassed the previous grueling summer in East Coast theaters. In Los Angeles Forrest enjoyed the attention of at least one Fanchonette, Mary Barth, or "Barthie" as she called herself. After receiving his picture, she promised to send hers and asked him not to forget her. He saved a glossy of his "good friend" Eleanore Whitney, who signed her photo with best wishes to "Cluff." Forrest also visited a cousin and several old friends living in California. Playing in the Rose Bowl had long been viewed by any college band as a crowning accomplishment and it capped a nine-year stellar career for Forrest as a trumpeter who, despite his infirmities, achieved national attention.

—⟩⟨—

Regardless of the exuberant time in Hollywood at the pinnacle of his musical career, Forrest had reluctantly determined during the previous East Coast summer that playing with a big-time band was a physical impossibility for him. He expressed doubts about his future in a letter to Parker Meredith, a former classmate and writer working at the MGM studios whom Forrest had visited on his November trip to L.A. Parker typed a lengthy letter to Forrest dated December 4, soon after SMU received word that it would be heading to the Rose Bowl:

> The news of your progress "in spite of your crutches" is a paradox, my friend. Forget not, that men are fabricated from the sinews of obstacles that strew their path, and if I heard of else than your success I should be sadly disappointed. Someday you may realize that your crutches are your greatest asset in that they have been the foundation of your personality and will.
>
> . . . . like yourself, I have had personal experience! Did you know that I . . . was as a child greatly handicapped by an accidental physical impairment that was in some ways a greater burden than your crutches? Did you know that I still suffer, sometimes intensely, and that . . . I have spent thousands for medical props upon which to lean this old frame? I don't think you did know it! [What Parker's problem was is unknown.]
>
> Why not? Because, like yourself, I have learned to smile, and my sense of humor, my will power, my ability to stand pain and discomfort, my habit of hiding my deficiencies and my determination have become the greatest advantages in making physically stronger men knuckle to my wishes. It is the same with you, my friend, and just you remember that your crutches are a greater boon to the popularity of that band than even the pretty figure and face of Betty Bailey.
>
> . . . . Pardon, my harangue . . . I know what you feel . . . once a man set me right about things and I just wanted to pass it along to one whom I think quite worthy. Never forget your value. Build to it! Use it! Let it urge you to be the superior man you are and never for an instant, not even in a letter to me, admit the possible suspicion of inferiority . . . . The more a man is given the privilege of overcoming, the better man he is. And I am right about that! Adjust your perspective now! Think about this, and write me. We'll talk about it New Year's!
>
> . . . . As to your queries about jobs, let's talk about that when I see you. Things out here are a bit difficult.

Forrest had long been using his friend's motto for living—both were leading lives as normal as possible, as society demanded that they do. Getting close to the day when he *must* find a job, Forrest had shared his feelings of discouragement, for jobs were still scarce in the sixth year of the Great Depression.

Controversy Angers Band Members. When Forrest returned to Dallas in January 1936, he settled right back into his family's home life near the SMU campus. Christmas greetings were waiting and, being a dedicated correspondent with friends near and far, Forrest surely pursued this pastime to ease the letdown from his California "high." At age 26 and no job in sight, Forrest worried what the future held for him since music was no longer an option.

Band director Tom Johnson had conversed with the NBC Artists Service, with whom the band was still under contract, about doing another tour the following summer. All the boys, Forrest included, looked forward to summer employment. However, in January band members were disappointed to learn that the SMU faculty committee on student activities recommended the band be brought under the School of Music rather than remaining an independent entity. Under this umbrella, the university could enforce strict eligibility rules requiring band members to be enrolled as students and to pass nine hours of course work in order to play.

Johnson defended his band in January 24 news clips: The reason ten band members were currently not enrolled was because tuition scholarships had not materialized for them. The band had terminated its summer NBC tour early to return to campus with the understanding that scholarships would be forthcoming for outstanding band members. However, only two half-tuition scholarships surfaced. Further, there were not enough capable musicians registered in the university to fill the needed positions, and the use of the outside men had been more from necessity than from choice. Johnson believed the new rules would alter the band's style of music that has secured theater and radio engagements.

The controversy apparently arose during the West Coast tour when "outsiders" were selected to make the trip while several student musician members of the band were not. On March 11, the *Campus* published an editorial stating the matter had been tabled until later in the spring over fear that Dallas could lose its "hot" but "too jazzy" band. The college newspaper felt it unfair to ask the band to help in the university's million dollar fundraising campaign while it still awaited this critical decision.

In the meantime, at the end of February four sides of the new Decca band recordings were released for sale in a nationwide campaign. At Shorty Wilson's, a local store, the record sold out on the first day causing the store to place another large order immediately. Always in need of funding, the band would receive a small percentage of the 35-cent retail cost per record.

Besides Fred Stulce, several other band members, perhaps some of the "outsiders," were lured away to dance bands. The band's tenor joined Richard Cole's orchestra at a hotel in Shreveport. Garner Clarke, the one-man band, was being courted by at least two different bands. One columnist writing about the band worried that Tom Johnson would not have enough fine musicians left to do the NBC summer tour scheduled to open in Asbury Park, New Jersey.

In early March, students, long frustrated by the administration's strict rules in areas other than the band controversy, staged an impromptu "folk" dance at the university's gymnasium.[63] Around 9 p.m. that night a group of male students arrived at the gym and opened it from the outside. Students filed in and an orchestra (perhaps including Forrest) began playing while more students arrived by car. When officials turned out the lights, the 500 students continued dancing by flashlight and to the beams of an automobile positioned at the gym door. Viewed as a peaceful demonstration to underscore their wishes for a relaxing of the rules, the gym hop lasted only one hour before the dean of students, President Selecman, and some police officers arrived to admonish them to leave the site, which they did quickly and without protest. Their point had been made. Dancing was finally approved by the SMU board in 1939 during the first year of Dr. Umphrey Lee's presidency, and the first all-school dance occurred in the gym in 1940.[64]

A more subtle finger-pointing at the conservative administration occurred the same week. After returning from California, Forrest had jumped right into rehearsals for the third annual student musical on March 4-5. Titled "Present Company Excepted," the "comic opera in two acts" was produced and staged by Charles Meeker, along with a librettist, and a composer. Set on a Gilbert and Sullivan-style mythical college campus where administrative excesses reigned, the obvious similarities between myth and reality tested the good sportsmanship of President Selecman and his colleagues. Hoping to leave the musical comedy an established tradition at

SMU, Meeker had already begun working as assistant manager and publicity director of the Palace Theater in Dallas but was allowed time off to wind up the last of his student musical shows. Another of Forrest's friends off to a career in show business.

Despite the demands of graduate studies, Forrest continued to communicate with people associated with the entertainment world. In response to his note, he received a nice letter from his friend, dance band leader Phil Harris, currently on stage at the Netherland Plaza Hotel in Cincinnati. Just five years older than Forrest, Phil was a singer and jazz drummer whose orchestra Forrest heard several times at the Adolphus Hotel in Dallas. Phil became music director in 1936 of The Jack Benny Show and went on with his actress wife, Alice Faye, to have a career in radio and in Hollywood.

Siyo Miller, one of the Fanchonettes, also sent Forrest a letter from New Mexico where she was traveling with her new 1936 Plymouth sedan named Crazy Horse after the famous Lakota warrior who was never wounded in battle. Though happily married, she teased Forrest about sending more letters to Mary Barth than to her.

For Forrest, it was the usual frantically busy spring. When did he have time to study? He performed in the 38-piece student symphony at McFarlin Auditorium before 1,800 people at the largest-ever-attended operetta performance at SMU. Amazingly, that same night Forrest made it to the Pi KA fraternity picnic at White Rock Lake with his date Mary Padgitt. Another night he attended a performance of the St. Louis Symphony Orchestra. In late April, he played trumpet in a Gilbert and Sullivan production of "Patience," put on by the Glee, Choral, and Arden Clubs of SMU, and went to Wichita Falls with the production in early May. Once again, the annual Sigma Delta Chi May issue of the Campus demanded Forrest's time and attention. He made no mention of graduation activities. He apparently completed courses for his MS degree that spring but still had a thesis to do.

All spring the controversy over control of the band's future continued to brew. In mid-May the boys received a major blow. Although many plans were laid and shows booked, the university council passed a resolution forbidding the Mustang Band to accept any summer engagements. Rather than inform the band directly, the University notified the NBC Artists

Bureau that the band's summer engagements were off, which angered the boys. To lose summer jobs that would have allowed them to pay a large part of their tuition and expenses for the next school year was a bitter pill.

Expressing his dismay, Eugene Key said he was "sorry the school doesn't believe in the band enough to trust it with the name of the University, for . . . we give the University much favorable publicity." Forrest is quoted as saying:

> Regrettable that the band cannot tour this summer, particularly because of pending contracts, and in the Centennial year, a time when SMU and the state of Texas could have used such publicity advantageously. I am sorry that when the University made the ruling against the band's trip, they did not express by resolution appreciation for the band's work last season.

Indications the university council did not appreciate the band's style of music may have been part of the reason for a turndown.

As an end-of-the-school-year gesture, the *Campus* asked 25 students what SMU needed and solicited a wide variety of opinions, from "beer in the co-op" to "some new dramatic talent" to "a new administration" and to "a million dollars." Forrest's response was more personal: *Ball-bearing wheelchairs and trolley service from the gym to Dallas Hall.* Another acknowledgement of the effort it took for him to maneuver around the campus.

Early June brought a Pi KA all-day picnic to Club Lake in Greenville. A photo shows Forrest sitting in a chair on the dock in vest, shirt and slacks with his crutches lying beside him. He is surrounded by bathing-suit-clad fraternity brothers and a number of co-eds. Even if he could not swim, he did not want to miss being with his new frat friends.

FDR's Visit to the Texas Centennial in Dallas.

After the band tour was squelched, President Franklin Delano Roosevelt's appearance in Dallas at the Cotton Bowl on June 12 was undoubtedly the biggest event in Forrest's summer. FDR came to celebrate the Texas Centennial Exposition six days after its opening at the Dallas Fair Grounds. It was billed as the first world's fair in the Southwest.

The Centennial offered the "Cavalcade of Texas," a historical pageant depicting four centuries of Texas history. Additionally, the Hall of Negro Life, an exposition milestone, was the first recognition of African American culture at a world's fair. The Texas Centennial Olympics held in the Cotton Bowl hosted the first integrated public athletic competition in the history of the South. The exposition was credited with helping Dallas buffer the Great Depression by creating over 10,000 jobs and adding $50,000 to the local economy. More than six million people attended before the Centennial closed on November 29.

President and Mrs. Roosevelt, arriving with their entourage at Union Station at 9:30 a.m., were greeted by Governor James Allred and the mayor of Dallas, among others. With his friend Joe Mansfield, Forrest in his wheelchair joined 50,000 others at the Cotton Bowl for FDR's address scheduled for 10:30 a.m. Surely the new facility must have had some ramps.

Forrest's snapshots captured military and naval men lined up before the speaker's platform and an Indian tribe from El Paso honoring the president with a chiefship. FDR, dressed in summer whites, waved his straw hat as he circled the field in an open-air sedan. Flanking FDR on his right side at the platform was his son, Elliott, age 25, who served as his father's crutch on that momentous President's Day. Reportedly an extremely hot day, where some fainted and were carried out of the stadium, FDR was praised for his strength and virility under such harsh circumstances.

After his speech, FDR toured the Exposition, refreshed at the Adolphus Hotel, and dedicated the new Robert E. Lee Memorial equestrian statue at Oak Lawn Park. Sitting in his car at the base of the huge monument, the President pulled the string to unveil the statue while addressing via microphone an orderly yet enthusiastic crowd of 35,000-40,000, all dressed up in whites despite the heat. An unflustered, smiling President shook hands with many children who broke through the ropes and swarmed his car before departing for Fort Worth around 2 p.m. This was only the third visit of a sitting president to Dallas.

While in Texas, the President and his entourage detoured to partake of the Marlin sulfur hot springs, about 120 miles south of Dallas.[65] After the 1891 discovery of the hot waters, reportedly 147 degrees F, Marlin became a popular medical spa town by 1900. In 1925 the Marlin Hot Wells Foundation for Crippled Children established a polio treatment hospital there that became a local alternative for polios seeking hydrotherapy when unable to go to Warm Springs, Georgia. One wonders why the family did not send Forrest to this rehab hospital? When it was established in the mid-twenties, he was still a teenager and presumably eligible for treatment in the healing waters. Given that he had been paralyzed for many years, it is questionable whether the healing baths of either Marlin or Warm Springs could have improved Forrest physically. His doctors may have suggested this and discouraged him from going. And it might have been too expensive for the family.

—˰—

FDR had a special relationship with Texas dating back to the 1932 Democratic Convention when both he and John Nance Garner, Texas Democrat and Speaker of the U.S. House of Representatives, sought the party's nomination for President. In that contested convention, FDR and others persuaded John Nance Garner to cast his votes for FDR on the 4th ballot in exchange for the VP position on an FDR-for-president slate. After that FDR was beholden to the Texas delegation who held exceptional powers on Congressional committees and commanded influence on legislation for more than 30 years. Besides Garner, both Sam Rayburn, a Texas Democrat from Bonham who later became Speaker of the House of Representatives, and Senator, Vice President, and President Lyndon Johnson from Texas were major benefactors of this deal cut in 1932 and were able to steer money to Texans and their pet projects.[66]

Shortly after taking office, President Roosevelt initiated the New Deal, which was a series of programs, public work projects, financial reforms, and regulations enacted in the United States between 1933 and 1936. It responded to needs for relief, reform, and recovery from the Great Depression. Texas Governor Allred, elected in 1934, was able to bring New Deal money and programs to aid various construction projects, such as the CCC (Civilian Conservation Corps) and NYA (National Youth Administration), which underwrote some student jobs at SMU. The largesse obtained from the Texas Congressional delegation over the years far surpassed that of other states. Likewise, the Texas medical community benefitted from New Deal initiatives, securing Works Progress Administration (WPA) and private monies to build two Houston hospitals (the Children's Hospital and the Negro Hospital) dedicated to crippled and deformed children.[67]

After seeing his hero in June, Forrest made several visits to the Centennial exposition that summer, at least one with his mother and sister. What other friends helped him get there? Robert Ripley, "Believe it or Not" creator, appeared as a guest star on legendary singer and dancer Rudy Vallée's Fleischman Variety Hour, which was piped from the General Motors Auditorium at the Centennial grounds to New York's NBC-WEAF radio network. Unable to obtain one of the few public seats for that broadcast, Forrest managed to get a 40-cent general admission ticket to see Vallée and actor Robert Taylor for the July 4 Cotton Bowl Queen's Night. One of the most spectacular fireworks ever staged in the United States lighted up Exposition park that evening.

Forrest struggled to locate employment after his college days were over. By then Depression-era shortages of food and other necessities were declining, but the job market had not yet recovered. It must have been disheartening for him to think he might actually have to continue living with his parents for the indefinite future. He had watched his brother and his college buddies leave town, find jobs, and get married. It would not be surprising if fear, panic, and depression were a part of his hidden psyche at that time of his life. The cocoon of college was behind him. He needed to emerge as a butterfly and try his wings. But how?

Fred Stulce wrote Forrest a letter that summer about the exciting places and engagements he had experienced with Dorsey's band. Constantly on the road, Fred "had been all over New England in every part of every state" and knew Pennsylvania by heart. Forrest's dad, G.O., en route to a meeting on the East Coast, had driven Stulce's car to Pennsylvania so Fred would have wheels. Fred was happy to be returning to Texas for a three-week engagement in San Antonio and four weeks at the Baker Hotel in Dallas. He planned to re-enroll at SMU in the spring semester but needed the fall's worth of tours to pay for his tuition and expenses.

Sorely disappointed to have lost fun and lucrative summer work, Forrest would now have to get serious about finding a real job. Forever networking for prospects, he wrote to Rudy Van Gelder, a drummer with Ted Lewis's band, whom he had heard play and was a member of Pi Kappa

Alpha (Pi KA) fraternity. Van Gelder penned a regular column for the *Shield and Diamond's* quarterly journal and mentioned Forrest in his column as a member of the famous Mustang band. Surely a good job prospect from his many contacts would come Forrest's way soon.

ENTERING RADIO AND FINDING LOVE: 1936-1940

CHAPTER NINE

SERENDIPITY PLAYS ITS HAND

It all started with a trip to Carlsbad Caverns, New Mexico, in August 1936, when I met Max Bentley, editor of Reporter-News, *Abilene, who told me about KRBC. We stopped at this resort Black River Village, and Bentley was there too.*

So begins *Scrapbook VI* as Forrest described the summer's family vacation to do some fishing and visit Carlsbad Caverns, which had come under US Park Service jurisdiction in 1927 after being discovered by local resident Jim White in 1901. The Cloughs were eager to see the caves. Forrest found the trip a welcome escape from the Dallas social life he must have experienced with mixed emotions. His friends were moving on, yet he seemed to be headed nowhere.

It was also a break from the intense summer training for radio announcing he had done with Charles Meredith, director of the Dallas Little Theater. During that training, Forrest prepared radio continuity and newscast items for recordings. Mr. Meredith then analyzed and critiqued recordings made of his voice.

As soon as he returned home from New Mexico, Forrest sent a letter to Max Bentley as well as to several radio stations in or near Dallas. He included letters of reference from six notable and well-placed individuals. Gene Heard, program director for KRBC, the Reporter Broadcasting Company in Abilene, wrote back to him on September 4:

Dear Forrest,
    Have received your letter and am glad to notify you that you have prospects of getting into the radio business. There is only one thing . . . that may interfere, that is salary. As you know, starting off a new station with no revenue is a hard job and we are going to be short staffed from the start.

167

I have convinced the manager that we need a good copywriter and announcer and that I think you can do the job.

Here is where your part of the bargain comes in. Write us the lowest possible salary you will accept. I hate to ask for the rock bottom, but it must be that. We can promise a raise as soon as we start making money.

Hoping to hear from you soon, I remain

Sincerely, Gene Heard, Program Director

It was Forrest's first and probably only bite—essentially an internship in today's parlance—but, in 1936, the opportunity to get a foot into a start-up station in the expanding radio broadcast field was a plum. The new station was located in a converted penthouse atop the Hilton Hotel in downtown Abilene, a north-central Texas town of approximately 25,000. A draft telegraphic response written on the back of an envelope in Forrest's hand reads:

Letter just received Stop Will begin work for actual cost of living Stop It appears best to stay in hotel Stop See what room and meals would cost Stop Fix pay and I will be satisfied Stop Want to prove my worth to you in this job Stop Don't let salary stand in way Stop

Gene Heard replied by cable on September 21: "Can offer twelve fifty week first month fifteen thereafter Stop Advise you accept and report immediately Wire answer today. Heard"

On the 23rd two news articles appeared in local papers, perhaps partially written by Forrest in a press release. *The Abilene Reporter*'s headline read: "Announcer for KRBC to Be In Abilene Today":

Forrest W. Clough, 27, of Dallas, who has battled nearly insurmountable physical handicaps through life and still achieved success, was on his way to Abilene today to become announcer and continuity writer for KRBC, the radio station of the Reporter Broadcasting company.

Paralyzed when four months old, Clough, son of Dr. G.A. [sic] Clough, Southern Methodist university's director of extension, went through high school and college in a wheel chair.

He took a B.A. degree in government, B.S. in journalism, and lacks only his thesis toward a Masters at Southern Methodist. The college work took him from 1927 until 1936 because of absences due to a nervous breakdown, appendicitis, and a venomous insect bite.

Despite his crippled condition—he cannot walk—Clough played in the Mustang band, as trumpet soloist. He travelled 60,000 [sic, 25,000] miles with the organization, including three coast to coast trips. During the summer he took special radio work and also a course in voice training with the Little Theatre of Dallas.

A similar, though more embellished, story appeared in *The Dallas Times-Herald* and included a professionally-made photo of Forrest sitting in a chair. The headline read: "Dallas Boy Overcomes Handicap of Paralysis, Obtains College Degrees, Enters Business World."

Forrest's hard work over the years had elevated him to one of thirteen staff members that Gene Heard, who had arrived from Ft. Worth's WFAA in September, selected after listening to 250 auditions for numerous positions at the station. Max Bentley likely put in a good word for him too, having met Forrest's parents and knowing that Forrest would not be destitute trying to live on a rock-bottom salary.

Forrest attributed his lucky break the result of the chance meeting with Max Bentley in Carlsbad. However, according to family legend but never confirmed by Forrest to me, Conrad Hilton himself was somehow involved in Forrest's good fortune. Having grown up and attending college in the territory of New Mexico, Hilton went to Texas after serving in France during World War I. During the oil boom, hotels were doing a brisk business and he saw a way to make money. After buying the Mobley Hotel in Cisco in 1919, he bought or built hotels throughout Texas. The Dallas Hilton opened in 1925 and the Abilene Hilton in 1927.

A keen businessman, Conrad Hilton surely knew that radio offered great financial opportunity and would have been involved in granting the lease to KRBC and the *Reporter-News*. Perhaps he even had a financial interest in the station. It is not improbable that Bentley, a key figure in getting the station off the ground, may have been at the Black River resort in order to meet with Hilton. At least he would have worked closely with the hotel magnate in getting the arrangement set up and perhaps consulted him about personnel to run the station. My mother contended he met Conrad Hilton while on the trip to the caverns. As much as Forrest talked about all the important people he met—dance band leaders, movie actors, and others—it is unlikely he met Hilton personally, since he probably would have recorded it in *Scrapbook*. More likely, Hilton, through Max Bentley, had a voice from behind the scenes in Forrest's selection.

On the Job at KRBC in Abilene. At Abilene's premier Hilton hotel, Forrest lived on the 8th floor (#801), ate his meals in the hotel restaurant or at Riley's café nearby, and supplemented his pittance of a salary with funds from home. He must have received some help from a hotel employee in the bath and in getting dressed. Each day he rode the elevator to the penthouse radio station with its two studios built in the latest design. Conrad Hilton and his associates had granted a 10-year lease to the *Reporter-News*, giving them permission to convert the hotel penthouse into the KRBC radio station.

The station's owners had also purchased ten acres at the eastern edge of Abilene to build its transmitter plant using the latest in Radio Corporation of America (RCA) product for 100-250 watt stations. Programs were carried from the studios downtown over wire leased from Southwestern Bell Telephone Company to the 182-foot transmitter tower that had four miles of copper grounding wire buried at its base.

An employee for only one week, Forrest jumped right in to help KRBC make its October on-air-debut. Parties to kick off the opening were the culmination of an 18-month effort in which the *Reporter-News* beat out three other applicants to build the first radio station in Abilene. The night before the gala event Forrest was invited to a buffet supper for technical and studio staff at the home of Mr. and Mrs. Bernard Hanks on Sayles Boulevard with its large homes and tree-lined median just south of downtown Abilene. Attendees included Gene Heard (program director), W.W. Robertson, Jr. (chief engineer, who lived in the transmitter plant), Max Bentley (editor of the *Reporter-News*), Harry Riley and Poole Robertson (advertising solicitors), Forrest Clough and Harold Moon (announcers and continuity writers), and five other employees.

Forrest and his colleagues orchestrated the two days of celebratory programming. A 30-minute dedication ceremony began at 6 p.m. Thursday October 1 in the penthouse studio followed by a galaxy of West Texas' finest talent. The public had the opportunity to participate in the debut with two dances, a floor show, and a jamboree of 15 entertainment features that alternated between the studio and the Hilton ballroom, lasting until after midnight. Various Abilene businesses and organizations sponsored short segments of the program schedule. The FCC allowed KRBC to return to the air from 6 a.m. to midnight on Friday, then the station picked up its regular schedule of 7 a.m. to 9 p.m. beginning on Saturday.

The November 14, 1936, *Radio Guide*, well-known in the broadcasting field, published "A Salute" to Forrest Clough, who was the first KRBC staff member to gain national recognition. The article ended with: "Forrest is an outstanding fellow. We hope you will listen to him and enjoy his broadcasts often. He's a scion of Dallas of whom that city may be mighty proud." Three weeks later Gene Heard, number two at the station and Forrest's boss, was honored in a similar fashion.

In mid-November, Forrest's former SMU buddy and editor of the *Campus*, Wilbur Cunningham, wrote a column for his employer, the *Dallas Times-Herald*. Titled "Former Dallasite Shatters Major Obstacles to Start Up Success Ladder in Radio," the article cited Forrest's "attractive personality and ample social, educational and cultural skills" as factors in his success. Forrest's friends were rooting for him.

Welcome letters and telegrams of congratulation arrived at the hotel. In a postcard his Aunt Lucy got right to the point, asking if he were lonely. Despite his rigorous work schedule, he managed to keep up a lively correspondence that likely helped stave off some of the loneliness he must have experienced in his isolated hotel room away from friends.

A letter from Tom Johnson, friend, former band director, and Minnard the Magician, surfaced among some old photos in 2016. Tom, hired as band director at Southwestern University in Georgetown, Texas, addressed his letter to "Mr. Forrest 'The Rat' Clough, Radio Announcer (of sorts)." Written five months into Forrest's assignment at KRBC, the letter revealed a lot about Forrest's repartee with fellow musicians:

> Dear Old Crip:
>   Well you little Bastard, I guess you thought we, Storey, Perk, and me had forgotten you didn't you. But we haven't you old son-of-a bitch, because in the first place your damn old picture is up here on the wall by my desk and every time I look up, I see you and me and . . . Goodrich on that damn ship's deck in Frisco [the U.S.S. *Polk* deck in fall 1933].
>   . . . . And we didn't get to congratulate you on your job. I am sure glad you got it and it is the very damn thing you needed. I suppose by now all the other Bastards in your studio are jealous of you for getting along with the female talent—that is if you still have the touch you had with Topsy, Three Queens, Fanchonettes, etc.

We have a fair band down here. We go on tour next week end, East Texas . . . and we will miss you and your goddam drinking. We still laugh at that night in Baltimore when you drank a couple of Tubs.

We can't get your lousy station down here in the sticks, but . . . I can see you sitting there in the studio, holding a script in one hand, and pulling up a girl's dress with your crutch. How is the new chair by this time??? It was a swell one as I remember.

Now, by God, we know you don't have to fuck around all the time so sit down and write me a letter. And don't make it filthy either. I might want some one to see it. Also, what the hell's the name of your station???

I must stop and send out some publicity. Write, write, write. Quick. Your Pal, THE MASTER [Signed] Tom

Upon discovering the letter, Forrest's grandson Nathan said, "Papa was a lot saltier than any of us ever imagined." The letter was not pasted into *Scrapbook* for judgmental eyes to see, but saved nonetheless because Forrest thought a lot of Johnson.

Forrest had no time off from his seven-day work week all fall other than a week out with the flu in late November. Someone had to fill in for him at the mike. His band buddy and Pi KA brother Joe Rucker, wrote him a group letter in December telling how they missed him and had heard he had been ill. The grinding schedule and getting KRBC to its next big step—broadcasting at 250 watts on December 8 in order to be heard in distant states—required Forrest to spend long days in the penthouse and solitary evenings in his hotel room. Good fortune, however, was shining on him even if he had not seen a raise in pay by Christmas.

Meeting the Girl of His Dreams. Many polios talk about their fear and the discomfort of immobilization for months in body casts away from family and friends, of painful stretching and bending treatments of their limbs, of needing the iron lung to breathe and then being frightened about being weaned off of it, of losing big hunks of school years due to hospitalizations, or of guilt for putting emotional and financial burden upon their parents. Polios were also embarrassed by being stripped down to a loin cloth and put on display in front of medical audiences, by lack of privacy in their overcrowded polio wards, by heavy metal and wooden braces and crutches that were often ugly, uncomfortable and hot in the summer, and by having to maneuver these bulky devices using strapped-on supports and holding on to something. The list goes on.

For those paralytic polios suffering in their younger years, it was doubly difficult during their adolescence. Their "different" appearance, their physical difficulty in keeping up with their classmates, and natural awkwardness in the dating game characterized the feelings of maturing polios. As Forrest grew older he likely felt the same inadequacies as other adolescent polios.

Easily comfortable with his male colleagues, Forrest especially wanted to be accepted by the opposite sex as well, but no serious girlfriend shows up in *Scrapbook* before he met my mother at age 27. Over his lengthy college career, he surely longed for a love relationship that would lead to marriage and family like most young men of his day. He even composed a song called "Foxtrot Sweetheart," about someone he was smitten over.

Having thought he wrote the song for my mother, I discovered he had copyrighted it in 1934, three years before Mildred entered his life. You can feel the depth of emotion in his heart as you read these words:

> *Year after year, I've been so lonely, Longing for someone to love,*
> *At last I have found my one and only, The one I'm always thinking of.*
> *Everything went wrong, Sweetheart, until you came my way.*
> *Now I sing a song, Sweetheart, each hour of the day.*
> *Castles in the air, I've built, are meant for you.*
> *Won't you say you care for me? My dear, please do.*
> *Skies are always blue, Sweetheart, because of your sweet smile.*
> *You've made my life worthwhile Every moment of the day,*
> *You can always hear me say I'm in love with you, Sweetheart.*

In July 1934 he obtained the words from the song "You Can Be Happy Again" (e.g., "Smile when your heart is aching. Smile when your heart is breaking...") by Lorraine Tombo that he heard on Capitol Theater's Family Hour from New York. He may have been pining over the loss of the love for whom he wrote "Foxtrot Sweetheart."

Scrapbook includes invitations to dances and parties, notes of thanks (for a gift or card) and friendship from women, as well as indications he had been someone's escort. His sister Margaret confirmed that Forrest went out on dates, but there was no serious girlfriend she ever heard about. She remembered him calling several girls once trying to get a date to some event and one girl turned him down because she said she was his second or third choice. Another time he must have been double-dating in the back seat of a convertible, and the top blew off during a rain storm, drenching everyone in the car. Amidst some photos of a particular mixed group outing to a lake, half of a photo had been ripped off and another was missing from that page. Could this have been the woman he wrote "Foxtrot Sweetheart" about?

Who would take on a husband who needed so much help with his daily self-care? Forrest must have feared more than anything a negative answer to that question.

—◦◦◦—

Sometime after the big opening, KRBC hired a new secretary. Mildred Wyatt, age 20, had arrived in Abilene two years earlier after graduating high school in McAlister, New Mexico, where she had grown up on her family's nearby dry land wheat farm. During the Depression, her father Charles had to work construction on the county roads to earn enough money to pay the taxes on his homestead to prevent losing it. When Mildred, the valedictorian in her tiny 1934 class, had the opportunity to go to Texas to take a two-year secretarial course at Abilene Christian College, she jumped at the chance. Her sister Verna, who was working at Abilene Printing Company as bookkeeper, would pay her tuition and help her with expenses. She knew that her parents would have one less mouth to feed and also saw no future for herself in eastern New Mexico. She had higher aspirations than those of a farmer's wife.

Mildred and Verna, five years Mildred's senior, lived with a couple named Bert and Ross Block. The young women cooked and cleaned for the Blocks in exchange for board and room. Ross was manager of the Paramount Theater in Abilene and knew a number of influential people in town. After Mildred completed her secretarial course, Mr. Anderson, Verna's boss, and Ross Block both helped her get introductions to job openings. Mr. Anderson was friends with the publisher of the *Abilene Reporter-News* who knew that KRBC needed a secretary.

Exactly when Mildred was hired is not known, but Forrest noticed the attractive, shy but talented young woman immediately. Nor is it known when he first asked her out but, according to Mildred, it was a double date with one of his work colleagues doing the driving.

Mildred first appears in *Scrapbook* photos with Maggie, G.O. and Margaret on the campus of Harden Simmons University during their late December 1936 visit to Abilene. By then the young couple were an item, and Forrest was eager to introduce Mildred to his family. On January 30, 1937, Forrest slipped an engagement ring on Mildred's hand and asked her to marry him. He wrote a letter to his parents telling them the news:

> *I'm very happy in a big way today. Yesterday was Roosevelt's birthday, and I celebrated in grand fashion. For some weeks I've been saving, planning, and last night I gave Mildred an engagement ring—a pretty little ring, old gold and three diamonds—one large and two small. She is tickled to death. It came as a complete surprise to her. We're hoping to get married before the end of the year. Ever since I met Mildred, I've been fully convinced that she is the only one for me. I'm hoping you all will be happy with me in my choice. She's a wonderful girl.*
>
> *. . . . In a few months, I'm hoping to start moving heaven and earth to get into a station in Dallas or Ft. Worth at a bigger salary, too, and then Mildred and I will tie the knot.*
>
> *Yesterday was a big day for Roosevelt. He's crippled like I am. I decided to make it a big day for me, and so purchased Mildred's ring and gave it to her last night. She was absolutely dumbfounded; I'll never forget how she looked . . . . I've paid about half of the ring price already, and have comfortable terms for the remainder . . . . Please I do not want any newspaper publicity about this there in Dallas yet—I've got to make more money before we can set a definite date. I'm happy—Mildred's happy—and we've got to bide our time now until I'm financially able.*

A large part of *Scrapbook VI* is devoted to the early years of courtship and marriage to my mother. Who wouldn't be ecstatic to find the love of your life! To Forrest, it was even more thrilling and perhaps unexpected. Since *Scrapbook* does not indicate he knew other disabled polios, he would not have known that most polios get married, have children, and lead happy lives despite their disabilities. Rest assured, Maggie and G.O. must have been relieved when Mildred came along to assume caregiving for their first born, for they would not be around forever.

Forrest's concern about making ends meet in order to marry Mildred was referred to in two letters from his parents in early February. G.O. states sentiments also reiterated by Maggie:

You must not worry about . . . not getting more pay. The station must not be making very much or they would make some raises. You are getting . . . experience. This you cannot do without and make progress. I want to urge you not to worry. Be glad everything is as well as it is.

. . . . We cannot come out there this month, for I am not able financially . . . just sent in a check for $274 on insurance, and I am rock bottom for the remainder of the month. I shall be able to send you the amount I usually send about the twenty-third of the month."

G.O. also mentioned he would talk with a "Dr. Smith" about opening up some contacts for him in Fort Worth.

In late February, Forrest received a response from family friend Glenn Addington about connections he might have in Dallas for him. Glenn thought continuity writing was a good choice for Forrest's future and suggested a couple of advertising agencies, one of which he knew had an opening. Forrest had scribbled the names of these agencies as well as WFAA and KFJZ at the bottom of Glenn's letter, so he must have approached those places about possible job openings as well.

The rigorous hours he was keeping as both announcer and continuity writer at the station were probably another reason for Forrest's decision to seek a new job. Perhaps continuity writing would be half as hard and time-consuming as both together. In a January 16 schedule issued by Gene Heard to him and to Mildred, by then serving as assistant program director, Forrest was on the mike from 7 a.m.-9:30 a.m., then 12-2 p.m., and 4-6:30 p.m., six days a week and on Sunday evenings from 5:30 to 8:00 p.m. In between the long hours on air each day, Forrest and Whisenant, another announcer, were expected to research and write their scripts. According to a news clip dated May 27, 1937, Forrest told the *Tyler Courier-Times*, in an interview he "worked from 10-12 hours a day at his radio job and for a time much longer."

Sometime after January 16, the station hired a third announcer named Doan, which took a major load off of Forrest and Whisenant, who was already a replacement for the fellow hired in September. Two others who had been hired with Forrest had already left for affiliate stations. In this new three-man schedule Forrest still opened from 7-9 a.m. and then worked the mike again from 1:15 to 4:00 p.m., and in between did his writing and "general handy man" chores. Under the new schedule each announcer got every third Sunday off. On the Sundays he worked Forrest alternated between the shorter evening 5:30 to 8:30 p.m. shift and the 12:30 to 5 p.m. afternoon shift.

Heard had realized for some time that the two announcers were overworked and hoped that hiring a third announcer would help. He had also gleaned that overwork put a hamper on quality:

> Announcers should have plenty of time to get all of their work done in a workday of eight hours. In the event one announcer becomes overworked (more than eight hours in the average day) another announcer will be assigned to assist him. Please do NOT attempt to do more than eight or nine hours work regularly, since with the new assignment of work, the natural expectation from you will be work of a better quality. Heretofore, it has been a known fact that the hours were much too long for work of the highest standard, but such is not the case now.

No wonder Forrest's fragile body rebelled. He was pushing himself to the point of exhaustion as he had done so many times during college. And with the new announcer, there was no hope for a raise. Admonishments from family and friends to take care of himself plus his desire for a better salary eventually forced Forrest's hand.

In the meantime, he and Mildred had a happy visit with Maggie, G.O., and sister Margaret on a weekend in early March. On Sunday they all lunched with Verna and Mildred's brother C.H. (Bub) Wyatt, who was attending a business school in Abilene, at the 226 Butternut house the three Wyatt siblings had recently rented together.

In a letter to his parents two months earlier, he had said, "Radio business fine, much better under Robertson's direction . . . . The grandest boss one could want." However, notes in *Scrapbook* indicate Forrest quit his "Abilene job and returned to Dallas on March 27, 1937," likely because he wanted to get back to Dallas in time for Stuart Sewell's wedding that evening. Robertson's leadership and the reduced hours were not enough to make things better for Forrest. He likely parted on good terms with management but it is not known whether he was living up to the standards they expected. According to Pi KA's October 1937 *Shield and Diamond* issue, Forrest "received the heartiest of recommendations at his resignation." There was no "office goodbye" but Bert and Ross Block held a farewell dinner for him and Mildred at their home. Forrest scribbled in *Scrapbook*:

Mother and a student from SMU came for me on Friday . . . . Mother, Mildred, and I had dinner at the Gem Cafe—then we took a drive and ended up at Mildred's. Mother left soon, and I returned to the hotel at 11:30 p.m—that evening, after a most wonderful time with Mildred—our last evening, for the present. After loading up early next morning . . . we went to Mildred's and brought her to work—a sad farewell, and we hit the trail for Dallas at 9:05 a.m., arriving at 2:15 p.m.

Only two weeks later Ancel and Adele drove Forrest out to Abilene for the weekend. In Mildred's first meeting with her fiancé's brother and sister-in-law, they took a picnic to Buffalo Gap, 18 miles south of Abilene. Three weeks later, Forrest hitched a ride with a Dallas friend he had met at the Hilton in Abilene and spent the weekend there with Mildred, returning home by bus on Sunday night. Describing each visit as "wonderful," he acknowledged that saying goodbye was difficult. But, Forrest still had not come up with a new job.

Back in Dallas for a Lengthy Job Search. Forrest spent the spring months networking and putting in applications. In late May he accompanied his parents to Tyler where his father gave the joint commencement address at Tyler High School and Tyler Junior College. While there Forrest was interviewed by the *Tyler Courier Times* for their May 27 edition. The article stated he was "exceedingly frail" and although he had loved his KRBC job, he had worked too hard and eventually had to give it up and return home to Dallas. Since leaving that job he "has been free-lancing at writing radio serial for advertisers, and has been having his stuff accepted with favorable comment." The article went on to say:

Forrest is interested in using his journalistic aptitude and training for the radio field . . . he intends opening offices in the Tower Petroleum building and going into business for himself as official representative for a large number of trade journals in the Dallas area. [He claimed he had already contacted 1,000 journals.]

Later, if he is successful, he will take on magazine subscription agencies, and if he is quite successful with his free-lancing at radio continuity writing he will devote more and more of his time to that field alone.

Forrest told the newspaper he felt thoroughly at home over the microphone and liked nothing better than talking to an unseen audience, that he had the "gift for feeling his audience and liking them" and hence they felt a kinship with him. He was determined to get before the mike again and if possible be a news commentator.

In the interview Forrest revealed his plans to attend a six-week radio school sponsored by SMU that his father was instrumental in bringing to Dallas. It was led by Ben H. Darrow, founder and director of the Ohio School of the Air broadcasting in Columbus. Darrow intended to teach students and teachers how to prepare copy for radio and how to meet the demands of the radio-listening public. Dr. Clough contended that radio was a "coming facility of education" and stu-

PHOTO MADE BY *TYLER COURIER TIMES* DURING INTERVIEW, 1937

dents and teachers needed technical knowledge about the field. Although SMU offered a "general interest in radio" morning class, Forrest attended the evening sessions for those eager to learn broadcasting, script writing, and the actual "workshop" of the radio. This obviously required someone to drive him there each way.

In the meantime, what was Mildred thinking about her future with this disabled guy who had a lot of dreams and plans but no actual job yet? Years later, after Forrest died, she confessed that her sisters tried to discourage her from marrying a man she would have to take care of all her life. She had been courted seriously at Abilene Christian College by a man planning to become a Church of Christ minister. But, as an admitted introvert, she did not want to be a preacher's wife with all the expected social responsibilities. Besides she was in love with Forrest and his outgoing personality. She likely felt he would show her a world she could never see back on the farm. Mildred would hitch her wagon to this up-and-coming radio star.

And Forrest was not going to let her forget him. Before he began the summer radio classes he visited Mildred in early June, taking the bus both ways, arriving at 3:30 p.m. on Saturday and leaving for Dallas at 11:20 p.m. on Sunday. A taxi or someone else had to meet his bus in Dallas in the middle of the night.

Mildred also kept up her end and made a surprise visit to Dallas the weekend of June 28, to help Forrest celebrate his 28th birthday. Forrest wrote:

> I was planning on my Sweetheart's visit, July 3-5, but to my great surprise, Mildred came on Saturday evening June 26 [leaving Abilene after her Saturday workday], to be here for my Birthday. She and Mother really played a trick on me. I was never so surprised. Big Birthday Dinner—Sunday, June 27—all relatives very fond of Mildred. Three glorious nights with Mildred, and two big days. Ancel, Adele and I carried her to Fort Worth Monday evening after picnic [at White Rock Lake, Dallas]. She left via train at 10:20 p.m. The grandest birthday I've ever spent because Mildred was with me!!

A month later, they had another "glorious weekend." Forrest says he

> . . . . went on train both ways arriving in Abilene at 6:25 p.m. Saturday and leaving at 2:35 a.m. on Monday August 2. Mildred sweeter as the days go by! We'll be together in Dallas Sept. 5, 1937!! Oh, Boy!!

Forrest meant that Mildred was moving permanently to Dallas. Having completed one year at KRBC, moving to Dallas to get married she felt would be an acceptable parting as far as her employer was concerned.

After radio school ended in early July, Forrest threw himself into several social and business activities for the remainder of the summer before Mildred arrived. He was one of 150 active members in the Pi Kappa Alpha fraternity alumni group in Dallas, getting named as membership chair.

Mildred arrived by train from Fort Worth late on the evening of September 6, since Forrest "couldn't meet her in Ft. Worth as planned because of rain." Maggie found Mildred a room in a house on McFarlin around the corner from theirs so that the young couple could see each other easily prior to their wedding, which they hoped would happen that fall. Mildred "landed a job at Universal Credit Co., on Sept. 11—only three days after registering at Cloud's Employment Agency—Also good prospects at WFAA, Dallas." At least one of them was employed. They celebrated

Mildred's 21st birthday on September 19, and Cluffie, Forrest's nickname for years, surprised her with an Elgin wristwatch.

In September he introduced Mildred to his Pi KA fraternity brothers at an Adolphus Hotel dinner party where 250 people danced to Glenn Miller's swing band. He re-instituted a monthly newsletter for the group and served as editor. Pursuing his passion of writing, editing, and news-gathering, this kind of volunteer work was one way to keep himself visible among colleagues. He also attended a Sigma Delta Chi journalism fraternity party, another good place to look for jobs.

Once again a volunteer, Forrest became involved as business manager in the opening of the new Southwestern School of Radio Broadcasting. Forrest placed stories in all the local newspapers and designed a slick black-and-white four-page brochure with photos. Beginning October 1, students would be trained at a downtown location in "all the phases of radio work." Experienced teachers actively engaged in radio program presentations would be hired. Prospective students would be "submitted to an audition and only a limited number picked for each two-month session."[68] The school did open, but to less enrollment than expected. Forrest penned into *Scrapbook*:

> *Quit Butler's Radio School on Thursday, November 4, 1937—No pay and No prospects there—to devote time to News Service till contact for permanent job is made.*

Forrest's own News Service, by then listed at home on Asbury Street, offered magazine subscriptions and renewals, radio script writing, news and feature articles, and trade journal correspondence. He hung out his shingle to any takers while he kept searching for that magic salaried job. During this self-employed stint, he wrote a radio program (U.S. copyright D52183, dated September 27, 1937, titled "For the good of humanity: episode 2, ...idea by Emil Michael Mancell, Dallas.") Mancell probably hired him to write the continuity.

Forrest must have gained inspiration from Glenn Addington, who had given him a few job leads. He was a well-known Texas advertising man with the Tracy-Locke-Dawson (TLD), Inc., ad agency. A December 1938, article in *Broadcasting* described Glenn's background and current situation. Titled "From a Bedroom Office," the article told how Glenn, for the last seven years, had been confined to his bed as a result of a severe spinal injury. Despite his invalidism, he "continued to produce a large volume of radio script, writing in bed with his typewriter on a lap table and checking auditions by telephone."

In the early 1920s Addington "began to see radio's commercial possibilities" through the sale of air time, which had not yet been tried in the Southwest. In 1925 Addington requested and received WFAA management's permission to provide a weekly program for one of his clients, "the client to supply the talent and the station to donate the time and allow commercial mention" by whatever company purchased the air time. Thus, the first "regularly scheduled commercial radio program in the Dallas area went on the air..." In another first, Glenn soon "committed the entire program to paper, a distinctive innovation for that time." Addington wrote script for clients, including Continental Oil, Imperial Sugar, and Dr. Pepper, for whom he produced the 182-week Pepper Upper series. Glenn had overcome the odds, just as Forrest hoped to do.

Forrest was indefatigable—putting himself out there, making contacts, doing volunteer work that gave him exposure to people of influence. He attended a Sigma Delta Chi luncheon in early October honoring his journalism professor "Dad" Henning, who had been granted a leave of absence from SMU in June because of illness. G. B. Dealey, president of the A.H. Belo Corporation, publishers of the *Dallas News*, praised Henning, who had formerly worked under him, saying that Henning demonstrated "two things vitally important to good journalism: accuracy and dependability."[69] Forrest wrote on the bottom of the invitation to the luncheon:

At this meeting, I met Mr. Dealey! He gave me a cigar and bought my lunch.

Forrest had faith that some day one of these important people he met would lead him to permanent employment, just as his old band, fraternity, and journalism friends had found: Bob Goodrich, a Methodist pastor in Port Arthur, Texas; Rolland Storey, director of religious education at another Methodist church in Port Arthur; Tom Johnson, band director at Southwestern University; Charles Meeker, assistant manager of the Majestic Theater in Dallas; Joe Rucker, art and technical director at Dallas Little Theater; Fred Stulce and Garner Clark, both with big-name dance bands; Bob Williams with Standard Oil; Stuart Sewell, Wilbur Cunningham, and

Eugene Key, all working at local newspapers. Forrest's determination, Mildred's love, plus his parents' financial and other support sustained him.

In the meantime, he had another gathering to attend "for old time's sake"—the SMU 1937 Pigskin Revue featured as its second act a reunion of the nationally famous 1934-35 Mustang band under Bob Goodrich's direction. His buddies came from all over the Southwest to perform. Forrest once again played "his drinking song." *Didn't miss a note!!* he crowed, and rejoiced in being with his talented, funny, jokester friends once again.

Wedding Bliss. Following the Revue held on Friday evening, Forrest's big day—one that he had longed for intensely over the past nine months—came on October 30 at a parlor in Highland Park Methodist Church. He and Mildred were married in the presence of a small group of relatives and friends. He did not have a job yet, but everyone must have felt it was the

FORMAL WEDDING PORTRAIT, 1937

right thing to do. Maggie sewed a royal blue velvet wedding dress for her new daughter-in-law. It was accompanied with black accessories and a bouquet of talisman roses. After the ceremony, the Cloughs entertained guests with a reception in their home.

Following the reception, Ancel and Adele plus several other relatives and friends took the happy couple downtown for a steak dinner. After eating, they drove around downtown, according to my mother, to look at Halloween deco-

rations before Ancel and Adele finally dropped them off at the hotel where they had a reservation. In the meantime, the other couples had thrown rice between the hotel sheets and partially filled the bathtub with rice.

Besides the excitement of their virginal bodies to keep them awake, the phone started ringing every few minutes. Answering it at first, they soon realized Ancel was playing tricks on them. Brothers will be brothers! The next day, G.O. picked them up before noon and took them back to Asbury Street, for Mildred had to work the next day. The newlyweds spent the second night of their married life in the front bedroom's double bed across the hall from Maggie and G.O.'s twin beds.

I would guess Mildred especially found this arrangement less-than-ideal, but the young couple could at least be together while Forrest hunted for a job and Mildred would not have rent to pay. She felt beholden to her new in-laws, for her own parents were unable to provide her support. It is doubtful her sister Verna or brother C.H. came to the wedding or it would have been mentioned in *Scrapbook*. At times it must have been quite lonely for her, but she had made her choice and was moving on.

After the October 1937 wedding and through the summer of 1938, *Scrapbook* documented Forrest and Mildred's life in Dallas while he continued to look for a job. On November 21 a *Dallas News* article announced the formation of the Texas School of the Air by representatives from at least 25 colleges in the state who met at the Baker Hotel in Dallas. The group, of which Dr. G.O. Clough was treasurer, sought a $126,000 Rockefeller Foundation grant to finance the school for two years. Destined to go on the air in September 1938 (but delayed until February 1940), the school would offer four daily programs for children and adults as well as radio workshops to be held at SMU, the University of Texas, and Texas State College for Women. Perhaps G.O., who had spearheaded bringing the 1937 radio summer school program to SMU, also thought this organization might provide employment for Forrest.

The winter season offered a few highlights but no job offers. Forrest put several ads in SMU's *Campus* during December:

> *Solve the Xmas Gift Problem the Smart Way, Magazines for All Members of the Family Will Turn the Trick! Call Forrest W. Clough . . . 5-7045.*

In early February Forrest's journalism professor A.F. "Dad" Henning died at age 60. A "self-made" man, Henning had no formal institutional training but spent his career printing, publishing, establishing, buying, and editing newspapers all over east Texas. A writer for the *Dallas News*, in 1923 he became professor of journalism and laid the foundation for SMU's School of Journalism. Literary editor for the *Dallas Times Herald* from 1927-1933, Henning published in 1931 "Ethics and Practices in Journalism" that became a standard work in the field.

Inspired by their role model, many of Henning's students went on to work at newspapers throughout Texas and the Southeast. Forrest used the skills he had learned from Henning to get a paid position teaching classes in news reporting, editorial writing and advanced news writing at Dallas College (his father's SMU extension school) in addition to running his News Service during 1937 and 1938.

A Waterborne Disease. While Forrest's polio disability was far from his mind at this time, efforts toward conquering the disease were moving forward. When the electron microscope was invented in 1938 and could detect tiny viruses, it was finally determined that the poliovirus developed in the digestive and not the respiratory tract. It enters the body via the mouth (by unclean hands, objects, and unsanitary food and water) and leaves in the feces. With the electron microscope, researchers were at last able to see large amounts of the virus in the fecal matter of polio patients.

The first symptoms begin to appear four to fourteen days after exposure and vary in intensity with many feeling they have only a case of the flu or a simple cold. Depending upon how well the body's immune system develops antibodies to the disease, the virus will manifest in one of four different ways. The mildest or "inapparent" form often includes fever, headache, fatigue and sore throat. "Abortive" polio may have similar symptoms with vomiting, abdominal pain and constipation or diarrhea in addition. [70] "Non-paralytic" polio may have some or all of the above symptoms but also a stiff neck and achy or sore limbs. Dorland's refers to these three as the minor illness. "Paralytic" polio is what Dorland's[71] calls the major, or fourth, illness, which involves the central nervous system, a stiff neck, pleocytosis (lymphocytes in the cerebrospinal fluid), and perhaps paralysis sometimes followed by muscle atrophy and contraction with permanent deformity. It is the most severe manifestation of the disease and is the form most feared worldwide. Estimates of paralytic polio cases as a percentage of all polio cases range from one to four percent,[72] [73] suggesting an average of 2%-3% that are paralytic.

In the more serious paralytic form of the disease the virus attacks the anterior horn cells or motor neurons of the spinal cord in the central nervous system, which control the body's muscles. If the virus causes paralysis in only the extremities, it is called "spinal" polio. If it affects the medulla oblongata that controls swallowing, breathing and circulation, it is called "bulbar" polio. A combination is called "bulbospinal." If it affects the brain stem and motor cortex, it is "cerebral" or "encephalitic" polio (polioencephalitis) (Dorland).[74] This third type was delineated as early as 1835 when Dr. J. Badham, in four of his paralytic patients in England, noted drowsiness, abnormal pupils, and, in one case, a derangement of the eye muscles, leading him to believe there was cerebral as well as spinal involvement.[75]

After the disease has run its course, many victims regain muscle strength to varying degrees following extensive therapy. For those whose breathing was seriously affected during the early, critical stage of the disease, death was often the result before the invention of the iron lung or respirator in 1927 by Dr. Philip Drinker. Although many escaped death by using the iron lung and eventually were "weaned" off of it, others were forced to remain on it, either full- or part-time, for the rest of their lives.

Medical authorities eventually concluded that the Industrial Revolution's improved sanitation and hygiene, as well as rural isolation, reduced children's abilities to develop natural antibodies to a virus that was endemic throughout society. The poliovirus affected middle class children as frequently as those living in crowded immigrant slums.[76] By the 1920s and 1930s polio was hitting communities with increasing frequency. It replaced tuberculosis as a primary public concern for finding a cure.

It had been a long haul of marginal income and uncertainty as far as Forrest's employment was concerned. But, his personal life had taken a massive leap forward during the year and a half after leaving KRBC in

Abilene. That start-up station in West Texas had offered a pivotal six-month opportunity that changed Forrest's life forever. He had found his life partner, but what was he going to do to earn a living that would support the family they both wanted to have? Once again, things were about to change.

CHAPTER TEN

KFJZ AND THE TEXAS STATE NETWORK

In the summer of 1938, Elliott Roosevelt, FDR's son and executive head of KFJZ Radio in Fort Worth, was ready to launch the new Texas State Network (TSN) of 23 stations. He envisioned TSN to be the largest radio organization outside of New York, Chicago, and Los Angeles, designed to bring better radio coverage to the state of Texas. TSN would be an affiliate of the Mutual Broadcasting System (MBS) and would compete with NBC and CBS, which were only slightly older than MBS. Roosevelt needed additional talented employees to staff the network headquarters and manage the transition from local radio station to the larger TSN network. He expected to move 50 families to Fort Worth.

Through an unknown mutual friend, G.O. made contact with attorney Raymond Buck at the Texas State Network, Inc., in Fort Worth. Little known nationally, Buck was general counsel of American Airways and wielded great influence within the Texas Democratic Party and for the increasingly powerful Texas oil oligarchy.[77] He also owned KTAT and the Southwest Broadcasting Co., which may have been the reason G.O. approached him.

Buck referred Forrest's papers to Roosevelt, who was impressed with Forrest's credentials. He likely could identify with Forrest's story because of his own father's struggles with the effects of polio. At last Forrest's and the family's networking paid off. Once again Forrest was positioned where he needed to be—on the front end of the young and expanding radio broadcasting business. Buck responded to G.O.'s letter a month after Forrest began work:

Dear Mr. Clough:

Absence from the city . . . has prevented me from writing you earlier with reference to your son Forrest W. Clough . . . . I want you to know, however, that I did take the matter up with Mr. Elliott Roosevelt, owner of KFJZ, and President of the Texas State Network, Inc., and recommended Forrest to him very highly. I am happy in the consciousness that my efforts gave Forrest the opportunity to obtain the position on his own merits . . . . Forrest is getting along fine, and the officials of the Texas State Network, Inc., are highly pleased with his work.

Sincerely yours,
The Texas State Network, Inc.
By, [signed] Raymond E. Buck

Mildred and Forrest moved to Fort Worth in late August 1938 and rented a furnished ground-floor apartment at 1109 College Avenue, which allowed easy access for Forrest and his wheelchair. They were thrilled to finally have their own place after almost a year living in Dallas with Maggie and G.O. About the same time, Mildred found a government job with the Public Works Administration (PWA) in Fort Worth. It paid $120 a month, and, after making only $70 a month at her job in Dallas, she found this pay exceptional. Forrest was making $30 a week, so to have $60 a week between them was heady. With this largesse, they started saving for a car while Mildred rode the bus (three rides for 25 cents) and Forrest took a taxi to work with his "cabbie" named Harvey.

Forrest began work as director of publicity and assistant civic program director on September 2. Both the *Dallas News* and the *Dispatch Journal* ran small articles about his new position, one of them mentioning that he had an MA in government from SMU. During his year and a half of minimal employment, he had managed to finish his thesis on the Federal Communications Commission (FCC), a New Deal entity created in 1934 by FDR to regulate fairness in the airwaves. In Texas in the 1930s-1950s the FCC played a major licensing role in all the buying and selling of radio stations by what Chris Hansen terms the "Texas Cabal."[78]

The company moved into its expanded quarters at 1119 West Lancaster on Saturday September 10 and made their first broadcast the next day. Two articles in *The Fort Worth Star-Telegram* describe KFJZ's move to their modern, air-conditioned, 18-room quarters equipped with the latest radio and sound equipment, 13 offices, two broadcasting studios, two control rooms, and an impressive lobby/reception room. TSN would be using four United Press teletype machines for their hourly five-minute newscasts.

Presumably Elliott Roosevelt oversaw the design and building of the new station. Given that his father got around in a wheelchair, one would think he would have constructed the bathroom door on the main floor (where Forrest worked) wide enough for a wheelchair to access. But not so. From 1938 until 1955 when KFJZ Radio moved to a new location, Forrest had to get out of his chair and onto crutches to walk down the hall to the restroom, a task that surely became more difficult as he aged.

During the first two weeks on the job Forrest tackled a mountain of work. He helped develop and circulate last-minute publicity for Texas State Network's elaborate inaugural broadcast scheduled for Thursday, September 15, from 6:30-7:30 p.m. The program offered a star-studded opener at the grand revolving stage of Casa Mañana's outdoor theater. Four- thousand people were expected and loud-speaker arrangements were made for anticipated additional numbers to stand outside the theater.

Coming from Hollywood for the inaugural broadcast, Bob Hope and Shirley Ross, movie stars, and Gene Autry, popular cowboy crooner, were joined by a Hollywood movie news commentator. Hope and Ross sang "Thanks for the Memory" and Autry sang some of his favorites. Everett Marshall, star of Casa Mañana for the 1936 and 1937 seasons, opened the show with the state song "Texas Our Texas," ending with a rousing "Eyes of Texas" with the audience joining in. A mixed chorus of 400 "Negro voices" singing "Deep River" and "Certainly Lord" was reportedly the largest chorus of its kind ever tried on a network

Governor Allred and governor-nominee W. Lee O'Daniel, among others, spoke at the event. Mr. O'Daniel, who had started his radio career at KFJZ ten years earlier, and his Hillbilly Boys did a number and also accompanied Gene Autry. Bob Hope, who was hosted at the Roosevelts' Benbrook ranch, delivered several jokes during the evening. The hour-long program was broadcast over TSN's 23-stations and 108 national outlets of the Mutual Broadcasting System (MBS), with which TSN was affiliated.

TSN INAUGURAL. L TO R: BOB HOPE, ELLIOTT ROOSEVELT,
GOVERNOR JAMES ALLRED, GENE AUTRY

Mutual added programs from four other stations around the country to make a 5-hour celebration of its 4th birthday, ending in Newport News, Virginia, with Jimmy Dorsey's orchestra playing.

Local Dallas/Fort Worth stations WBAP and WFAA and the NBC network ran special programs to give Elliott's TSN inaugural event a little competition, including the Rudy Vallée Variety Show at 6 p.m. just as the TSN Mutual Broadcast was beginning. As Elliott would see, these older networks were out to get him.

More than 8,500 people turned out at Casa Mañana for the big event. After the hour-long broadcast, the stars appeared on a stage outside the theater and later at two theaters downtown so the overflow audience could see the celebrities who had come to town. A column in the *Star-Telegram* congratulated Roosevelt and his associates for the precision they exhibited to put over TSN's first show from Casa Mañana—better than air shows put on from Radio City and Hollywood.

On September 15, 1938, *The Fort Worth Press* ran glowing articles about TSN. The new staff was introduced with brief bios of five of the top brass, beginning with Elliott, then next in line, ahead of ten others, was:

> Forrest W. Clough, publicity and civic program director, formerly Dallas correspondent for *Broadcasting Magazine, Radio Daily*, and *Advertising Age*; newspaper and radio business about four years, was former announcer and continuity writer at KRBC, Abilene; holds a B.S. Degree in journalism and M.A. degree in government from SMU.

Apparently, Forrest's advertising credentials as an independent news service provider had also caught Roosevelt's attention. Many of the listed colleagues became Forrest's good friends and household names around the Clough family home over the years.

Roosevelt had assembled a professional and talented organization. Of course, it did not hurt that he had stellar parentage to assist with his big splash into network broadcasting at the young age of 28. On the surface, one might think that Roosevelt money was behind Elliott's venture into the radio broadcasting business, but apparently not. An intriguing backstory may help one understand why Elliott's tenure in the Texas radio business was problematic.

Elliott moved to Texas in 1935 in an effort to get a new start after his ill-fated involvement in the aviation fiasco when the government tried to bring the airlines under its control.[79] Seeing radio as a new and exciting field, he became President of Hearst Radio, Inc., in late 1935 and eventually acquired four radio stations for Hearst. He wanted to buy a string of stations himself and began a dual role as VP for sales for the Southwest Broadcasting Co. that owned KTAT & other radio stations. He also befriended wealthy Texas oilmen (e.g., Amon Carter, Sid Richardson, Clint Murchison, Jesse Jones, Charles Roeser), many of whom owned radio stations. As a loyal son, he likewise jumped into the Texas Democratic party. There he encountered resistance because many, although Democrats, were more conservative than FDR's "New Dealers."

These Texas oligarchs saw Elliott as a useful conduit to the president and the government bureaucracy because of their increasing concerns about oil industry regulation and their need to obtain FCC licensure for their radio stations. In September 1937 Elliott bought KFJZ, a small 100-watt station that quickly became a 250-watt enterprise with money loaned him by Murchison and Richardson as well as his wife Ruth Googins. Over time they and others reportedly loaned him approximately $500K to help him purchase the elaborate 1500-acre Dutch Branch ranch (a place to entertain his father and his new Texas associates). The loan also helped build the state-of-the-art KFJZ and TSN headquarters in Fort Worth in 1938 as well as funded another adventure in 1939-40. The ranch and livestock were heavily mortgaged and held in his wife Ruth's name as a shield against creditors.

By 1938, Elliott's lavish lifestyle and overextension into the radio business began to be a point of contention with many investors who held stock in the new enterprises. Reportedly, his new TSN had lost $105K by September 1938, just at the time Forrest began his $30/week job. According to Hansen, in only a few months after experiencing major operating losses and an inflated overhead, Roosevelt could not make payroll and was on a desperate search for new financing.[80] In his well-researched book, Hansen details complicated wheeling and dealing that helped keep Elliott afloat a while longer and also created a heavy Texas Democratic influence on governmental politics all the way through Lyndon Johnson's presidency.[81]

The TSN inaugural broadcast, as gay and spectacular as it was, occurred against a backdrop of ominous activity in Europe. Along with TSN's broadcast, *The Fort Worth Press* reported that 14,000 Czech reservists had been "called to colors" because of the recent fighting in the Sudetenland where 50 Czechs and Sudeten Germans had been killed. *The Fort Worth Star-Telegram* that day showed photos of Czech soldiers doing maneuvers at Milovice in Bohemia, since the Prague government felt that hostilities would break out following Adolf Hitler's belligerence in the Sudeten controversy. Switzerland, which later claimed neutrality, was also doing military maneuvers in the Bernese Alps, ready to put 500,000 men under arms in case of another war. Meanwhile, with Elliott busy at TSN, FDR was in Rochester, Minnesota, where his older son James had undergone surgery for a gastric ulcer. The President told supporters at the train station he was returning to Washington, DC, due to the critical European situation.

On the US home front, diverse but less menacing issues appeared in local headlines. A member of the National Labor Relations Board noted a decline in strikes since 1937 due to improved labor laws, but he expected resistance from the business sector. In Louisiana, a Negro was being held in an attack on a coed and her escort parked near a country church early in the morning. Several governors planned to attend the Tyler Rose Festival. Seventy-six Texas towns were invited to send "duchesses" to the Texas Cotton Festival scheduled for October 5. And, finally, novelist Thomas Wolfe, famous for his epic-length books, died of pneumonia at age 37 in Baltimore.

Early Days on the New Job. Affairs in Europe were far away from the thoughts of a happy bridegroom in a new position. Forrest needed to become better acquainted with all aspects of radio broadcasting, radio advertising and publicity in particular. The TSN opening forced him to be a fast learner and draw on his innate talents as he hit the ground at top speed.

Elliott Roosevelt appointed International Radio Sales, Inc., a Hearst Radio subsidiary, as exclusive national representatives for the newly formed TSN and 19 of its 23 TSN stations. By the first of October, TSN was offering 17 hours of programming daily to its network, including Mutual (MBS) programs, and had contracted with several companies to sponsor its programs. Forrest likely spearheaded preparation of an elaborate brochure telling TSN's coverage story.

Forrest attended the Advertising Federation of America Convention at Hotel Texas in Fort Worth in late October, a ripe opportunity to recruit advertisers to the new network. Advertising and radio publicity were a niche in radio broadcasting he could not have identified as an SMU student performing his first trumpet solos over KRLD. Copies of many of his press releases and some of the ads he created during those early months on the job found their way into *Scrapbook*.

FIRST WEDDING ANNIVERSARY

— ˅ ˄ ˅ —

Family and friends also drew Forrest's attention during the fall. Mildred's sister Verna, her uncle, Homer Wyatt, and her brother Mack paid visits. The young couple celebrated their first anniversary, and Forrest attended the 1938 Pigskin Revue at SMU's McFarlin Auditorium. He went fishing with a KFJZ colleague at Eagle Mountain Lake, catching six fish but throwing back five that were not long enough.

Ancel and Adele attended the SMU-TCU game in Fort Worth in late November with Forrest and Mildred. The next day they all celebrated Thanksgiving together in Dallas at their parents' home. Presumably Ancel and Adele drove Forrest and Mildred to Dallas and took them back home on Sunday evening. Ancel was not working with IBM at this point and soon would open his "Clough Whiteway Service" station in Dallas. Forrest was happy to have his brother close by again.

MILDRED IN PI K A LOCKET

December brought other milestones. On December 17, 1938, Grandmother Mary, 82, and Samuel M. "Popee" Johnson, 88, celebrated their 64th wedding anniversary. Forrest and Mildred sent out their "Mr. and Mrs." Christmas cards and flew out to New Mexico on Braniff Airlines. It was the first airplane flight for each of them and Forrest's first meeting with Mildred's parents.

Forrest made two photos of Mildred at home in their apartment in early January 1939. In one, her curly brown head is bent over a book. In the other, she is happily wearing the Pi KA mother of pearl locket Forrest had given her along with a smile of contentment and joy as a still-young bride (only 23) in her own home and away from the in-laws. It beat being a farmer's wife.

Job Promotions. In January 1939 after four and a half months with TSN, Forrest was promoted to the publicity division of the merchandising, promotion, and publicity department. On March 22 he was elevated again to educational director of that department, which was likely a newly created position with more responsibility but no increase in pay. He was in charge of all college broadcasts, educational features for secondary and elementary schools, and broadcasts of statewide civic interest. His promotion generated a press release and several announcements in local papers and radio industry publications.

The *Ennis Daily* ran a comprehensive article about Forrest and his family of Ennis origins. It was the only publication to mention his handicap:

> For a man who will never admit defeat, the world has only respect and honor . . . . After suffering from infantile paralysis, Forrest Clough determined early in life that he would not permit this handicap to make any difference to him in his career . . . . Many others would have been satisfied with making an excellent scholastic record but not Forrest. He joined the Mustang band and became one of its star soloists . . . . Still not satisfied he was getting the utmost from his opportunities, Clough obtained a job as SMU correspondent for the *Dallas Morning News* and stories of his fine work are still told on the campus and in *The News* office . . . . Handicaps? Never mention them to Forrest W. Clough for he does not believe in such things.

On March 1 he attended the initial meeting of the Pi KA alumni chapter in Fort Worth and a few weeks later a Fort Worth-area banquet of the SMU Ex-Students Association honoring Dr. Umphrey Lee, the incoming SMU President. He let Dance bandleader Phil Harris know he tuned in to his orchestra on the "Jello Show" each Sunday and got a welcome response. Engaging with people and his community was Forrest's natural modus operandi. Who knew what his various activities might lead to, if only to obtain more TSN advertising spots and new topics for his educational programs?

On March 10 a special person visited the radio station—Elliott's mother, First Lady Eleanor Roosevelt. She was interviewed in a 9 a.m. broadcast by Gail Northe, director of women's activities and an authority on ladies' fashions from WFAA. Forrest watched the broadcast from behind the plate glass audience viewing area at the studio and took several photos. While Forrest never met FDR, he was happy to have rubbed shoulders with his hero's wife and son.

ELEANOR ROOSEVELT COMES TO KFJZ, 1939

Forrest also got to know his work colleagues, taking photos of them like a kid excited about a new toy. In fact, in news clips concerning his TSN appointment, he reported photography as his biggest hobby. There's a shot of Forrest with a cigarette in his left hand, sitting in the reception room at TSN with a colleague who is smoking a pipe. While the majority of Americans smoked cigarettes at mid-century, he only occasionally—to my knowledge—smoked a pipe. In mid-April 1939 the young couple hosted their own party at home with KFJZ colleagues sitting around their living room smoking and drinking hard liquor.

Elliott Roosevelt hosted the First Annual Barbecue and Gridiron Dinner at his ranch near Benbrook Lake on Sunday evening April 23, 1939. The mimeographed invitation included an agenda for the event titled "A Calm Day at the Texas State Network:"

Act 1. "Texas under six flags and a flour sack" followed by Interlude*
Act 2. "Texas in the world news" followed by Interlude*
Act 3. "Are network officials necessary?" (KFJZ staff) followed by Interlude*
Act 4. "Doctor 'Cure-All' Pope" (an antidote) followed by Interlude*
Act 5. "When the Northe Gail blew South" followed by Interlude*
Act 6. "Where the V.P.s were on the day of September 16" followed by Interlude*
Act 7. "What happens behind closed director's doors" followed by Interlude*

* Interludes marked with an asterisk denote "surprise acts"

Jack Gordon, a *Fort Worth Press* columnist, described the lively party. In a circus tent set up for the festivity, an impromptu stage provided the platform for a gridiron performance that "roasted" several well-known folks. Recently-elected Governor W. Lee "Pappy" O'Daniel fumed that he and his Hillbilly Band had been cut off the radio. Elliott Roosevelt was declared an authority on "Texas in the News," sociology, theology, anthropology, geology, ideology and obstetrics (Roosevelt, one year younger than Forrest, and his wife Ruth had two young children). An 8"x10" glossy shows Elliott on his knees, pointing his six-shooter at four vice-presidents of TSN and saying, "It's tough to be famous." Startling the audience with a live bullet or a blank in one of the Interludes, Roosevelt shot a hole through the hat of a TSN official who asked for his autograph.

ELLIOTT ROOSEVELT AT KFJZ BARBECUE

More than 55 attendees poured into the ranch's tent, the large majority dressed in Western attire. Costumes included bloomers made from Hillbilly flour sacks and slacks with the mastheads from a dozen Texas newspapers pinned to them. Forrest wore bib overalls, a kerchief, and a straw hat. Mildred can be seen sitting beside him half way back in the jam-packed tent, also in a pair of overalls.

McDonald Observatory Dedication. On May 4 Forrest piled into a car with Clyde Fulks, announcer, and Truett Kimsey, chief engineer. They headed to the Davis mountains in West Texas to attend the dedication of the new McDonald Observatory, operated jointly by the University of Chicago and the University of Texas (UT). The threesome, along with a number of other TSN technicians, planned a 25-minute broadcast the next day as part of the annual meeting of the Southwestern Division of the American Association for the Advancement of Science (AAAS).

Forrest and company stopped in Abilene overnight en route to Ft. Davis to visit KRBC. An *Abilene Reporter-News* clip stated that Forrest, an ex-KRBC announcer and continuity writer, had arranged the observatory broadcast as a feature presentation of his TSN education department. Traversing over a gravel road in a black sedan, Forrest, riding shotgun—and donned in suit, tie and hat—photographed the scrub-brush-covered lands of the Davis Mountains. The observatory, housing the second largest telescope in the world and "equal in height to a five-story building," sat atop 6,791-ft. Mt. Locke, 16 miles from Ft. Davis.

Arriving by noon from Abilene, Forrest relished a "real chuck wagon dinner" put on by the Warner & Swasey Company, builders of the impressive facility. Principal speakers at the mid-afternoon dedication ceremony were the presi-

TRUETT KIMSEY AND FORREST AT MCDONALD'S OBSERVATORY

dents of both universities, the chairman of UT's board of regents, and Professor Otto Struve, observatory director, who gave TSN an exclusive interview. The broadcast was carried over the TSN network using the private telephone line of five ranch houses between Ft. Davis and Mt. Locke. Astronomers from five nations attended the following day's Astronomical Symposium on Galactic and Extragalactic Structure where Dr. Edwin Hubble of Mt. Wilson Observatory near Tucson gave a talk.

With their role completed, the three TSN colleagues left the observatory and headed to "Old Mexico" (Forrest's label) and into Villa Acuna at midnight, where they spent one hour. At 4:30 a.m. on the 6th they arrived in San Antonio. By 6:45 a.m. they had reached Austin where they spent the day sightseeing around the State Capitol and other places. Finally "the boys" made it back to Fort Worth at 11 p.m. Saturday night, likely exhausted after 40-plus hours without sleep. According to a TSN news release, the broadcast of the historical dedication was considered "one of the most important in the history of the network."

Forrest and Mildred were eager to go places on their own. Forrest filled two *Scrapbook* pages with information about the Crosley, the "car of tomorrow...the very car for us!" A convertible sedan with a $350 price tag appealed to Forrest. It weighed less than 925 pounds and had a possible gasoline economy of 60 miles to the gallon at 30 miles per hour. However, for him the Crosley remained a pipe dream. Mildred's more practical nature led them to purchase a used black 1937 Chevrolet sedan in mid-June, a big step up from taxis and buses.

Forrest's boss, Elliott Roosevelt, leaped into the national media arena on June 3 with a 15-minute broadcast three times a week over the Mutual network in Boston, New York, and Washington, DC. Dividing his time between Washington and New York, Roosevelt posed problems to listeners and asked for their solutions, awarding gift radios for the best answers. Was this a way for his father to get a pulse of the people? His absence from Fort Worth left TSN under the direction of H.A. Hutchinson, one of its vice-presidents.

In mid-August Mrs. Elliott Roosevelt bought KTAT for $101,570 (i.e., her stock in the Tarrant Broadcasting Co.) from Raymond Buck (the lawyer who had facilitated Forrest's hiring at KFJZ). To make the purchase, she had to surrender the license for the smaller KFJZ as a condition set by the Federal Radio Commission, putting that 250-watt station out of existence. KTATs powerful 1,000-watt station was to be the key outlet for TSN, of which Elliott was still the general manager despite his absence.[82]

This move allowed the new KTAT, re-designated KFJZ by September 1, to be on the air 24 hours a day, to retain KTAT'S commercial programs, and to continue its own programs, including baseball broadcasts. However, the purchase also called for the dismissal of all but one of the 27 KTAT employees. *Broadcasting*[83] listed Gene Cagle (also an investor in TSN) as KFJZ manager under the new ownership, with Forrest Clough, the fourth mentioned, as publicity and educational director. With the change the entire KFJZ staff moved into the KTAT quarters in the Hotel Texas until they were allowed to return to their own Lancaster Street building, which by then had a second floor. On its first anniversary, the higher-powered KFJZ signed new contracts with 23 stations, three of which were substitutions for the original members of TSN.

Forrest's Educational Programming. Believing radio was a superb tool for education, Forrest inaugurated a new series called "Current Affairs Forum" in cooperation with SMU's Institute of Public Affairs along with leading Texas colleges and universities. Forrest's monthly schedules included a range of topics to appeal to diverse audiences: a series of half-hour musical and dramatic broadcasts from Baylor University; national MBS programs such as Elliott Roosevelt's "America Looks Ahead;" "American Wildlife Talks;" "This Wonderful World" from the Hayden Planetarium; and US Army Band concerts from Washington, DC.

State or local-affiliate educational programs made up the remainder of Forrest's line-up, such as "Friendly Chats" with Governor O'Daniel, from the governor's mansion in Austin; and "True Adventures in Texas History," dramatizations for children featuring the Lone Star State's colorful history.

Besides scheduling and coordination, Forrest's job had promotional and publicity functions as well. He wanted to involve TSN with the new Texas School of the Air, due to begin in 1940 under the auspices of the State

Department of Education. The new school was designed as a statewide supplementary curriculum aid for children in schools with radio-equipment. The proposed reach of the Texas School of the Air from its broadcasting centers in Denton and Austin could be expanded through TSN's statewide network.

Thus, in the fall of 1939 Forrest produced materials about how TSN could serve the Texas School of the Air. With 1,033,500 radio homes linked together by 24 TSN stations in the fourth largest radio network in the world, the new school promised to get wide exposure for any locally developed curricula for children and adults, e.g., programs about specialized industries such as cattle in Amarillo and beef packing in Fort Worth. These programs would be fed with no line charge throughout the network and receive promotional assistance from affiliates and the radio station's central offices.

On the Home Front: Fall 1939. In mid-October Mildred and Forrest moved into a ground floor, unfurnished apartment at 1909 8th Avenue. The new place had a wooden ramp allowing Forrest to roll into his home on his own steam. Maggie, being a real horse trader, negotiated with a local furniture store to take $160 cash instead of the $200 required for installment payments on living and dining room sets, a stove, and an icebox. Mildred's job with the PWA had been eliminated shortly before they moved and finances would be tight for about a year.

Soon after their move, the old 1933-35 SMU band had a second reunion and performed at the annual Pigskin Revue under Bob Goodrich's direction. Forrest once again played his solo "drinking song," joining 22 of his band buddies who appeared in the second act of this popular three-act show. That weekend, he also attended the University of Texas-SMU Homecoming game and Dr. Umphrey Lee's inauguration ceremony as the fourth SMU president, the first with an earned doctorate degree.

At the band reunion, the group decided to publish a quarterly newsletter so members of the famous 1932-36 band could stay in touch with each other. Appearing in January 1940, the first edition probably involved Forrest in producing the column titled "Remember When?" For example, "Clough, reclining on his cot backstage at the Earle Theatre in Philly, was so beautifully shocked by the tall blonde in the Rickey Brothers' act?" Or, remember when "the band slept through the Rose Bowl game" or when "Stuart Sewell combined a malted milk, four beers and a cigar all over the floor of the bus one night?"

The newsletter also featured a list of band firsts: to travel transcontinentally, to make a guest appearance on a coast-to-coast network, to play swing, to travel farther than any college musician has ever traveled, to have stayed after football games to entertain large crowds of people, to habitually make the sports columns, to originate a style of music, and to be the envy and ideal of the current 70 SMU band members. Over the years the band's membership had little turnover—they were a group of musicians tied together stronger than any fraternity.

Finally came Christmas 1939, the end of an era. H.A. Hutchinson, who managed TSN operations in Roosevelt's absence, thanked Forrest for some "smokes" he had gifted. Maggie and G.O. sent a telegram wishing Mildred and Forrest a Merry Christmas. As New Year's rolled around, this young couple was riding high, though they must have noted the dark clouds hovering over Europe. Little did they know the new decade was about to change the world forever.

CHAPTER ELEVEN

BIG CHANGES FOR KFJZ AND TSN

On Halloween 1939 Elliott Roosevelt announced a new project—the formation of the Transcontinental Broadcasting System (TBS) to be the nation's fourth national network. Little more than one year after launching the regional Texas State Network (TSN), Roosevelt wanted to form his own network and sever TSN's national affiliation with the Mutual Broadcasting System (MBS). The anticipated 114-member chain of independent radio stations, ranging from 250 to 50,000 watts, but chiefly low-powered stations, would include all TSN stations in the chain. It would also be a competitor to the three current major networks (NBC, launched in 1926, CBS in 1929, and MBS in 1934).

News clips in the *Star-Telegram* and the *Press* pieced together plans for this new network. John Adams, a vice-president of TSN, would be president/director of the new TBS. Although "one of the leading spirits" behind TBS's formation of the new organization,[84] Roosevelt would hold no formal office. TBS hoped to go on the air January 1, 1940, with the exclusive broadcast of the Cotton Bowl game as its debut and 35 hours per week of paid-for programming. TBS's management set up offices in the General Electric building in New York City with a skeleton staff and stated it expected to earn $6 million a year.

A New Coast-to-Coast Network? Roosevelt was frustrated with his lack of independence vis-à-vis the Mutual Broadcasting System (MBS) and hoped to give himself more leeway by running his own network. At least that was the plan.

Officials justified the new network because of the numerous and artificial restrictions placed on radio stations by the existing major networks, citing the onerous terms of radio versus newspaper advertising. The Chicago firm of Blackett-Sample-Hummert (BSH), Inc., the nation's top ad agency in dollar volume of radio placements, was a backer of the new network. Some of their clients were frustrated by the various barriers, rate and otherwise, they had encountered.

Thus, the bold step of taking on the three established networks. If they would not play ball, then Elliott and BSH would build a new team. The new TBS offered other incentives beyond removing barriers to its member stations, including a more generous remuneration rate than what other networks offered. Payment to stations for commercials was based on a sliding scale varying with power and potential audience, which established each station's card rate. For example, the advertising rate cards saved by Forrest showed KFJZ's rates moving upward over the year because a station could command a higher fee from advertisers with increased wattage and therefore a wider audience.

Likely watching in amazement, but also trepidation, Forrest clipped articles between November and February from local newspapers and two industry periodicals (*Broadcasting* and *Advertising Age*) that documented the risky undertaking. Perhaps Forrest applauded Elliott's reasons for trying to get TBS off the ground. He knew TSN's ability to increase revenue, and hence employee salaries, was being hampered under the old arrangement with MBS.

But, what if it did not succeed? Would he lose his job?

The four primary actors in the controversy were: TBS's senior management, which kept playing musical chairs, with Roosevelt himself first on the sidelines, then in, and finally out; TSN's and MBS's affiliate radio stations; the network's financial backers, primarily BSH and its clients; and the Mutual Broadcasting System (MBS). The latter two actors fought back.

A smoldering brouhaha between Roosevelt and primary backer BSH led to BSH pulling over half of its sponsorship. Elliott Roosevelt resigned from TBS network on December 21,[85] apparently because of his "failure to produce the $175,000 outstanding on his pledge of $245,000, on which he had deposited $70,000 with the network."[86] With TBS's loss of 15-to-20 hours of sponsored air time and the missing $175,000, it was impossible to go on the air without the needed financial backing, which would postpone the network's start until February 1.

With TBS's delayed start, MBS, whose affiliate stations were being raided by Elliott's new network, jumped in, revamping and expanding its efforts to solve the problem. This led to at least eleven of Texas State Network's 24 stations pulling out of the new TBS affiliation. In the end MBS made adjustments, including exclusive five-year contracts with each of its affiliate stations, to counter the new competitor's plans to lure MBS members into the TBS fold. With its realignment in Texas, by February 1, 1940, MBS had a new lineup of 118 stations.[87] This included canceling its contracts with TSN as an entity and signing 12 Texas stations, including Fort Worth's KFJZ, as individual outlets as well as the addition of several new stations. MBS also planned to strengthen its competitive position by establishing package discounts to advertisers buying blocks of time on a large number of MBS stations.

Mutual Broadcasting's realignment managed to prevent the proposed network's opening. In the end the Transcontinental Broadcasting System (TBS) simply failed to materialize. *Scrapbook* contained no further information about this "ghost-to-ghost" network, as some called it.[88] The unnecessary outlay of money, unsuccessful maneuverings to get financing, and obvious hard feelings left many who had supported Elliott outraged. However, these wealthy tycoons needed Elliott and covered up the debacle to prevent it from becoming a public albatross around his father's neck in the upcoming election. How the loans were paid off (or not) and by whom would not be fully revealed until 1945 Congressional hearings about Elliott's finances.[89]

One fortunate outcome for KFJZ and its employees was that the TBS fiasco had forced the more favorable MBS adjustments not forthcoming earlier. In the end Forrest was surely relieved that TSN, though smaller, was still intact, that MBS got Elliott's message and made adjustments, and that he still had a job.

The stress of this new venture put Roosevelt into Cook Hospital "for a rest" in late November 1939 and perhaps caused a minor car crash he and his wife were in on December 4th. Two months later a *Star-Telegram* photo shows Elliott and Ruth standing beside their well-stocked automobile in Tucson, Arizona, en route to hunt big game in Mexico. The quixotic boss would escape his critics—and his creditors—for awhile.

—◦◦◦—

On January 20, 1940, *The Fort-Worth Star-Telegram* ran a full-page personal sketch[90] of Elliott's father, FDR, the man who had lived seven years in the White House. It featured two photos of the president taken of the same face angle, one made in 1933 and another in 1939. The article focused on FDR the man, many of his daily habits in the White House, the family's changes and happenings over seven years, deaths and tragedy among several friends and those in his administration. He had only gained five pounds in the seven years, from 182-187, stayed at his desk from 9-6 daily, had friends to lunch in his office, then dinner at six, often inviting the last visitor on his day's schedule to join him. He was an avid collector of stamps (25-30,000 of them), naval/seafaring prints, and ship models (77 scattered around the White House and his office). He was in excellent health and swam daily to keep fit.

FDR once told an old friend that the "weakened legs that infantile paralysis left him," were his greatest handicap but also his greatest asset because they kept him working at his desk all day and he was not tempted to get up and walk around. This mention of his disability came toward the end, almost as an afterthought. Both FDR and Forrest saw their handicaps as unimportant and found ways to enjoy life that did not require the use of their legs.

Texas School of the Air and Some Good News. In the midst of all the activity around the TBS fiasco, Forrest managed to stay focused on his educational radio programming, probably wondering from one day to the next which network would be carrying his programs. Both Fort Worth newspapers reported on January 9 that Texas School of the Air would begin in February carrying three series of 15-30-minute programs per week for sixteen weeks to more than 3,000 Texas schools.[91] Forrest's promotional efforts to the Texas School Superintendents had paid off and TSN got the contract. His School of the Air programs finally took flight, although everyone was still waiting to hear the outcome of Roosevelt's new TBS network.

The programs would be planned, written and produced by three organizations: The University of Texas, in language arts for juniors and seniors; the Dallas Radio Workshop, on social relations of living together in a democratic society for the intermediate grades; and the joint sponsorship of North Texas State Teachers College and Texas State College for Women, on elementary science for the lower grades. His February TSN public service schedule showed 30-minute programs being aired five days a week for the different levels of students. Because KFJZ now had an individual contract with the Mutual Broadcasting System (MBS), Forrest was able to continue carrying and expanding the original MBS network programs in his schedule as well.

Forrest developed five pages of double-spaced cue sheets for the inaugural broadcast of the Texas School of the Air, set for 1-1:30 p.m. on February 4, 1940. He had scheduled, to the second, when each of five different TSN stations would begin to feed its part of the program. After announcer John Hopkins introduced the show at KFJZ in Fort Worth, 20 seconds were allotted to the theme song of "Texas Our Texas" by W. J. Marsh. Then Forrest came on the air as TSN's representative in Elliott Roosevelt's absence and read a 2.5 minute script he had written informing the public of how and what the school programs would consist of each week. Educational leaders contended Forrest's series of programs was "the most progressive step in Texas educational history."[92]

Eager to be behind a mike again, Forrest wrote and broadcast the public service program "Crime and Death Take No Holiday" for 15 minutes each afternoon. He gave news and statistics about traffic accidents and death by other unnatural causes in cooperation with the Texas State Department of Public Safety.

He was also invited to play his trumpet with the TSN orchestra on the Budweiser-sponsored show on March 8 titled "The Perfect Host Entertains." Jimmy McClain of the station introduced Forrest with laudatory comments and ended with:

> Now his fine work as Educational Director of the TSN leaves him only 'hobby time' for his beloved trumpet. But as ever, there's a thrill in his every trill! Listen, as Budweiser, the Perfect Host, presents Mr. Forrest Clough.

FORREST AT MICROPHONE, 1941

After Forrest's presentation with the orchestra, McClain read a script he had written about two kinds of people: happy versus unhappy. Wealth had little to do with which category a person belonged to. Referring to it as the "disease of unhappiness," McClain suggested the first cure for this ill is a smile. Just as a singer smiles because it can be heard in the tone of his voice, a smile from the heart is felt by everyone and they are more likely to be friendly and companionable. Since this had been Forrest's practiced philosophy throughout his life, he may have helped his friend write the script.

A welcome surprise arrived on Forrest's desk on April 9—a letter on TSN stationery from Elliott Roosevelt, back from Mexico:

Dear Forrest:
    I have just been going over the KFJZ statement for the month of March and I . . . am highly pleased with the progress being made.
    KFJZ has just experienced one of its greatest months since going on the air about 15 years ago. Such progress cannot be made without the

wholehearted cooperation of each employee.

I have instructed the Accounting Department to add a 5% bonus to your check this week, as a token of my appreciation for your loyalty and cooperation. I am convinced that the station can . . . continue to do such a good job that I can, from time to time, give you other bonuses, and I hope in the near future some much-needed permanent general increase in salary.

Sincerely, Elliott Roosevelt, President

To KFJZ employees, this letter meant that MBS's changes with improved remuneration rates and other incentives were working to KFJZ's and TSN's advantage.

Following on this good news, Forrest received another letter on May 9 from TSN general manager H. A. Hutchinson:

Dear Forrest:

It has been the desire of this company to restore salary cuts as quickly as possible. To date, as you perhaps realize, this has been impossible to do in line with the revenue that the company is receiving.

Mr. Roosevelt is now on the air again as commentator for one of the large national advertisers, for which he is receiving a talent fee. Out of this talent fee he is allocating a certain amount each month which he wishes to be passed on to his employees as an expression of his appreciation for their special loyalty and cooperation since the streamlining of KFJZ and the network.

Effective this date, an amount equal to 10% of your regular salary will be . . . included in your . . . paychecks, beginning May 15.

Sincerely yours, H. A. Hutchinson

Author Chris Hansen told us why there was insufficient revenue as early as late 1938 to meet payroll. However, *Scrapbook* contained no mention of the original salary cut or whether a 10% increase made up for it. This must have been hard on the couple during Mildred's one-year lay-off from her government job. Roosevelt's misadventures—TSN's overextension in 1938 and the TBS fiasco a year later—had put all of his employees at risk.

Forrest attended the Conference on Education by Radio at the University of Texas on August 7-8, 1940. Someone, perhaps not from KFJZ, had to drive him to and from Austin. His talk titled "Future Prospects for Educational Broadcasting over the Texas State Network" highlighted accomplishments thus far. In the nine months from September 1939 to June 1940:

.... *exclusive of the numerous 'public service' broadcasts fed our stations from the Mutual Broadcasting System, we consistently originated upwards of forty . . . [educational] programs per week from our various stations over the state.*

He cited the monthly educational bulletins mailed to increasing numbers of school and civic leaders statewide.

And then there was his prize—Texas School of the Air—which was broadcasting regularly after six months to approximately 750,000 Texas school children. As for the periodic forums on national and international concerns, he gave a word of caution: it was essential that TSN ensure that

.... *both sides of controversial issues are presented by authorities on the subject ... in order that Texas may be served in a democratic way.*

On TSN's two-year anniversary (September 15, 1940) Forrest issued a press release reviewing the star-studded inaugural ceremonies and many of the network's achievements in programming to date. He listed current advertisers, including BSH's two clients who had pulled their ads and were partially responsible for the TBS failure, who were back on the MBS and TSN bandwagon.

On the Home Front in 1940. On February 25, Forrest took Mildred to the Melba Theater in Dallas for a Sunday matinee of the movie *Gone with the Wind*, starring Clark Gable as Rhett Butler and Vivian Leigh as Scarlett O'Hara. Tickets cost $1.20 each, a splurge on one $30/week salary. Mildred was so impressed that three years later she wanted to name her daughter Melanie after Olivia de Havilland's role, but Forrest said no.

On March 2 the *Press* announced new officers for the local alumni chapter of Pi Kappa Alpha with Forrest elected Secretary-Treasurer. In early April he returned to Dallas for the funeral of his 82-year-old Grandmother Mary Ross Johnson, beloved poet, pianist, and spiritual inspiration to Forrest.

The May 1940 "Midnight Oil" publication at SMU's Dallas College dedicated its edition to Dr. G.O. Clough for his sympathetic understanding of the needs of students. G.O. had served for six years as the first Director of Extension of an expanded downtown college with a residence credit program. The school had started as a struggling non-credit night school in

MAGGIE'S PARENTS, MARY AND SAMUEL JOHNSON, 1937

1920 with classes held in various downtown buildings before locating in the YMCA Administration building at 1709 Jackson Street. Under Dr. Clough's direction, it had become a self-supporting, growing and thriving downtown college where Forrest had taught radio and journalism classes during his 1937-38 job-search-hiatus.

In late May Forrest received a memo from Hutchinson approving his request for his vacation from June 9-23. Two weeks plus federal and state holidays was the maximum vacation time that Forrest ever received from KFJZ in his 32-year career there. As on this and many future vacations, he and Mildred headed their car to New Mexico, an increasingly popular tourist destination, this time with sister Margaret along.

Forrest celebrated his 31st birthday soon after returning from the trip, which was mentioned in *Radio Daily* on July 5. Life was good for the newlyweds, though Mildred had not yet returned to work.

Another Roosevelt Surprise. On May 29 the *Press* featured five outstanding Fort Worth residents who were listed in Who's Who in America. Elliott Roosevelt and Texas Governor W. Lee O'Daniel were two of them along with TCU's head coach, the editor of *The Fort Worth Press*, and a local violinist. Roosevelt's tribute mentioned that he bought KFJZ in 1937, organized Texas State Network in 1938, and was President of TSN as well as of Tarrant County Broadcasting Co. The article also stated his news commentaries were broadcast over the national Mutual Broadcasting System.

No mention was made of the TBS fiasco. Local movers and shakers surely wanted to stay in Elliott's good graces, and hence his father's, even though at this time he reportedly was laying low to avoid his creditors. Raymond Buck, who had been instrumental in Forrest's hiring at KFJZ, once said that Elliott was a great salesman but stank as a businessman. By 1940 TSN stock had become worthless.[93]

Three months later, and only a week after the two-year anniversary of TSN, KFJZ's employees were taken by surprise. On September 21 the *Star-Telegram* announced that Elliott Roosevelt had returned home to wind up his business affairs before reporting October 7 to Wright-Patterson field in Ohio for duty in the procurement division of the Army Air Corps.

In early October both local papers announced that Roosevelt had given up his $76,000 annual pay at TSN to be a Captain in the Army Air Corps (USAAC) for $316-416 a month, depending on which paper one read. Only men between 18 and 35 without dependents were eligible for service. He was married, had three children, and could not enlist as a private. Elliott had no choice but to seek an alternative service and went to see family friend Brigadier General Henry "Hap" Arnold, head of the Army Air Corps.

Although Elliott hoped to become a pilot, he failed the physical due to poor eyesight and his excessive height (6'3"), weight and age for new pilots. Instead, by signing waivers, and on Arnold's recommendation, Elliott qualified as a captain and received a reserve specialist assignment in procurement. He traveled to Dayton, Ohio, with his family and lived in a house off base.

Other reasons not publicly offered were behind Elliott's move to the military. Congress had passed a military conscription law in September 1940. Even though Elliott had dependents and was exempt from the draft, by enlisting he would have a choice. Besides, it was only six weeks until the election, and voters might react negatively if the President's sons did not serve, even though the US was not yet at war. Eleanor felt all four of her sons should serve, and all eventually did. James became a captain in the

Marine Corps. Franklin and John, the youngest sons, received reserve commissions in the US Navy, FDR's favorite service. Given his interest and past experience in the aviation industry, Elliott chose the USAAC.

However, more pertinent to this story according to Hansen:

> A catalyst for his sudden fit of patriotism . . . was his failed broadcasting business and the several hundred thousand dollars he owed and couldn't repay. The loans, some of which were obtained through the considerable persuasive powers of the president, would become a toxic issue five years later when Congress investigated his financial affairs.[94]

Joining the USAAC would keep his creditors at bay while he was in the service. He would get out of radio while, on the surface, he appeared to be at the top of his field. Elliott went on to a meteoric rise in rank to that of Brigadier General, had an illustrious military career in air reconnaissance, and made significant contributions to the war effort.[95] However, Elliott Roosevelt was plagued with scandal throughout his life, and his controversial role in the airmail scandal and failed radio businesses were just the beginning.

Forrest clipped news articles about his boss (and his boss's father) every time they appeared. Whether he was just an extremely loyal employee and fascinated by the Roosevelt mystique or because of his personal identification with FDR is not clear. Perhaps some of both. Forrest was likely also worried about the future of KFJZ following Elliott's departure.

KFJZ under New Management. Meanwhile, H.A. Hutchinson remained in charge as general manager of KFJZ, with no increase in pay according to newspapers, and officially became Forrest's new boss. With the ten percent raises to employees just a few months earlier, the station must have anticipated enough revenue through advertising and the new MBS arrangements to continue operations despite the loss of Elliott's talent fee shared with employees. Gene Cagle, became KFJZ's president and, along with Texas backers, turned the station into a profitable business.[96] *Scrapbook* contained no further mention of salaries, promotions, or Elliott Roosevelt. Henceforth, Forrest would look up to Gene Cagle.

On October 8 *Radio Daily*, an 8-page 5-cent New York newspaper, announced Forrest's TSN plans to launch the Texas Inter-Collegiate

Broadcaster's Council to coordinate the best radio program possibilities from each institution. The inaugural conference for this organization met at TSN headquarters in Fort Worth with representatives from 12 leading colleges and universities in attendance. Forrest was named president and coordinating chairman, while vice-chairmen included representatives from Baylor, TCU, SMU, the University of Texas, and the Texas State College for Women. Forrest made a presentation, titled "Importance of College Radio Workshops to American Broadcasting," at North Texas Agricultural College at Arlington.

The *Radio Daily* also covered another topic—television—and provided news of the Radio Manufacturers Association meeting on October 8 in New York. The head of General Electric's radio and television department reported on the progress of the recently formed National Television Systems Committee, which hoped to recommend standards for the new industry by early 1941. Forrest was eager to learn more about this new medium that could enhance his educational programming. He was carving his niche in radio broadcasting and hoped to expand that when KFJZ radio added television to its domain.

Although Forrest attended the fall 1940 Pigskin Revue, this year band members from his era did not perform. The popular *Collier's* magazine[97] offered a summary of the band's history to date under four band directors, three of whom added their own touches to Cy Barcus's original new swing style he had used to recruit students to play in the band. All three carried on Barcus's tradition of playing their popular theme song:

> Whether it is Peruna that makes the SMU band or the band that makes Peruna, there is no doubt that the band is in a class by itself among college tooters. Boy, they swing it! . . . . the Methodist maniacs are in tune with history.

Apparently, some band member had gone to east Texas and:

> . . . . observed the natives in the act of drinking Peruna, a bottled tonic [medicinal, with a heavy dose of alcohol].[98] He also brought back the east-Texas version of "They'll be Loaded with Peruna When They Come,"

which he surreptitiously taught the other band members. They began playing it, the students began singing it, and SMU soon had its theme song.

By 1940 Frank Malone recruited band members for the ten scholarships he had to give each year as carefully as Matty Bell recruited football players. Musicians were choosing SMU in order to be in the band, unlike the band's struggling early days when there were no scholarships and student band members did a lot of extra work because they liked music. Proud of his affiliation, Forrest had helped make music history at SMU.

When the national draft legislation was passed in September, the Selective Service mailed out booklets entitled "Bulletin of Information for Persons Registered 1940." Dating his booklet "October 10, 1940," Forrest clearly fit into Class IV: "those persons deferred from service either by the law itself or for physical disability or other reasons." His brother Ancel was listed as Class I—"those persons available for training and service in the land or naval forces." However, Ancel flunked his physical due to flat feet. He was also about to become a father at age 29, which would have made him ineligible as well.

Ancel proudly wrote a letter to his brother on November 13 from the Electric Accounting Machine Division at his Dallas office of International Business Machines (IBM), the company for whom he worked as a top salesman his entire career:

> Dear Bud:
>   Don't faint, don't pass out, don't lose your head, don't fall out of your wheel chair, don't announce the shock over the radio, but prepare yourself for a surprise, and take it like a man. Next May we will have a new arrival in our family. Yes, you will be an <u>Uncle</u>. I will be a <u>daddy</u> and Adele, a mother. So we are very happy. Started to tell you Sunday, but just didn't. Just told Mother the other day.
>
> Your bud, Ancel

What a joy. The next generation of Cloughs was about to begin. And Ancel and Forrest, both ineligible for military service, would be around to enjoy the little one. Meanwhile, Forrest and Mildred celebrated their third wedding anniversary.

AFTER THE SCRAPBOOKS
END: 1940-1983

CHAPTER TWELVE

THE HOUSE ON WILLING AVENUE: 1940-1949

Scrapbook VII's final entries in December 1940 indicated Forrest was thriving two years into his job as educational director at KFJZ Radio. Why he stopped making scrapbooks is anyone's guess—whether it was the growing war in Europe, the departure for military service of the boss who had hired him, the pending war effort at home, or just a busy home life. Once married, Forrest focused his energies on making a living to help support his family—and enjoying what he had worked so hard for. Perhaps making scrapbooks had been his form of therapy, a way to stoke his ego as well as his self-esteem in the face of such uncertainty about his future.

The last 43 years of my father's life are pieced together from several photo albums made in the 1940s, fifties, and early sixties, from my own recollections, numerous conversations with my brother, and interviews with family members and friends of his. Forrest would leave no more commentary about the war or the post-war era—where life was comfortable for the first time since before the Great Depression.

In October 1940 Forrest and Mildred began building their first home at 2924 Willing Avenue in south Fort Worth. Although Mildred had taken the Civil Service exam before being laid off at WPA the previous year, her name did not surface to the top of the Civil Service register for twelve months. She went back to work for the government just before construction began on the new house, believing it had been worth holding out for a federal job that paid almost double what she would earn in the private sector.

FORREST PAINTING THE FENCE

The new home was a two-bedroom, one-bath frame house with a one-car garage—a house Forrest always claimed had cost only $3,500. A cement ramp to the back porch and one inside the garage gave Forrest easy access to his new home. In March 1941 they moved in. A colleague from KFJZ along with a Pi K A fraternity brother helped build a picket fence around the backyard, and friends and relatives pitched in to paint it white.

While Mildred had waited for a government job to materialize during their second year in Fort Worth, she was able to drive Forrest to and from work in their used Chevrolet. When she went back to work, Forrest presumably resorted again to taxis to accommodate her schedule. With her salary, they could finally afford to create a home to their liking after three years in two rental apartments and living with Forrest's parents.

In May 1941 Forrest became an uncle when Ancel Michael was born, the first grandchild for his parents—a nice Mother's Day present for Maggie, then in her early sixties. Forrest filled photo albums with pictures of his nephew Mike on each monthly milestone. He was a proud uncle, biding his time while he and Mildred built their nest in the hope of having their own family one day.

In mid-July Forrest and Mildred, accompanied by Maggie, G.O., and Margaret, piled into their new second-hand Chrysler Royal sedan and headed to Colorado for a two-week vacation. US entry into the Second World War would not occur for another five months, so gasoline rationing did not deter their travels. Staying in motor courts, they visited Pike's Peak where they found snow, Cave of the Winds, Garden of the Gods, Denver, Trail Ridge Road on the western side of Estes Park (more snow, something unusual for these Texans), and crossed the Continental Divide. The family must have enjoyed revisiting some of the places they had seen during G.O's summer teaching at the university in Greeley. En route home they spent several days with Mildred's family in eastern New Mexico, just as the wheat harvest was coming in. It was the first time Maggie and G.O. had met Ethel and Charles Wyatt.

After the bombing of Pearl Harbor on December 7, 1941, several family members and friends were called up, including Mildred's brother Corban (C.H.). With both Forrest and Ancel ineligible for military service, the war would go on without them. However, the family would be subject to the gas and food rationing and other domestic inconveniences that affected all Americans during the lengthy war in Europe and the Pacific.

By late spring a dog house appeared in the Willing Avenue back yard for their new cocker spaniel named Mac, and Mildred was pregnant with me. In September, she was "showing" and, as a government employee, not allowed to work, so she quit and took the train out to New Mexico for a 2-week visit with her parents. Presumably, Maggie came to stay with Forrest while she was gone. Maggie and Margaret gave her a "stork shower" in Dallas on November 14. The couple, at the height of "stork anticipation," spent a cozy Christmas at home with a roaring fire, Mildred, sitting comfortably, sewing, and Forrest, in his wheelchair, smoking his pipe and reading.

In the wee hours of February 6, 1943, Mildred went into labor. As pre-planned, Forrest called Johnny Smith, who worked at KFJZ, single, and, according to Johnny, still a teenager. Johnny came right over and helped Forrest into the car. Mildred had a few housekeeping chores to finish, including letting Mac out to relieve himself, before her mother-in-law arrived to take care of Forrest while she was in the hospital. Johnny swore in a 2001 interview that once he had loaded my father into the car and he was patiently waiting in the driver's seat, Forrest said, "Well, Johnny, let's get going!"

Johnny's reply: "Well, don't you think we should wait for Mildred?!?"

KFJZ COLLEAGUES DAVE NAUGLE (L) AND JOHNNY SMITH (R)
PERUSE SCRAPBOOKS WITH SUSAN, 2001

According to my mother, they arrived at the hospital about 5 a.m. and she was given an injection of "twilight sleep." When Maggie arrived from Dallas, she joined Mildred in the labor room, while Forrest was forced to wait outside.

Susan Melinda Clough arrived at 11:07 in the morning. I weighed 9 lbs.10 oz., a large size for my 5'3," 110 lb. mother. As was the custom of the day, the anesthetist put Mildred completely out. She did not remember a thing, and I arrived drugged and slept much of the first three days of my life, uninterested in nursing. My drowsiness and indifference to her milk caused Mildred to develop mastitis. We stayed in Harris Hospital for more than a week before coming home, probably due to the inflammation. My grandmother, who had stayed to help Forrest, hired a nurse for three weeks. Although protocol called for breast-feeding in 1943, my mother only managed to nurse me for two-and-a-half months.

When I was 13 months old, Mama took me by train to Abilene where we met Aunt Verna and her new husband O.T., who possessed enough gas rationing stamps to drive us to New Mexico to visit my Wyatt grandparents. Mildred had not seen her parents in over a year, and she likely left Forrest in the hands of his mother while she was away.

Numerous visitors—neighbors, KFJZ colleagues, friends, and relatives on both sides of the family—graced our family's doorsteps in my early years. These included: Wally Blanton (from KFJZ) and his family, Aunt Margaret and her handsome Navy lieutenant fiancé Robert J. LaPrade, Jr., and Mary Lou MacBeth, my mother's college friend, whose lieutenant junior grade husband Mack was away on naval assignment, and her young daughter. My parents also managed to find enough gas ration stamps to make periodic trips to Dallas to visit my father's extended family.

My reign as queen of the household came to a halt on Wednesday, January 10, 1945, when brother George Hamilton entered the world a week early. Forrest was ecstatic to have a son whom they named after both grandfathers. Apparently, my biggest indignation at the arrival of this competitor was missing Aunt Margaret's wedding on January 12, where I was to have been a flower girl.

My father could not attend his sister's Friday night wedding due to the logistics of getting him and, hence, me to the Highland Park Methodist Church in Dallas. Although Margaret has no idea who stayed with my father and me while my mother was in the hospital, she believes Maggie came to Fort Worth on Saturday morning right after the Friday evening wedding. Margaret remembers visiting us on Sunday the 14th before she and Bob took off for San Diego and Bob's deployment to the Pacific where the war would continue for another half year. Logistical planning was a constant ingredient in my parents' relationship. Someone always had to stay overnight to help Forrest.

Pictures of baby George's first few months dominated Forrest's photo albums, though I showed up in a few places. Reticence would best describe my expression as I peered over my three-month-old brother's baby carriage. Who was this new person I was going to have to share my parents with? That May we greeted aunts Gladys and Jess, visiting from New Mexico. Uncle Bub (C.H.) stopped over in November 1945 en route home from the war in Europe, where he had served as an army paymaster and was in the Battle of the Bulge.

In the meantime, the National Foundation for Infantile Paralysis (NFIP) and the March of Dimes were still going strong. In 1945 the March of Dimes raised $18.9 million for NFIP. A volunteer army of millions of mothers marched through neighborhoods one night a year in January collecting for the organization. Movie theaters and sports events across the country routinely passed the hat to collect for the cause. The NFIP had over 3,000 local chapters of volunteer helpers.

—✦—

At the beginning of 1946, the usual birthday celebrations occurred in January and February—George's first with a big cake and a visit from Aunt Margaret, whose new husband was still away in the Pacific, and my third with the Blantons' twin daughters at my party. Just as we did every spring, Mike and I pulled our Easter eggs in a little wagon around our grandmother's backyard in Dallas. By then, according to my mother, my father was calling me "Suzie Q," a moniker that embarrassed me later when I entered my tomboy stage in elementary school.

With war and rationing behind us, in June 1946 my mother drove our family of four to New Mexico, beginning what would become an almost annual vacation to the state through the mid-fifties to see her family. We usually stopped overnight in Abilene to visit Verna and family then continued on the next day to Aunt Gladys' at the crossroads of McAlister,

New Mexico, and to the family homestead seven miles north in the tiny community of Jordan. On that first trip for our foursome to the flat, high plains of eastern New Mexico, we watched Uncle Ben harvest his wheat fields, and I accompanied my grandfather to his Quonset hut barn to milk the cows.

It was this summer of 1946 when Forrest made family movies and stellar black and white photos of Charles and Ethel. One photo could have been an award-winner—reminiscent of Dorothea Lange, herself a polio survivor who had the disease in 1902 and walked with a serious limp. Ms. Lange left the world iconic and

CHARLES AND ETHEL WYATT

poignant images of dust-bowl families and of the Japanese internment camps in California. In a 1960s University of California oral history by Suzanne Riess, Lange offered a brief statement of polio's impact on her.[99] Polio "was the most important thing that happened to me . . . formed me, guided me, instructed me, helped me, humiliated me." Lange maintained her disability was an asset wherever she went because people were more considerate of her.[100] Forrest saw his disability similarly.

Professional Activities. Forrest's lifelong interest in people would not allow him to isolate into his marriage, family, and job, and live a quiet life of contentment. He had hooked up with Sigma Delta Chi's Fort Worth chapter and his old friend Walter Humphrey soon after arriving in Fort Worth in 1938. The organization was made up mostly of people working on newspapers but would become an important social outlet for Forrest over the years. Also, he either initiated the development of or was heavily involved with local chapters of SMU and Pi Kappa Alpha (Pi KA) alumni groups. Although he used his networking skills to organize these people into groups, he often needed Mildred to pack us kids into the car and ferry him to evening meetings.

An excellent newspaperman and organizer himself, Humphrey, editor of *The Fort Worth Press*, instigated the annual Sigma Delta Chi Gridiron dinners in 1946, usually held in the spring. By then Forrest was serving as treasurer of the Fort Worth chapter and handled ticket sales for the dinner "roasts" of dignitaries, proceeds of which supported scholarships for journalism students.

Forrest received a letter from Walter Humphrey thanking him for handling the tickets and finances for the second Gridiron Dinner held on April 1, 1947, All Fools' Day, at the Texas Hotel for $5 a head. Humphrey's note came on Shoreham Hotel stationery from Washington, DC, where he had witnessed "the original Gridiron before a house of 547, all in white tie and tails! It was a good show and worth coming to Washington for. The President, all the main candidates but Dewey, and most of the big shots in Washington were on hand." Forrest would have loved to attend that high-end Gridiron Dinner in the nation's capital.

The annual Gridiron Dinner in April 1949 summoned all invitees to surrender themselves to be "grilled, roasted, toasted, parboiled and fried, all in the interest of the public welfare." Texas politicians from Governor-elect Allen Shivers on down were raked across the coals. Walter published a four-page rag called *The Yellow Jaundice* that gave a preview of The Gridiron Follies for that year. Forrest apparently arrived in costume as Mr. Moneybags.

Forrest sold tickets to these Gridiron dinners held from 1947 through the late fifties, handling sales of 500-700 tickets each dinner. When George and I were in elementary and junior high school, we remember our dining table covered with checks from attendees and helping Daddy address and stuff tickets into return envelopes.

In the spring of 1948 both local newspapers announced the founding of the Fort Worth SMU Alumni Club, with 39 charter members and Forrest elected as president of the organization. Likely initiating the club's start-up effort, Forrest recruited Ancel to the three-man publicity and arrangements committee. In mid-June he orchestrated an SMU alumni club barbecue picnic at Sycamore Park.[101]

Three years later Forrest invited head SMU football coach H.N. (Rusty) Russell to address the SMU alumni club of 70 members at the Triple XXX Restaurant in Fort Worth. He relinquished his presidency to another alum at that meeting, but likely attended meetings as long as the group met. These professional meetings were the major way gregarious Forrest could make new and revive old friendships.

Forrest also reactivated Fort Worth's Pi KA alumni group, which had been organized with his help in the late 1930s. Their reconstituted group held its first monthly meeting in April 1949 at a local restaurant not far from our home. Naturally, Forrest, was elected President and the 19 actives began a membership drive. Unless Forrest provided constant cheerleading, I wonder how long this second effort continued. Five years later, a local attorney made a third attempt to organize 62 Pi KA alums ("Pikes") living in the Fort Worth area.

Life at KFJZ in the Late Forties. Little appeared in the photo albums to offer clues about Forrest's work life at KFJZ Radio. There is no indication when he gave up or was moved from educational programming (his position in 1940), which he enjoyed so much. He was designated "traffic manager," who scheduled programs and ads the salesmen brought in, sometime in the late 1940s. His earlier career enthusiasms took a back seat to family considerations. Broadcasting was out, but he did mention a few events that happened over the years, including this WRR Radio photo.

BUCK RUSSEY, TRUETT KIMSEY, MRS. KIMSEY, MILDRED, FORREST – WRR CHRISTMAS PARTY, DALLAS, 1947

In one July 1946 adventure for the station, he made a plane trip to New York City, staying five-nights at the St. Moritz Hotel at 50 Central Park South for a total of $28.29. Someone named Carl Haverlin at the New York office he was visiting (likely a radio station) made his reservations that were confirmed by telegram. He saved a breakfast menu from the hotel and a dinner menu from Sardi's on W. 44th. The expense report shows that he paid excess baggage fees (presumably for his wheelchair), traveled around the city by taxi, gave numerous tips to those helping him, and a $14.80 "courtesy gift," perhaps to a colleague he took to dinner. Ten years after he lived on his own at the Abilene Hilton Hotel, he managed a solo trip to New York City. If a colleague accompanied him, he left no record of it.

Missing George's birthday two years later, Forrest spent two days in January visiting KCRS in Midland, Texas. Taking numerous photos, he must have accompanied someone from KFJZ who did the driving, likewise on a second trip in August. KCRS was probably a new TSN station.

In August 1948 our family attended a KFJZ picnic at Barnes Place, a pleasant tree-covered spot on a small lake in the River Oaks area of Fort Worth. This was the first KFJZ "social" documented following Elliott Roosevelt's bar-becue almost ten years earlier. KFJZ's new management was back in the black, a relief to Forrest.

In early April 1949

```
EXPENSE ACCOUNT TO N.Y.
  JULY 30-AUGUST 3, 1946

7.25.46    Travellers Checks    2.25
7.29.46    Smokes, Gum           .75
7.29.46    Tip & Insurance       .75
           Excess Baggage       3.75
7.30.46    Taxi, tips, foods   18.60
7.31.46    Taxi, tips, foods    5.26
8.1.46     Taxi, tips, foods,
             Entertainment      25.66
8.2.46     Taxi, tips, foods,
             Entertainment      49.52
8.3.46     Hotel bill           28.29
           Entertainment, taxi,
             tips, meals        55.65
           Excess Baggage        4.76
           Courtesy Gift        14.80

                      T O T A L  210.00


AMT CARRIED    $350.00

AMT RETURNED    140.00
```

NEW YORK CITY EXPENSES, 1946

Forrest went on a 3-day fishing trip to Possum Kingdom Lake near the Oklahoma border with several of his friends from the station. Pictured at the KFJZ camp consisting of two cabins were four colleagues and an African American man named Lonnie, who had a cooking pot in his hand. I am sure Forrest was delighted to be included in outings like this even though someone always had to help him get what he needed.

Family Life. At Christmas of 1946 Santa brought not-yet-two-year-old George his first electric train with a figure-eight track. Probably reminded of his band days, Forrest finally had a young son with whom to share his enthusiasm for railroading. He likely wanted to be a playful father unlike his own reserved academic father who had no hobbies, according to Margaret.

More relatives—my mother had 26 first cousins—came to visit in 1947 as well as Forrest's old SMU friend Bob Williams on home leave from Saudi Arabia. There were the usual birthday parties and Easter egg hunts in Dallas. In July, when I was four and George two, our family motored on to Colorado after stopping to see my Wyatt grandparents. We visited the great sand dunes near Alamosa, where Daddy sat in his chair on the edge of a small stream taking photos of us frolicking in the biggest sandbox we had ever seen. He probably wanted to join us. We did our first mountain hiking, caught a view of "fourteener" Mount Elbert, tallest of the fifty-three 14,000-plus-feet mountains in the state, and traversed the 1,052 ft. high bridge suspended over the Royal Gorge. We rolled my father across in his chair and looked at the Arkansas River passing rapidly below.

By October 1947 Ancel and Adele had built a new home in Fort Worth where Ancel was transferred by IBM. Forrest was happy to see his brother more frequently. Besides recruiting him to help with the SMU Alumni Club, he went with Ancel to the SMU-Rice football game, one of very few he attended over the years because he could not get there under his own steam. In December, while my father sat at the curb and made photos, George and I made our first visit to Santa Claus whose elevated sleigh was parked in front of Mrs. Baird's Bakery. As a 5-year-old, I was excited at the prospect, but George cried and would not sit on Santa's lap.

Forrest and Mildred bought a Plymouth in spring 1948, the first new car they had ever owned. Mother's Day was spent in Dallas that year, and G.O. retired as head of SMU Extension in June. In the summer we headed in our new car to Red River, New Mexico, and the cabin my Aunt Gladys and her husband Ben were building. Red River was a sleepy little town then, with only a roller rink and a community center for square dancing and non-denominational church services. At that time, a downhill ski resort was far from anyone's mind in this beautiful pine-and-fir-tree-covered valley of the Sangre de Cristo mountains. We probably stayed at a cabin motel in town.

Fall 1948 photos revealed our TV set. Reportedly, we were one of the first five families in Fort Worth to obtain one. Many neighbors came into our living room to watch the initial test pattern and a Four Roses ad when WBAP-TV went on the air in September as Texas' first television station. Forrest naturally wanted to be one of the earliest to embrace this new and exciting technology.

As was our custom each Christmas Eve, George and I placed a note for Santa and some cookies beside the fireplace. On Christmas morning, we found the cookies gone and a note from Santa, handwritten in script, which I eventually realized was my father's cursive. For Christmas 1948 Santa brought George a plywood board with new track attached for his electric train. He could enjoy more hours of fun with Daddy. He also received some Lincoln Logs that I persuaded him to share with me, while Santa gave me a clown doll and "girlie" things.

At a family gathering in Dallas in late May, Ancel announced they were moving to Corpus Christi (or simply "Corpus" to our family), Texas, 400 miles away, where he would take on a new sales territory for IBM. An exciting prospect for Ancel but undoubtedly a disappointment for my father, who would miss his brother. By July Ancel, Adele, and Mike were ensconced in their white brick, ranch style home on the Gulf Coast of Texas and we were eager to visit. My parents and I drove to Corpus while brother George stayed in Dallas with our grandparents.

In that coastal town with its palm trees, sea breezes, and balmy weather, Forrest enjoyed his brother's company and reconnected with his former journalism mate Wilbur Cunningham, who was managing the Breakers Hotel. Next came Laredo, Texas, where the MacBeths lived. Marilou's husband had traded his WWII navy uniform for that of a US border patrol officer. Although the MacBeths had come to Fort Worth several times, this was our first opportunity to visit them in Laredo, a town with a population of about 51,000 founded by colonial Spain in 1755.

We ventured with the MacBeths south of the border to Monterrey, Mexico, for two nights at the Regina Courts. This was a big first for Mama and me, who had never been out of the country. My father purchased an automobile insurance policy for August 9-11, the two days we planned to be in Mexico. That policy cost $3.30 and indicated my parents had paid $1,605 ($17,315 in 2019 dollars) for their 1948 Plymouth sedan. Monterrey, founded in 1596, was located in the striking setting of the Huasteca Canyon completely surrounded by mountains. We experienced our first "old world architecture," so unfamiliar to those of us from the north. What I remember most is eating at the then-popular Sanborn's, where my mother allowed me to order a rare treat of hot cocoa. En route home we overnighted in Brownwood with Daddy's cousin J.D. King, who was superintendent of schools and a favorite relative of Daddy's.

In late August 1949, Maggie and G.O. celebrated their 45th anniversary and shortly thereafter I entered first grade at Daggett Elementary School, a yellow brick two-story building with a hipped roof of red clay tiles. Built in 1926, today it is the oldest elementary school still in use in Fort Worth.

Revisiting Willing Avenue Memories. From early childhood I wanted my parents' approval and knew not to create trouble for my mother's difficult, caregiving life. One infant memory occurred after learning to crawl. I circumnavigated the dining table legs a time or two while unraveling several of my mother's spools of thread I had grabbed from her apple green sewing box. What I remember is the tongue lashing by my mother that showed her unhappiness with me.

Sadly, some of my early memories before the age of six are of times when I felt undesirable or got reprimanded. As a student at Mrs. Massey's

kindergarten near our house on Willing (fall 1948), we performed the play of "Sleeping Beauty" for our parents, wearing elaborate costumes that someone's mother had made for us. I so wanted to be Sleeping Beauty, but alas was relegated to being one of the ladies in the court. Not one photo of me in my satin and net ball gown shows a smile on my face. That was perhaps the first of several early disappointments where I learned that one's physical appearance and popularity often spoke louder than one's abilities.

A few other memories surface from living on Willing: Driving with my mother twice daily down Eighth Avenue to

DISAPPOINTED "LADY-IN-WAITING"

take my father to and from work on W. Lancaster, 3.3 miles each way. My brother and I getting spanked by our mother in the back seat of the car for not posing nicely for a professional photographer. Finding the bathtub full of water one May 1949 morning and my mother having a fit that I might let the water out. (The Trinity River had flooded overnight, threatening the city's water supply, killing ten people and forcing 13,000 homes to be evacuated.

The bathtub water was for drinking until the crisis passed.) Seeing my grandmother, who was sleeping on a rollaway bed in the living room, getting undressed and wondering what that funny thing around her middle was (a corset).

At age five or six, two neighbor boys, Wayne and Chip, and I set up a lemonade stand three houses to the north in front of Chip's home. We also tried to smoke grapevine behind his garage. Later I was mad at Chip for some reason and rammed the fin of my metal jet mobile into the back of his heel, almost severing his Achilles tendon and then being forced by my parents to apologize to him. (Wayne and I are still in touch but Chip went to jail for murdering someone.)

CHAPTER THIRTEEN

THE HOUSE ON RYAN PLACE: 1949-1955

My first through sixth grades

Deciding they needed a larger home to give my brother and me separate bedrooms, my parents bought a lot at 2728 Ryan Place Drive, a few blocks away from our home on Willing and a 4-block walking distance to Daggett Elementary. Construction on the one-floor, three-bedroom one-bath house began in early November 1949. Built to their specifications, the ranch-style home included a cement wheelchair ramp from the one-car garage into the house. Ecru brick with green trim, it had a living room picture window, in vogue at the time.

We moved into the new home just in time for Christmas. Like magic, a decorated tree with lots of gifts, including a cowgirl outfit for me, appeared in the new living room. But I was

SUSAN AND HER NEW BIKE, 1949

235

disappointed at not finding a bike. As we usually did after gifts at home, we drove to Dallas to be with my grandparents where Santa had left other surprises. My grandmother insisted that my parents and I go to her garage soon after we arrived where I was thrilled to discover my first bicycle—a used 24-inch girl's bike she had painted blue. I was so proud of that bike—as well as of the doll baby she gave me, dressed in her hand-crocheted sweater, bonnet, booties, mittens, and a smocked dress with bloomers.

After beginning the 1950's with photos of birthday parties and family visits, Daddy once again turned his attention to the 1950 Gridiron dinner held at the Blackstone Hotel. Walter Humphrey published another edition of *The Yellow Jaundice*, which gave some juicy photos of several of the stars of the show dressed in drag. The Gridiron invitation read:

> A hot seat that fits your specifications has been reserved at the griddle. It takes us a whole year to get the lowdown on the highups of Fort Worth and Texas—but we dish it all out in one night. And whatta night!

That year Forrest saved a Gridiron song sheet with lyrics only a Texan in 1950 would appreciate. Two songs though had relevance on a national scale. Harry Truman was the first president to propose the idea of universal health care soon after his inauguration, but got nowhere with it in Congress. The Gridiron poked fun at the President and his push for what many called socialized medicine. Although our family may not have had health coverage until my mother went back to work for the government, my father likely sympathized with his colleagues. Just as the concept still encounters fierce opposition today, these journalists, both Republican and Democrat, were not enamored with the idea and expressed their feelings in these catchy songs.

HARRY'S RAG TAG BAND

Come on along, come on and join
Mr. Truman's welfare state.
Come on along, come on and join,
Harry's waiting at the gate.

He will greet a new born child with a pass
that's good for life.
If you've got a poll tax he'll help you get a wife.
That is the welfare plan what am,
Voter man . . . .

DOCTORS IN THE WELFARE WONDERLAND

Taxes high, they'll get higher,
Your old doc you can't hire.
Too late to beware of.
You'll get your share of
Doctors in our welfare wonderland.

Socialized, you'll be sicker,
You will die, a lot quicker,
You'll get the same pills
For all of your ills.
Living in our welfare wonderland.

In the White House you can count on Truman,
Though he bawls you out in each campaign,
He intends to see that every human
Stays well enough to vote for him again.

Later on, if you're laid up,
We'll be there if you are paid up.
We're socialized today.
Welfare state's here to stay.
We're doctors in the Welfare Wonderland.

This song provides one explanation why so many Texas Democrats helped put Republican President Dwight Eisenhower in the White House two years later. There would be no more talk of national health care until the Social Security Amendments of July 30, 1965, established Medicare and Medicaid under Democratic President Lyndon Johnson. Republican President George W. Bush's administration added drug coverage to Medicare in the early 2000s. Since 2016 it has been the Democrats who champion healthcare for all, fighting Republican efforts to repeal Obamacare.

My father always said he voted for Wendell Wilkie, who ran against FDR in 1940. That election occurred only two short months after Elliott left

KFJZ and joined the military and about the time Daddy's scrapbooks ended. Why the change in loyalty I do not know. For 31 years he had voted Democratic, as had Mildred, whose family of poor farmers were staunch Democrats. He also supported Thomas Dewey in 1944 and 1948.

Even if his dream of being an on-air announcer had faded, Forrest managed to do behind-the-scenes broadcasts to TSN's 16-member network—reduced by a third from its initial membership. The 15-minute program, the only one of its kind in Texas, was aired on closed circuit from Fort Worth at 4:30 p.m. Monday through Friday and at 10:30 am on Saturday. He began each broadcast with:

This is a TSN closed circuit. Not for broadcast. Engineers monitoring please see that this does not go on the air.

These programs informed stations of special public interest events planned for regional broadcast. Or, they asked certain individual stations to report back their availability to run a national network show not previously scheduled. Listeners could not talk back to "the voice" but they could if necessary call or write Forrest.

Calling them Forrest's "ghost broadcasts," KFJZ salesmen jokingly said it was the oldest program on the air without a sponsor and threatened to "peddle his broadcasts" commercially. So Forrest wrote the script, made his broadcast every day, but was not heard by the public over the air. Since his listeners were paid to listen to him, he knew his Hooper rating—the radio industry's major audience rating system during the 1930s and 1940s—would always be the same.

Some Happy Memories. Summer 1950 found George and me at Forest Park's circular swimming pool cooling off on a very hot Father's Day. Apparently, there were no worries about polio that year because my parents allowed us to go swimming in a public pool. Forrest labeled a photo of himself as "The Old Man" just a few days after his 41st birthday.

In August both sets of our grandparents joined us in Red River. The cabin was finally completed after two years of hard work by Uncle Ben and his son Aaron. Constructed with three bedrooms and an empty room for an eventual bath and shower, the cabin was positioned amidst the tree-covered mountainside overlooking the town from the north side. Uncle Ben had built a steep ramp for rolling Daddy up to the porch and into the house and also placed for him in the future bathroom a straight back chair with a hole in the seat and a bucket below. The cabin offered an open floor plan with a bar separating the kitchen from a large living-dining area. Instead of a refrigerator, the cabin had a screened window storage cooler opening in the kitchen and protruding over the roofed back porch, where it could get quite cool on a summer night. An outhouse and extra beds in the open area and on the front porch for the younger generation completed the living space.

That summer we rode horses for the first time, visited Taos pueblo with its tribal dances, and played in mountain streams. My father exhilarated in parking his wheelchair on the front porch and absorbing the majesty, cool air, and scent of the pine and fir trees. For all for us, to relax and play in this idyllic place certainly beat the summer heat and humidity of Texas.

In the forties and fifties the Red River Pass (9,852 feet) was a gravel road with treacherous switchbacks. Family members worried about vapor locks in their cars at high altitude and were always relieved when they completed the descent into the valley or finished climbing the pass to Eagle's Nest and Cimarron. Nerve-wracking for my mother, she had to traverse it once each trip to visit the cabin and enjoy Red River's peace and beauty. The state finally paved the road in the sixties.

Before we were born, Forrest and Mildred had made friends with a childless older couple, Jim and Elsie Gallacher, who owned a grocery store near their old home on College Avenue. Akin to a local set of grandparents, we picnicked and socialized with them for many years. Our parents often took my brother and me to their house for overnight babysitting. For several years when we were young Elsie took George and me on a city bus downtown to buy presents each Christmas for our parents—for us, a very special adventure. They both passed away in our elementary school years.

All four of us attended Sunday School, followed by church service at Matthews Memorial Methodist Church on Berry Street, a church my parents had joined sometime in the early forties. My mother parked the car in a special spot right next to the sanctuary's east side entrance with no stairs. There my father could easily roll his wheelchair into the church. He sat in the right hand aisle facing the pulpit near that side entrance and we sat in the pew right next to him. On a few occasions an African American pastor would attend, sitting on the front row and pointed out by Reverend Sterck as a "special visitor." To my knowledge, the church was not integrated when my parents left Fort Worth in the mid-1970s.

Watching TV was a favorite pastime once we were in the new house. *Howdy Doody, Ed Sullivan, The Lone Ranger, Roy Rogers, Leave It to Beaver, Father Knows Best,* and *I Love Lucy* were TV shows we enjoyed watching with Daddy, while Mama tackled the kitchen or read the newspaper. I have warm memories of sitting on the wooden foot piece of Daddy's wheelchair watching TV in the evenings after we grew too big to sit in his lap. He would remove his pants and braces in preparation for bed, often sitting in his boxer shorts. This left room for me or my brother to perch on the foot piece between his thin, limp legs. His firm left hand on my shoulder, once I was seated on the foot piece, offered one of the few physical intimacy expressions he was able to give. He could not lavish us with caresses, much less firm bear hugs, like other fathers.

We always loved going to Grandma's house in Dallas. As soon as we arrived, we invaded her refrigerator stored on the back porch behind her tiny kitchen. We each grabbed one of the Dr. Peppers she always kept on hand because we were not allowed soft drinks at home. Instead, my mother had all of us, Daddy included, drinking Brewer's Yeast in our orange juice and eating Blackstrap Molasses rather than jam on our toast, though occasionally we got honey. Mama was a fan of Gaylord Hauser and Adele Davis, two early nutritionists who saw our soils and food quality going downhill, long before "eating healthy" became popular.

Grandma Clough, on the other hand, had no problem with sugar. She always cooked a delicious dinner, serving it on a dining table that could expand to seat her three children, their spouses, her grandchildren, and often additional relatives. What I remember most were her ambrosia salad, sweet potatoes with marshmallows on top, and her angel food cake made with eight egg whites that we put strawberries over. These accompanied a ham, roast, or turkey and dressing.

My parents did not socialize often, except with family, probably largely because of Mama's work and so many household responsibilities. Being an introvert, she did not appreciate parties in the way my father did. However, on Ryan Place, we frequently shared a weekend evening meal with the Brownlows, friends who lived up the street, or had a cookout with our next door neighbors, O.J. and Emma Johnston and Emma's mother, Granny B. The Johnstons, also members of my parents' church, had two parakeets but no children. George and I saw them as another set of grandparents. Occasionally, we stayed overnight where I shared a room with Granny B. When I got my driver's license much later, I helped Emma drive on two-or-three-day trips to Oklahoma and north Texas with her nieces who were my age. These trips increased my eagerness to see more of the world.

For his 6th birthday in January 1951, George received some miniature houses and other buildings to go with the new American Flyer train set delivered by Santa. In order to lay out a town surrounding the train, its tracks, and station, someone from KFJZ created a masonite board stabilized with fir strips around the edges. It conveniently sat atop my mother's dining table, only used when guests came. George and his dad could "play train" to their heart's content. That train still runs perfectly sixty-plus years later.

FAMILY OF FOUR, SPRING 1951

As in the previous winter, snow covered our new neighborhood whose trees were still midgets and would not reach full size for many years. We delighted in Mama's homemade snow ice cream with vanilla and sugar. At Easter, Ancel, Adele, and Mike once again traveled from Corpus Christi to Dallas. Cousin Mike reminded me recently that Grandma always hid a large decorated goose egg and whoever found it got a prize of candy. He was upset that year because George, not he, found the goose egg.

In August 1951 Ancel, Adele, and Mike joined us in Red River. Ancel's car experienced a vapor lock climbing the steep roads at the 10,000-plus altitude to Cabresto Lake. This bubble in the fuel line forced us to cool our heels along with the car's engine for awhile before returning to the cabin. Besides cookouts, those of us who could hiked to an abandoned mine behind the cabin and up Mallett Canyon. We also wandered down the mountain from the cabin to the valley below. Ancel, always looking after his brother, drove Daddy downtown and maneuvered his wheelchair through the grass up to a stream bank so they could fish together.

In early September 1951, I entered third grade and George first. We celebrated Christmas at our house first and then at my grandparents' home in Dallas. Once again, George and I received new cowboy clothes and boots, standard attire in Texas, to accommodate our growing frames. Those were the days girls had to wear dresses to school and were only allowed in pants for one day at the time of the winter fat stock show and rodeo.

I was also in a Brownie troop and able to commandeer 17 girlfriends to my birthday party when I turned nine in February 1952. On an April week's vacation to Corpus Christi, we crossed a causeway to Padre Island where we enjoyed a motor boat ride in the Gulf waters. That was the no-so-happy time Ancel agonized in pain for most of the day from a jelly fish sting and George got a miserable sun burn. En route home to Fort Worth we stopped at the Alamo in San Antonio to re-imagine the 1836 historic battle. Only a month later, I faced the biggest trial of my life to date.

My Bout with Polio. In early May 1952 near the end of third grade I attended a joint Brownie/Blue-Bird party at St. John's Episcopal church across the street from Daggett Elementary. Afterwards I retreated to Kaye Brownlow's house. She lived with her parents and younger brother in the next block up the street from us. We had met riding our bikes when she moved into the neighborhood in the second grade and had become instant best friends. We created a "science club" in her garage to inspect bugs and do experiments, went to Girl Scout camp together one summer, shared many sleepovers, traveled to California by train in our teens, and are still in touch today.

While using the see-saw in Kaye's backyard and later climbing up on the roof of her garage, I felt my back aching and neck a little stiff, similar to flu symptoms. The pains gradually worsened and by evening I had added a raging fever that lasted through the night. I distinctly remember a hallucinatory dream in which I was Alice in Wonderland tumbling down through a black vortex where I was met by Tweedle Dee and Tweedle Dum.

The next morning my mother transferred my father to the front seat of the car, dropping him off at work for his half-day Saturday shift, and then taking me a few blocks farther to our pediatrician, Dr. Weir. Although weak, I must have walked, perhaps aided by my short, small-boned mother, to the car because she could not have carried my tall gangly, nine-year-old body. A number of polio survivor narratives describe their inability to walk soon after the fever, stiffness, and delirium occurred. For some, though not me as I recall, nausea hit before ever getting to the hospital and being diagnosed. I lay on the backseat of the car staring at my father's wheelchair, which was always positioned in the floor behind the bench seat up front. I worried about what could be wrong with me, as I felt sicker than ever before.

Dr. Weir took one look at me, suspected polio, and sent us immediately to the City-County Hospital, designated for all Tarrant County polio patients. There he met us to perform a spinal tap, the only way he could confirm his diagnosis. In a room in the hospital's isolation ward Dr. Weir had me lie on my side and assume a fetal position while he put a large needle into my spine to extract spinal fluid. He was removing the fluid to determine if there was a "notable increase in the white blood count and protein levels."[102] I do not remember extreme pain from the procedure that other polios describe. Dr. Weir's diagnosis was correct. To this day I cannot remember feeling scared or worried about this polio diagnosis or that I would end up like my father in a wheelchair.

Only my father, who was immune, and my mother, who had been given a gamma globulin shot, were allowed to visit me. George also received the shot but medical staff would not admit him to the isolation ward. After World War II, doctors began giving injections of a concentrated portion of the serum that had been extracted from convalescing polios. They gave this anti-body-containing gamma globulin serum to anyone exposed to polio with the hope of boosting their immune system temporarily for a number of weeks and preventing contraction of the disease. Gamma globulin definitely provided "some benefit in reducing cases in an epidemic,"[103] which 1952 turned out to be.

I spent a week in that room until my fever subsided and the infectious stage of the virus had passed. During that time I received the experimental Sister Kenny treatment of hot wool packs (large wool cloths) wrapped around my legs several times a day. Reportedly, heated in water up to 140 degrees, the packs were put through a washing machine ringer before nurses wrapped our limbs. Oh, how the packs burned my skin and smelled of hot boiled wool, an odor that still hangs in my memory.

Sister Kenny Treaments. Prolonged immobilization in body casts and splinting of paralyzed limbs were methods carried to excess on polio victims in the 1930s. These treatments inadvertently encouraged a certain amount of neglect by nurses and prevented patients from aiding themselves in the restoration of muscle function, representing a real nadir in treatment of paralyzed patients.[104] The country thus was ripe for new ideas and techniques for helping polio victims.

The breakthrough came with the arrival of the Australian nurse, Sister Elizabeth Kenny. She had no formal training, yet was allowed to serve in WWI where "sister" was the rank of a lieutenant. Finding little enthusiasm in Australia for her ideas about polio treatment, she came to the States in 1940 where she found doctors to support her theories about hot pack therapy, especially during the acute, contagious phase of the disease, and the use of massage, whirlpool baths, and muscle stretching to reduce spasms, stiffness, and hence paralysis.[105] She traveled around the US, finding the most support in Minneapolis where the Sister Kenny Institute (later renamed the Kenny Rehabilitation Institute) was established in 1942. When the National Foundation for Infantile Paralysis (NFIP) failed to give a large grant to the Kenny Institute, the Sister Kenny Foundation was set up three years later to fund research in all areas of poliomyelitis, including some oral polio vaccine trials conducted in 1957-59.[106]

Most newly-diagnosed polios in the 1940s and 1950s experienced the Sister Kenny hot packs and exercises, which became standard treatment throughout the US until the disease was eradicated in this country. People who were fortunate enough to get her treatment no longer had to endure the earlier tradition of immobilization in splints and body casts and stretching of taut, shriveled muscles. Not only was her treatment more humane, but many patients regained mobility far better than those who had had the earlier painful treatments. Sister Kenny believed that patients could become or do anything they wanted if they just set their minds to it.

My stay in the hospital isolation wing was the first time away from family at night. I remember being introduced to a bedpan and sitting up in bed to eat my meals, but not whether I was allowed to attempt walking. My favorite recollection is that of seven gifts my Brownie troop and school friends sent me, one to open each day of the week until—hopefully—I would be released from isolation. These thoughtful gifts, probably arranged by Mrs. Brownlow and neatly displayed on the window sill nearby, got me through what must have been lonely days. I remember most the ViewMaster with several wheels of slides of national parks and fairy tales that allowed me to escape my confines. Unlike many polio victims' toys and other possessions, my gifts did not have to be destroyed under the earlier common belief that they were virus carriers and could affect others.

According to the May 1952 *Fort Worth Press* article titled "Polio Sufferer, 9, Busy With Her Mail," I was diagnosed on a Saturday and therefore missed my promotion to the junior department at Sunday School. Brother Thomas Sterck, our pastor at Matthews Methodist, was allowed onto the isolation ward to present me with a Bible. He reported finding me engrossed with cards, letters, and gifts from my friends. Seclusion away from family was not as bad as I may have feared it would be.

From isolation I was transferred into a ward with several other girls who were exhibiting various stages of paralysis. One teenager named Rosa Estes slept in an iron lung at night but was able to sit up in bed and do wood-burning designs into leather belts by day. My father loved chatting with her when my parents came for visits. I remember hot whirlpool baths, physical therapy exercises, walking the hospital corridors, talking with the girls in my ward, especially after lights out, and attending two birthday parties, both of which made the newspapers. The Fort Worth articles listed me as an attendee at Adele Alldredge's party in the girls' ward (only hours after she was released from isolation, lying in her bed with hot packs on her back, neck, and thighs), and Gene Caulfield's party in the boys' ward. My brother was allowed to visit me in the ward as well as one classmate who had had polio a year earlier and was therefore immune.

The newspapers listed me as the 27th polio case in Tarrant County so far that year. The polio season was still young but would turn into the 1952 epidemic that afflicted 3,984 victims in Texas alone. Of the 57,879 people who contracted the disease nationwide, 3,145 people (or 5.4%) died,[107] and 21,269 (more than one third) were left with some degree of permanent paralysis.[108] I was one of the lucky two-thirds.

FORREST EXITING HELICOPTER, 1952

While I was still in the hospital, my father took a work-related helicopter ride on June 4, 1952. An anguished look masked his face as he was lifted from the Bell helicopter in Fort Worth into his wheelchair. Why he was riding in it remains a mystery. We heard over the years that he made a trip to New York City for KFJZ in 1952, but I could find no official record of it. Perhaps family legend mistook the 1952 trip for his well-documented one in 1946. Although barely home from my hospital polio bout that June, I would surely have remembered sharing in the excitement of his going to New York.

Returning home from the hospital after what officials termed a "mild case," I left 37 other polio patients behind. The doctors requested I sleep with a piece of plywood under my double mattress for firm support of my back. Before store-bought weights became common, I was instructed to do exercises holding a five-pound rock in my right hand. My discharge papers indicated my right side—knee and right shoulder—was weaker than my left. I did those exercises and regained strength over the summer.

Life after Polio. Except for my father's helicopter ride, a six-month gap in photos appeared after my spring bout with polio, the very same disease that had felled my father 43 years earlier. Caught up in the largest epidemic in US history, I recuperated fairly rapidly. However, my parents did not want me—despite being an A student and one of the oldest pupils in my class—to be double-promoted. They feared I would be too weak. Thus, I entered Miss Casburn's fourth grade class at Daggett Elementary in September. Experiencing no noticeable residual effects from the polio, I soon ran 7th station on our girls' elementary school relay team. For me, life jumped back to normal.

My parents supported Dwight Eisenhower in the fall 1952 election. My father disregarded Adlai Stevenson and all that he stood for. I too got caught up in his "I Like Ike" fervor, playing on the piano the general's campaign theme song that began: "V stands for Victory with General Eisenhower..." He felt Eisenhower could best deal with the Russians in the growing Cold War.

For Christmas 1952 I received a blue parakeet named Billy. My parents had decided dogs were not a good idea when our adopted stray dog Butch bit the postman. A few years later, however, George and I persuaded our parents to let us keep Buster, a stray who attached himself to us on Kenley Street. After awhile Mama complained that George and I were not dependable in providing Buster food and water or cleaning up his messes in the yard and gave him to someone at KFJZ. A bird was easier to maintain than a dog, so Billy was a source of joy for my family for seven years, until he died when I was in high school. Sad to lose Billy, I buried him in a shoe box in our back yard.

The summer of 1953 we made our usual trek to New Mexico. After leaving my Aunt Gladys' home that had indoor plumbing for Daddy, and my grandparents' homestead farm with its outhouse and Sears catalogs, we traveled to Red River through Questa, the less daunting route. My father's fishing license issued in Tucumcari, NM, that summer described him as being age 44, 5 ft. 3 in., 140 pounds, with blue eyes and brown hair and no mention of his disability. He had gained 15 pounds since college.

Maggie and G.O. spent their August 1953 anniversary weekend at our home in Fort Worth where we picnicked on the round redwood table with lazy susan we kept in our family backyard. Daddy watched the charcoal grill and could holler "Mama," which he often called her, when meats were done. It started out "Mama," followed by "Mildred" if she didn't respond immediately. Later that month the MacBeths arrived on Braniff Airlines for a visit and we all went swimming at Forest Park Pool, again no polio scare that year and, anyway, my parents believed I was immune.

History came to life for me in September 1953 when I entered 5th grade and began Miss Rutha Cooper's Texas history class. It became even more intriguing on my mother's 37th birthday later in September when we attended a big Clough family reunion in Lancaster, Texas, with approximately 75 relatives, including children. Ancel and my father helped organize it and my grandfather presided, reading from a one-page typed history he had compiled of our Clough lineage that began with his grandfather. George Washington Clough was born October 7, 1820, supposedly in Georgia, according to G.O., though census records indicate his birth in Virginia. History was fascinating when I could harvest my own ancestral roots from it.

Over the next decade I followed my father's genealogy efforts working with an Amarillo cousin. Daddy would roll up to his sturdy homemade desk with glass top, and I would pore over his shoulder at charts and letters he had accumulated. We were trying to determine exactly who were George Washington Clough's parents. We knew only that he was orphaned at a young age, in either Virginia or Georgia, and lived with a man who was in the horse-racing business. When a small boy, he was tied on a horse and made to ride in the races. As a teenager, he ran away and went to Mississippi where he met Ancel Heard, whose friendship prompted the name Ancel to enter our Clough lineage. The two young men moved to Rusk County, Texas. George married Mary Polly Cooper there and began the lineage that had gathered in Lancaster.

In December 1953 we made a fortuitous Christmas trip to New Mexico, driving out for a week to attend my cousin LaVern's wedding on the 24th. My brother was ring bearer in the at-home ceremony in McAlister, located between Clovis and Tucumcari. Back then it boasted a general store, post office, two churches occupied only when circuit ministers materialized, and my Uncle Ben's gas station and garage. Three small adobe-covered homes, one of which belonged to my Aunt Gladys, situated themselves in the immediate vicinity where state highway 252 and 312 intersect.

That Christmas we stayed at my uncle Bub's home with his family only a mile east down a dirt road from the old homestead. My 78-year-old grandfather Charlie Wyatt was not feeling well when we were visiting, had long had a case of ulcers that restricted his diet, and declared that his time was at hand. He had already picked out the suit he wanted to be buried in, leaving it hanging in his living room closet under the attic stairs. Charles and Ethel held court with children and grandchildren sitting at their large round kitchen table, all savoring Grandma's famous biscuits and gravy. My grandfather passed away on January 5, 1954, in a Tucumcari hospital after a short illness, according to the local newspaper. My mother traveled to the funeral to support her mother and siblings while my grandparents came from Dallas to care for Daddy, George, and me.

The March toward a Polio Vaccine. Eddie Cantor made notable contributions to the polio crusade before his death in 1962, making Forrest forever his fan. In the late 1930s, Cantor had joined with President Roosevelt as a prolific fundraiser for polio and the search for a vaccine. Coining the phrase "the March of Dimes" from the March of Time (popular radio series, 1931-45), he encouraged his radio listeners to send a dime to the White House. Well over two million dimes flooded the White House postal service.

Between 1931 and 1949, three distinct immunologic types of polioviruses (designated Type I "Brunhilde," II "Lansing," and III "Leon") were identified on the basis of specificity of neutralizing antibodies being separated into these three serotypes.[109] The poliovirus was no longer a single virus but a family of individual serotypes. Not only did each of the three types have its own "special antigenic" attributes but also its "characteristic biologic attributes."[110] This discovery changed the way everyone viewed the virology and immunology of polio, and would make it possible to attempt a vaccine that would protect against all three types.

However, other discoveries had to be made before developing a vaccine. Although a Swedish team of clinical virologists had isolated poliovirus from intestinal excreta in 1912, no other researchers pursued this direction until the late 1930s. In 1941 Albert Sabin (at University of Cincinnati) and David Bodian, working with Dr. Howard A. Howe, both at Johns Hopkins, disproved in separate studies the long-held belief of the nasal portal of entry, thus making the alimentary canal the entrance for the poliovirus. Next, Dorothy Horstmann at Yale and David Bodian each were able to detect poliovirus in the blood, during the brief period of incubation in which the virus developed the very antibodies that would destroy it.[111]

Another discovery would eventually facilitate greatly the ease of making a vaccine. In 1936 Sabin and Peter Olitsky at the Rockefeller Institute successfully cultivated for the first time the poliovirus outside the body. They did it in the nervous tissue of human embryos with the Type II strain that had been passed cerebrally for 20 years from monkey to monkey. But nervous tissue was hard to come by, and the monkey was essential in proving whether a virus had grown or not.[112]

Then in 1948 Dr. John Enders, Dr. Thomas Weller, and Dr. Frederick Robbins (at Children's Hospital in Boston) managed to grow the Lansing Type II poliovirus in human embryonic non-nervous tissue. For the next two years they were able to cultivate strains of all three serotypes of poliovirus in various non-nervous human tissues. Along with this success was the even more important discovery that the growth of polioviruses was accompanied by a characteristic change within the infected cells that researchers could detect and determine through a light microscope whether poliovirus existed in a given culture.

Also, this team learned that neutralization tests could be performed in vitro. Being able to more easily handle polioviruses for a variety of purposes made it feasible to develop a vaccine. The use of non-nervous tissue culture instead of monkeys as hosts made all the difference. All these discoveries opened up the possibilities for making both inactivated (killed) and attenuated (live) poliovirus vaccines.[113] In 1954 the trio of researchers were awarded a well-deserved Nobel Laureate for their work.

In 1947 Dr. Jonas Salk was hired by the University of Pittsburgh to study viruses. With support from The National Foundation for Infantile Paralysis (NFIP), Salk's Pittsburgh lab participated in the immunological typing program (1949-1951) that identified 192 strains of poliovirus each classified as either Type I, II, or III. Having worked on an influenza vaccine during WWII, Salk moved naturally from the typing project into developing a "killed virus" vaccine for polio, made from the live viruses that had been grown in a laboratory and inactivated by formalin (a clear, aqueous solution of 40% formaldehyde). Salk's vaccine was first tested on humans in 1952, with 5,000 Pittsburgh school children getting the vaccine before the field trials were held.

The country was still searching for a vaccine in the early 1950s when Salk was doing field trials of his vaccine. The NFIP needed additional money to complete the trials and inoculate young people, students in particular.

In September 1953 Forrest accepted the post of State Radio Chairman of the 1954 March of Dimes. Interviewed by the *Tyler Courier-Times-Telegraph* and something called *Texas Polio Gram*, Forrest made a statement re: his new position:

> *I plan on doing everything within my power and among the wide circle of friends I have in Texas radio to see if this won't be the year in which we get polio reeling backwards. More than many other people, I know what polio can do to a person.*

How that 1954 campaign transpired in Texas is unknown. Texas was the scene of polio epidemics yearly from 1942-1955, and local citizens across the state confronted the challenge as volunteers and fund raisers. From 1938 through 1954 the Texas March of Dimes volunteers raised $67 million.[114]

When named 1954 March of Dimes Texas State Radio Chairman, Forrest told an interviewer for *The Polio Gram* that he did not let his confinement to a wheelchair keep him from "looking at the rosy side of life." Even here he put a positive spin on his disability: polio was not a big deal for him. Forrest continued:

FORREST IN MID-1950'S

I made three coast-to-coast trips with the S.M.U. band as solo trumpeter during my college days when our football team was hitting the high spots. Perhaps I didn't mind my wheelchair because I never knew any other way of getting around.

Between 1938 and 1962, the NFIP's annual income averaged about $25 million a year, over half of which stayed in the local communities to pay for hospital care of polio patients in the days when few families had health insurance. The remainder of NFIP's funds paid for educational programs, advertising and promotion, and research to develop both the Salk and Sabin vaccines; for conducting the Salk vaccine field trials; and for funding the purchase of the first batch of killed-virus vaccines from six pharmaceutical labs for American school children in April 1955.[115] Between 1951 and 1955 alone, the March of Dimes raised $230 million to help fund the field trials and pay for the initial vaccines.[116]

The January 1954 national campaign raised a record-breaking $55 million to support Jonah Salk's inactivated vaccine field trials. And, when funds were running short late in the summer, it raised another $20 million. No public health experiment involving so many children and so many thousands of volunteers (both professional and non-professional) had ever been tried before, and was akin to a nation mobilizing for war.[117]

That spring, under sponsorship of the NFIP but independently directed by Dr. Thomas Francis at his University of Michigan-based Poliomyelitis Vaccine Evaluation Center, 1,349,135 lower elementary-age children participated in the largest public health field trials ever undertaken. Well over 200,000 volunteers nationwide participated, including doctors and nurses. Salk's vaccine was administered to over 600,000 children throughout the country by injection, 95% of them getting three injections over two-three months. More than half of the participants were part of the control groups who received placebos rather than the killed virus. Despite the Supreme Court's de-segregation ruling that year with Brown vs. the Board of Education, black children in Montgomery, Alabama, received their injections on the lawns of white public schools because they were not allowed inside. It took almost a year to collect, evaluate, and release the results.[118]

In spring 1954 there were the usual family visits between Dallas and our home in Fort Worth, with a big Easter gathering at my Grandma's well-laden table. In June, loaded down with luggage tied on top of our Plymouth, we trekked to Aunt Jess's in Arkansas before heading to East Texas and Houston to see more relatives. In Houston we toured the Battleship Texas and the San Jacinto Monument, grounds where General Sam Houston defeated Santa Ana and the Mexican Army in 1848. Next came Corpus Christi with the highlight of that visit being the pillow fight. Always playing pranks on his brother, Uncle Ancel had the brilliant idea to fold my father up inside the rollaway bed, leaving his head hanging out one end. Pounding the folded bed with pillows, we watched the feathers fly everywhere and all laughed hysterically, including my father. Although we had to clean up the mess afterward, that pillow fight left a happy childhood memory.

In July when I was 11, my brother and I, feeling very grown-up, traveled by train to New Mexico to visit our Wyatt relatives. I remember the sleeveless flowery sundress I wore and carefully doling out our sack-lunch food to make it last. We arrived in Tucumcari, a town of about 7,000 founded in 1901, at the oldest Spanish-style train station in New Mexico. Coming from a big city, it was hard to believe that Tucumcari, 35 miles north of the old homestead, was the first real town my mother ever saw at age eight. This town was where our relatives did their weekly shopping.

When we accompanied them we often bought milkshakes at the local drugstore with its wooden "Tobacco Indian" statue standing out front. We visited our grandmother Ethel, who continued to live alone on the isolated homestead after my grandfather died, something she would do for another four years before moving to a little house next to Gladys and Ben. Since my parents had already had their two-week vacation, George and I took a train home from Tucumcari, stopping in Amarillo to visit Aunt Virginia and her infant twin girls.

ANCEL, FORREST AND MARGARET WITH THEIR PARENTS AT 50TH ANNIVERSARY CELEBRATION

On August 25, 1954, Maggie and G.O. celebrated their 50th Wedding Anniversary at the SMU Student Union Building. Three hundred guests, including three people who were at their wedding 50 years earlier, attended the celebration. Everyone was thrilled with the outcome. By that fall of 1954 Aunt Margaret and family had moved into their new house on Tulip Lane in Dallas, and we used their place as the family gathering spot at Christmas.

With polio behind me, my pubescent body emerged in fifth and sixth grades after my fourth grade teacher had shown us "The Kotex Show," imploring the boys to stop teasing us girls about our changing bodies. I soon began to view the opposite sex in a light different from my earlier tomboy days. Eight of us sixth-graders joined a square dance group and were driven one night a week by someone's parents to the dance class, stopping at a local drive-in for milkshakes afterwards. My mother took her turn, fortunately able to leave Daddy alone when she needed to go out. All eight of us would squeeze onto the bench seats of a Ford sedan with fins while the driving parents politely sat together in another car. I exchanged ID bracelets with my first love Paul in that group and also had school girl crushes on two of the neighbor boys.

I have many happy memories of our life on Ryan Place: the freedom we had to run all over the neighborhood, riding our bikes, climbing trees, playing hide and seek, or joining neighbor kids in someone's front yard for softball. We lived close enough so that I could walk or ride my bike to elementary school, one time falling over on my bike and cracking the school's cello I was trying to carry. I also set up a make-shift school in my bedroom with me as teacher at a desk complete with an apple on its corner. All the younger neighbor children were my students.

But reprimands occurred during those carefree days as well: my last humiliating spanking in the third grade—this time with a belt by my father—for something really terrible I must have done, because Daddy usually never laid a hand on us. My mother was the disciplinarian who occasionally used switches made from the peach tree in our back yard.

In my first encounter with "the authorities," my friend Kaye and I were scolded by a policeman for dropping green prickly horse or hedge apples from a railroad bridge down onto the street below. Fortunately we never hit a car or we would have been in big trouble. To this day, I bend over backwards to avoid encounters with lawyers, policemen, and other authorities, just like my father did.

A Polio Vaccine at Last. On April 12, 1955, the ninth anniversary of Franklin Roosevelt's death, it was announced that the Salk vaccine was "safe, effective, and potent"[119] at a ceremony at the University of Michigan in Ann Arbor. Forrest saved a tape recording of that momentous ceremony. Although neither George nor I received the Salk vaccine, once the field trials were successfully completed, it was administered by injection to school children throughout the country. This vaccine, and later Dr. Albert Sabin's cheaper and easier-to-administer oral live vaccine, forever changed the face of polio in America. The number of US cases dropped 85-90%, to twenty per year by the mid-1960s.[120]

CHAPTER FOURTEEN

THE HOUSE ON KENLEY STREET: 1955-1961

My seventh through twelfth grades

In the spring of 1955 my parents built a new house at 4016 Kenley Street, one mile south of US 30 where KFJZ had recently constructed its new TV station on the West Freeway's access road. Again built to my father's unique specifications, the house was situated on a concrete slab with only one step up to the kitchen from the double carport. Someone, probably from KFJZ, built a long wooden ramp so Forrest could roll his wheelchair by himself into the house. Because the land sloped slightly, there were three steps up to the front porch of this pink brick three-bedroom, one-and-a-half bath home. It had linoleum flooring throughout except for the living-dining carpet area. We moved in June to get settled before school started.

KFJZ Moves into TV. In the late 1940s when WBAP-TV went on the air, my father became enamored with the new medium seven years before KFJZ added a television station. Not only an early owner of a TV set, Daddy also provided behind-the-scenes exposure to this new entertainment world for my brother and me. Through his contacts, he managed to get George and me onto a kid's show at WBAP-TV with Mary Parker, a local personality associated with the Howdie Doodie TV show. We loved seeing ourselves on the television screen and were excited about our father working at a TV station.

For a few months during 1954, Forrest, concerned about his future, had followed media coverage of TSN's application to the FCC for a license to become Fort Worth's second VHF TV station, joining WBAP's Channel 5. The Texas State Network's principal owner was Sid Richardson, who acquired it in the mid-1940s after Elliott Roosevelt's debts were settled. Reportedly the richest man in America at the time, Richardson was a Democrat, an important player among the Texas oil barons, and a friend of FDR, Truman, and Texans Lyndon Johnson, Senate Majority leader, and Sam Rayburn, Speaker of the House. In 1941 Richardson befriended General Dwight Eisenhower (Ike), becoming a major financial backer of his run on the Republican rather than the Democratic ticket for President in 1952. Richardson was one of many prominent Texas Democrats who supported Ike.

Amon G. Carter owned WBAP-TV, the *Fort Worth Star-Telegram*, and other local corporations. Carter and Richardson had long been friends and business associates, and Richardson was competing against two other wealthy groups of people for the Channel 11 license. One competitor filed a formal request to the FCC that Richardson and Carter disclose their business dealings with each other. Although it was known publicly that Carter and Richardson were joint owners of the Texas Hotel and of the airport in Fort Worth, the request alleged the two men had other joint enterprises. Granting TSN the license for Channel 11 would give the two wealthiest and most influential men in Fort Worth control of both TV stations to the detriment of the public interest. The FCC examiner ordered Richardson to provide information on three of seven points requested by the competing group.

On August 12, 1954, after a six-month battle, the competitor gave up efforts to obtain the TV license, thus paving the way for Richardson to construct the new Channel 11 TV station. It was also disclosed that TSN had agreed to pick up all costs its competitor had invested in the application process, because otherwise the battle could have dragged on for years, thus denying Fort Worth a needed second TV station. The new station would push local sports coverage and host a 1,000-ft tower and 360,000 watts of power.

With license in hand, President Gene Cagle initially announced that construction would begin at a location in Meadowbrook, in east Fort

Worth, near WBAP. My parents drove us around on weekends to look at housing and lots to build on: first, in the Meadowbrook area, and, later in west Fort Worth after the decision was made to locate at 4800 West Freeway instead. The station opened in the summer of 1955.

As for Forrest's position at KFJZ and TSN, by 1951 he held the title of traffic manager with no mention of the educational programming he had loved so much ten years earlier. He was listed as traffic and promotion manager for both KFJZ Radio and TSN in a news clip in September 1953. He survived the expansion of KFJZ into television in 1955 and worked for both KFJZ-TV and radio, though in what capacity is unknown. Gene Cagle, also a principal owner of TSN along with Richardson, remained Forrest's boss.

To supplement his modest salary over the years, Forrest set up a mail-order sales business. Incremental raises promised ten years earlier had likely evaporated. Forrest advertised in magazines and sold such things as bird tweeters, Yahtzee game sets, telephone receiver shoulder supports, and a large wooden key that could be fixed to the wall with hooks to hold seven keys. Attempting this business for several years, he probably made negligible money. The business disappeared after my mother returned to work in the mid-fifties.

—◦❀◦—

In July 1955 my brother and I rode out to New Mexico with Kaye, her brother, and parents who were on their way to California in their new air-conditioned '55 Chevy. We stopped at a motel over-night to visit Carlsbad Caverns and I remember how delighted I was to swim under water at the motel pool, hanging onto

GRANDMA ETHEL AND SUSAN, 1955

the shoulders of Mr. Brownlow, something I could not do with my own father. They dropped us off at Aunt Gladys' in McAlister.

As a tall, thin, gangly, 12-year-old, I spent a bucolic month on the old homestead with Grandma. I sewed doll clothes on Grandma's treadle machine, picked fresh vegetables from her lush garden watered by the large cows' tank nearby, watched Grandma churn butter and wring a chicken's neck to kill it for supper, and daily walked a half-mile each way to the mail box while earning points for my Girl Scout hiking badge. Later I accompanied cousin LaVern (seven years older and able to drive) to Red River and took square dancing lessons at the Community Center. Aunt Gladys sewed me a "squaw" dress with a tiered skirt complete with rick rack patterns, perfect for the a la main lefts and do si dos. My parents, at last settled in their new home, came out in August to visit and take us home.

Emancipation at Last. Since our new home was only a mile from my father's work, he sought independence and found an electric-powered wheelchair that would propel him down Sanguinet Street to work. This would allow my mother to return to work full-time and not have to drive my father to and from the office everyday as she had done for the 15 years they lived in south Fort Worth.

Forrest learned from a magazine that electric outdoor chairs were manufactured by the Stevens Company, located in Kansas City, Kansas. He ordered his emancipation ticket and was soon driving his motorized "scoot buggy," as he also called it, to and from work each day. Once every few weeks he ventured another ten blocks farther to get a haircut, and transferred into the barber chair via his portable board (of well-polished hardwood, 2.5-ft. long by 8" wide). His electric chair, which weighed 268 pounds and cost $495, got its batteries charged overnight on our carport and at the radio station during the day. He transferred to a manual wheelchair both at home and at work.

To handle cold weather, Forrest's KFJZ buddies in the carpentry shop installed a plastic windshield to reduce winter's sharp air and mounted a roof as a buffer against the rain. He wore a fur-lined cap with visor and earmuffs, gloves, a heavy jacket and scarf, and put a blanket over his lap. Occasionally, if it were bitterly cold or raining hard, a colleague would take him to work or bring him home by car.

Everyone knew Forrest and managed to avoid hitting him as he hugged the edges of the asphalt pavement each way to work and home, something he did for fifteen years until he retired in 1970. He became such a familiar

Forrest Clough . . . in compact compact.

EMANCIPATION "SCOOT BUGGY," 1961

sight that reporter Bob Trimble took this photo and wrote an article about him and his electric "voltswagen" for *The Fort Worth Press* in 1961. Trimble's article stated the electric chair was "powered by two 12-volt car batteries, hooked in series to give 24 volts."[121] Steered by pushing a drive control operated by his strong left hand and connected to a back guide wheel, the chair had two speeds and reportedly averaged eight miles per hour. Brakes activated simply by releasing the drive control. Forrest proudly claimed he once beat Wally Blanton in a drag race across the station's parking lot, though Wally maintained his go-kart had apparently failed to function properly. Loyal to his employer, Forrest pasted only one bumper sticker on the back of the buggy: "Drive safely—says KFJZ 1270."

Feeling so successful with his new freedom, Forrest wrote his own story, which he submitted to *Reader's Digest* about his life and new-found emancipation. It was never published and sadly discarded long before I began to write this biography.

—˃⎪⎮˂—

In fall 1955, I entered the 7th grade at Stripling Junior High and my brother the 5th grade at Arlington Heights Elementary. We were at last old enough to fend for ourselves after school each day when my mother went back to work. By then I was earning a small allowance each week vacuuming the carpet and doing the family ironing after school, including Daddy's polyester-cotton shirts and our flat bedsheets and pillowcases. These chores were almost enjoyable because I could watch TV's Spin and Marty and the Mouseketeers at the same time. At first my mother worked part-time at an insurance company while she renewed her Civil Service credentials to get back into a government job. She eventually obtained a GS-5 Clerk-Stenographer position with the US Soil Conservation Service, where she worked for about 25 years. I often got rides to school with two neighbor girlfriends whose mothers did not work outside the home.

After moving to the west side of Fort Worth in 1955, my parents continued driving across town to Matthews Memorial Methodist Church on Berry Street. My father began serving as Program Chairman of the Methodist Men in the mid-fifties at their church, and both parents were active members of the Kum Duble class, several of whom appeared at my parents' funerals in 1983 and 1997. Once we made friends on the West side, George and I convinced our parents to drop us off and pick us up at Arlington Heights Methodist Church where our school friends attended. We were both very active in our church youth group during our junior and senior high years.

When my mother went back to work for the government in the mid-1950s, our family obtained group health insurance, which had become popular during the war years when wages were frozen and employers were allowed to offer health benefits to attract workers. In 1940 the US population was 132.1 million and only 15 million people had health insurance. A small private employer like KFJZ, barely able to pay a living wage, likely did not provide health insurance initially. The station may have done so by 1950 when the country's population was 152.3 million and 82 million had commercial or Blue-Cross-Blue Shield insurance. My parents each had brief hospitalizations for minor surgeries while I was living at home, but medical costs were minimal compared to today. The National Foundation for Infantile Paralysis (NFIP) paid for my month-long hospitalization in 1952 as it did for many other polio victims in the 1940s and 1950s.

—\l/—

In early July Charles B. (Charlie) Jordan, a former Vice-President of TSN and then general manager of KFJZ-TV when it went on the air, relinquished his demanding duties due to health concerns. This left Gene Cagle as both president and general manager of all TSN operations, as well as general manager of KFJZ-TV. Forrest was fond of both men and was sad as well as disturbed to see Charlie leave. Forrest believed these two men were his guardian angels, and with Charlie gone, that meant Gene Cagle was his only remaining management ally. Forrest viewed Cagle as his "protector" in an increasingly competitive, cutthroat business.

Forrest had wonderful friends among his peers at the station. When George was old enough to participate in the soap box derby, KFJZ-TV sponsored him and his car in 1956 and 1957 in the local derby race down W. Seventh in front of the Will Rogers Coliseum. My father sat in his chair and my mother, relatives, and I on the curbs both years to watch the race. John Perry, head of the TV station's carpentry shop, gave advice on the construction and painted George's car with KFJZ logo. He also helped fine-tune some of the mechanical rigging on the unmotorized race car. Internal weights and a streamlined design without pedals, plus skill on the part of the driver, propelled the car down the low-grade hill to the finish line. George had such fond memories of his derby races that years later he helped three of his grandchildren build cars and enter races in their early-teen years.

Extra special were the times my father got us into the TV station back stage during star-studded fund raisers for various charities. I obtained the autograph of movie actress Jane Russell, at the time married to football great Bob Waterfield of the Los Angeles Rams. Leo Carrillo, the Spanish American actor best known as Pancho in *The Cisco Kid*, arrived decked out in cowboy attire along with his equally-adorned horse. My brother and I thought our dad lucky, rubbing shoulders with all those famous people.

A major change in TV station ownership occurred around 1960, a year after Sid Richardson's death. Movie star Bing Crosby and associates bought out the TV station, and renamed it KTVT-TV, Channel 11, which it remains today. KFJZ Radio was not part of the deal, and there was no place for Forrest under their regime. That is probably the time Forrest became director of FM Radio. As long as Gene Cagle was around, there would still be a place for Forrest in radio.

Daddy's Daily Routine. In each if our houses, Daddy's management of his disability was similar. At bedtime he stood up in his braces and leaned on his desk while my mother helped him get his pants off. Sitting back down in his chair, he then took his braces off, locked them, and parked them standing against his solid green desk. He rolled his wheelchair next to his bed and scooted himself along his trusted board right into bed and maneuvered his legs into the correct position for sleeping.

The next morning he got up the same way, first sitting up in bed, swinging his limp legs to the bedside, and them sliding on his board to his chair. In the bathroom, he slid back and forth from his locked chair right onto the toilet seat. Back in the bedroom, he buckled on his braces, pulled his pants up to his knees, and stood leaning over the desk. He called my mother from the kitchen, who then pulled his pants up the rest of the way and helped him tuck in his shirt that he had buttoned with his left hand.

To take a bath at night after removing his braces, he undressed, slid from his chair to the open toilet seat and then onto a 6x12" stool, probably made by a carpenter at the TV station, to reach the smooth-top edge of the bathtub. From there he moved his legs over the side and slid into the tub and turned on the water. To get out of the tub, he grabbed the rim of the toilet seat and pulled himself up onto the stool and toilet seat and then into his wheelchair via his board. There were no grab bars that are so common today.

We ate all our meals at the fake-green-marbled chrome kitchen table, where Daddy lifted a fork with his bad right hand and ate like the rest of us. He could hold a knife in his good left hand to cut meat and other foods. Daddy was as self-sufficient as he possibly could be—he did not want to rely on my mother or George and me any more than he had to.

—⟩⟨—

After Forrest gave up handling the annual Gridiron ticket sales, our family of four continued to enjoy the Gridiron dinners and shows during my junior and senior high school days. I found them great fun and felt grown-up being included with Fort Worth and Texas dignitaries. Those Gridiron dinners helped stoke my interest in government and journalism as possible career fields. Forrest thoroughly enjoyed his association with this journalism fraternity that offered him more affirmation and recognition than his employer did.

I remember one evening when we left in plenty of time to attend the Gridiron dinner, for my father always gave us a short warning when we went anywhere: "We need to leave in five minutes, Mildred. I am going to the car (or back door/breezeway/ramp, etc.)." He knew how much extra time it took us to help him and his chair into the car. To this day I am anxious about getting places on time or ahead of time, a legacy from Daddy I do not always appreciate. I plan, make lists, even pack days in advance, because I cannot abide last-minute rushing to get to an airport or to make an appointment on time.

That evening we drove downtown for the event and parked on the street not far from the hotel. After we had maneuvered my father from the car and into his wheelchair on the sidewalk, he was taken aback, perhaps embarrassed, when two young African American girls came up and offered him a dime. They saw that he could not walk and wanted to help him in some way. A proud individual who wanted no sympathy, he naturally refused the dime but thanked the girls profusely for their concern. What irony in the life of this conservative, educated, Southern white gentleman that these girls showed such grace and generosity to someone who seemed far worse off than they. Needless to say, we were not late for the dinner and show.

Goodbye to Maggie and G.O. In January 1957 my beloved grandmother Maggie suffered a stroke and was hospitalized for about three weeks before she died. My father saved all the condolence messages, as well as post cards and letters written to him by both parents the last few years of their lives. He owed so much to them for giving him the opportunity to live as normal a life as possible in his formative years.

My grandfather and his increasing dementia were a big challenge for my grandmother, with her worries over him exacerbating her own decline. Grandpa went to a nursing home in Dallas for a year, dying two days after his 80th birthday in February 1958. I remember visits to his private room on Turtle Creek Boulevard, but fortunately his dementia prevented him from understanding that Maggie had died. He would always ask when we visited, "Where is Dutch?"—the name he called her throughout their marriage. At this point Forrest quit making photo albums and turned to slides.

⚬⚬⚬

Other than taking in a ballgame or two, Forrest had little contact with SMU on-campus events until the 1961 Pigskin Revue. For its 25-year reunion, the famous 1935-36 band took over the second act of this Revue. My father rehearsed in our living room for weeks. I was amazed to hear Daddy playing like the young, enthusiastic, "smooth-style" musician of yore, since he rarely got his trumpet out. For one last time he played his hallmark solo "Drink to Me Only with Thine Eyes." All the old band members who could be assembled got together after their performance for dinner at the Topper Restaurant in Dallas.

After that, Forrest put away his horn forever. Was it his music that kept him sane and capable of dealing with his young adult fears about ever having a normal life, with career, wife and family? Once his dream was accomplished, he did not need to lose himself in music anymore. I also suspect that after twenty-five years of little practice, he got winded and found it difficult to sustain the long notes he had been known for. By 1961 post-polio syndrome, not yet identified in the medical literature, was likely creeping in, the poliovirus having compromised his respiratory system years earlier.

In addition to his weakened lungs, my father also had to make some adjustments as his aging arms lost strength. His back and its scoliosis must have been hurting because I remember him in his chair with a pulley contraption above his head that, with chin in a strap, pulled his neck and head upward. At age 46 when we moved to the Kenley house, he could roll himself up the long six-inch-high sloping ramp. Going down the ramp, he could hold onto the front tires of his wheelchair and brake himself. As the years wore on, he needed assistance getting up and down the ramp. Before they left Kenley, he had advanced to an electric wheelchair with a joy stick to start, stop, and turn.

More Distant Vacation Trips. School and Girl Scout summer camp activities filled photo albums I made during junior and senior high school. They showed little of family life other than our vacation trips. We branched out on our family ventures beyond New Mexico after my grandmother Ethel moved to Abilene to live with Aunt Verna and began spending time with us during the winter months in Fort Worth. We no longer needed to visit her in New Mexico.

Working for the federal government, Mildred eventually accrued up to 26 days/year of annual leave. During my elementary and junior high school years, we ventured as far as we could by car and back home in two weeks. Not only did Forrest and Mildred want to see new places, they also wanted to give George and me unique experiences that Fort Worth and Dallas did not offer.

My mother, brother and I had only been in six states surrounding Texas the fall before I entered ninth grade, and we were raring to see more. In 1958 we visited Aunt Jess's family in central Arkansas before heading to the mountains of northwest Arkansas, southern Missouri, and eastern Kansas. We stopped by the Stevens Company so that Daddy could thank them personally for the freedom their motorized chair had given him.

The following summer (1959), we ventured to the Atlantic Coast via New Orleans, visiting my father's old friends in Mobile, Alabama. We explored Sumter County, Georgia, from where the Wyatts emigrated to Texas after the Civil War. Next we headed south to Thomasville, Georgia, close to the border with Florida. We wanted to find the "plantation" farm house of my grandmother Maggie's Ross ancestors. Carrying a small photograph Daddy had, we found the unpainted rundown farmhouse. The African American man who answered the door responded: "Well, my name is Ross, but I ain't got no plantation." Almost a hundred years after the notorious institution was abolished, we were talking with a descendant of one of our ancestor's slaves, thankful he had inherited the old home place and it was still in the family, so to speak.

Next we visited the Battle of Atlanta museum, gaping at the Civil War murals on every wall that depicted battles and even the notorious Andersonville prison. We stopped at Stone Mountain east of Atlanta to see a bas relief of Confederate heroes Stonewall Jackson, Robert E. Lee, and Jefferson Davis carved on its north face. We swam in the Atlantic Ocean not far from our motel in Brunswick, Georgia, where George encountered a sting ray. In North Carolina's Blue Ridge Mountains we visited Daddy's dear friend Stuart Sewell and his wife in their trailer home atop a pine-covered mountain overlooking Asheville. At Lake Junaluska in Maggie Valley we discussed how much Grandma Clough would have liked it. Traveling through the Great Smokey Mountain National Park and Pigeon Forge, Tennessee, we made our way home.

By then I had my driver's license and could spell my mother on this lengthy trip, which certainly took some strain off of her. To make any of these family trips over the years, we all had to pitch in to assist my father— the occasional help with his self-care that my mother ministered on a daily basis; helping him in and out of cars, over curbs, through doors; stopping by the side of a two-lane country road so he could relieve himself out the shotgun seat where he sat or to urinate in the oval-shaped glass honey jar he always kept at his feet. We could never take a motel room as a family without first checking that the bathroom doors were wide enough for his wheelchair. I have a sweet memory of the times when riding the lonely two-lane roads in eastern New Mexico where it was "safe" for my father to steer the car with his strong left-hand and forearm resting on his briefcase next to Mama. Keeping her foot on the gas pedal, she would put her arms up behind her head while we all sang songs like "Clementine," "Oh, Susanna," and "She'll Be Coming 'Round the Mountain . . ."

In summer 1960, at the end of 11th grade for me, we headed north to Winnipeg, Canada. We stopped in Omaha to see an old Pi Kappa Alpha friend of my father's, went through Fargo, North Dakota, boated across Lake of the Woods in northern Minnesota, and plunged our feet into the 50-degree waters of Lake Superior before wending our way back to Texas. While in Winnipeg, George and I took a bus across town to see a professional football game. During junior high, I had a school girl's crush on several Southwest Conference football players, sending fan letters and receiving autographed postcards in return. Everyone in the Clough family was crazy about the game, including my father, and I still know better than to telephone Aunt Margaret in the middle of an SMU or Dallas Cowboys game on TV.

Forrest and Mildred must have savored this trip to Canada. They probably realized it was their last as a family of four, since I would be going away to college the following summer.

Later in summer 1960, I funded a train trip to southern California with money I had saved from my part-time work since 8th grade at Montgomery Ward and Edison Jewelers. Traveling with Kaye, who was going to see a good friend, I visited my junior high girlfriend Leslie who had moved to Solana Beach. In California I met a young woman who attended Whittier College near Los Angeles and learned that Whittier had a study-abroad program in Copenhagen. I wanted to get to Europe, so applied and was accepted, receiving a partial scholarship to this private liberal arts school that at the time charged $1,500 per year for room, board and tuition.

What would I major in? What career field should I pursue? From my vantage point, my father worked a 9-5 desk job, and my mother was a secretary. Perhaps because my parents seemed to have unremarkable jobs, I never aspired to do anything exceptional or unusual. My mother assumed that as a woman raised in the 1950s I would become a teacher, a secretary, or a nurse. Indeed, she insisted I take typing in high school to qualify for the civil service register. She believed I could always get a job as a typist, and I have used that skill throughout my life. Teachers were respectable and with a four-year degree she felt I could find a teaching job as long as I picked up my credentials, which I did eventually. I followed my mother's practical advice and completed the basics to assure myself a job—she told me in no uncertain terms that I could not rely on a man to support me, something she had learned early in her marriage.

Whether to please my parents or my own will to succeed, perhaps both, I was always a straight A student. I loved social studies, writing, history, literature, and the arts. Maybe I could become a journalist like my father or a college teacher like my grandfather Clough. Selected for Who's

Who my senior year in high school, I was voted Most Studious female, along with my high school sweetheart John, who was chosen Most Studious male. High school showed me I had to prove myself in ways other than the popularity/status game, and I chose academics.

The Sabin Oral Vaccine. The spring of my senior year, my classmates and I lined up outside behind Arlington Heights High School (AHHS) and swallowed our sugar cubes with a small amount of Dr. Albert Sabin's "live" polio vaccine on it. I was supposedly immune from polio, but the authorities wanted me to take it anyway.

While Salk's inactivated vaccine had been approved in 1955 for use and was being given to thousands of school children in the United States, Sabin had been working to create a different vaccine. He believed that a live or attenuated oral vaccine "tamed through serial passage in tissue culture"[122] rather than an injected killed virus vaccine would be more effective. He began work on this in 1952 at a time when Salk was already doing human trials with his inactivated virus vaccine. Although the NFIP provided funding to Sabin, the foundation and others paid little attention to his efforts, instead throwing their support to Salk, whose vaccine was almost ready for distribution. And the public was clamoring for it.

However, an incident at Cutter Labs in 1955 gave everyone pause. Two hundred four children, their families, and community members around the country contracted polio from a bad batch of killed virus vaccine. Thus, safety and quality control protocols had to be developed before people were satisfied and felt safe with Salk's killed virus. Because of this concern, people began to turn their attention to the live vaccine that Sabin was perfecting.[123]

In the years prior to 1955, there was great competition between Salk and Sabin, who discounted Salk's abilities as a researcher. Besides, Sabin wanted to get what he believed to be a better, more protective vaccine out to the public before Salk did. However, that was not to be. Sabin did field trials on 180,000 school children in Cincinnati and on more than a million students in the Soviet Union from 1956-1960. Sabin's vaccine and two others were used in a total of 20 independent field trials in 15 countries. Two international conferences declared the live vaccine had shown no signs of poliomyelitis in any of the vaccinated subjects but there were delays in getting it officially approved in the US. The vaccine was finally licensed by the US Public Health Service for use in 1962,[124] although many of us ate our sugar cubes in 1961. At last the public had a safe and effective attenuated vaccine that could be administered to school children.

It was eventually determined that Sabin's oral vaccine was easier and cheaper to administer. It also killed the poliovirus in the intestines before it could reach the central nervous system, something the Salk vaccine was unable to do. To attain immunity, simple sugar cubes handed out by volunteers replaced periodic injections by trained personnel. Even though there were always a few cases of polio developed as a result of administering the live vaccine each year, Sabin's oral version became the preferred vaccine for the next fifty-plus years. To this day it is still administered to all young children in the West. The US witnessed its last case of polio in 1979.

With the advent of Sabin's vaccine, teams were mobilized around the country to administer the vaccine-laced sugar cubes. For example, in 1962 Dallas pediatrician Dr. Percy Luecke spearheaded a drive to give Sabin's sugar cubes to nearly a million people on two summer Sundays with the aid of 4,500 volunteers in 90 schools.[125]

Texas, a Leader in Treating Polios. Texas and California, especially Harris County (Houston area) and Los Angeles County, competed from 1930 onward for hosting the most polio cases each year. The oil boom in Texas between 1901 and 1960 brought in thousands of immigrants, who carried viruses with them and increased exposure of the vulnerable, largely agrarian Texas population to infectious diseases. The boom saw small towns in west Texas doubling in size every decade.[126] Additionally, the warm Texas climate was a natural incubator for the poliovirus. With the onset of WWII, polio epidemics increased tremendously in Texas with the influx of people working for aviation manufacturers, military training facilities and other war-related activities that sprung up around the state. Texas recruited the highest number of military personnel of any state[127] and the virus attacked an above average number of these enlistees and their families.

Texas was something of a pioneer in adapting to the needs of those afflicted. The boom in immigration to Texas encouraged the establishment of medical, philanthropic, civic and fraternal service organizations, all of which geared up to treat the overwhelming number of polio victims. A few examples: The Texas Scottish Rite Hospital became the premier facility for all polio patients in Texas when it took over a smaller Shriners hospital in Dallas in 1926. It had the latest advances in physical therapy, bracing and orthopedics. The Texas Society for Crippled Children was established in 1929 as an advocate for victims, securing increased funding and establishing diagnostic and treatment centers around the state. The Southwestern Poliomyelitis Respiratory Center in Houston, which got its first iron lung in 1931, became one of fourteen such facilities around the country.[128] The Center managed all critical care patients in Texas during the 1952 epidemic and contributed greatly to the reduction of the bulbar and respiratory polio death rate.[129]

Texas was a leader in another area. Opened in 1941, the Gonzalez Warm Springs Rehabilitation Hospital in Ottine, Texas, 65 miles east of San Antonio, was established on the site where a company some years earlier tried to sink an oil well but instead discovered the 106-degree waters. Similar to the Warm Springs facility in terms of services to polio victims, it had the advantage of doing its own local fundraising and could avoid political considerations that FDR and his program could not. For instance, unlike the Georgia facility the Texas center was integrated racially just like the Scottish Rite Hospital in Dallas.

Memories from Kenley Street. Happy memories of junior and senior high school remain as well as the natural awkwardness of those teenage years. This period was the time when our bodies morphed into adulthood, hormones exploded, and we began to discover who we were and what we wanted to do with our lives. I remember my first formal dance in the 8th grade when parents drove us on dates; my first car date when the young man did a 180-degree skid on an icy street that fortunately came out okay without our parents finding out; and our Methodist youth minister's cousin Fess Parker visiting our church in his Davy Crockett outfit and singing "Born on a mountain top in Tennessee...." I experienced eight summers of adventures with the Girl Scouts at Camp Timberlake on Eagle Mountain Lake near Azle, a small town north of Fort Worth. My parents would drive me out on a Sunday after church and pick me up two weeks later. I joined my high school's Moral Rearmament Group in the post-Sputnik scare (when

Russia launched its first rocket before the US could send one up).

Like our parents, my first steady boyfriend John and I supported Richard Nixon in his bid for the US presidency in the fall 1960 elections, even skipping school one morning to attend his downtown rally. My American History teacher wore a black arm band the day John F. Kennedy was elected president. She did not want a Catholic in the White House.

John helped my high school days feel secure and enjoyable before we went to opposite sides of the country for college. He was a football player and hung out with the top jocks in our school. We were included in plenty of social activities, many of which centered around friends from my Methodist youth group. We never lacked for fun things to do, parties and dances to attend. Dating and getting along with the opposite sex were not particular issues for me upon graduation.

However, junior and senior high years were socially difficult for me as a female, exacerbated by the fact that my parents had little money and no social status—a feeling that went all the way back to kindergarten. Many popular girls at school came from families whose parents were wealthy and prominent locally or statewide, with some serving later in President Johnson's administration. Our school had four social clubs for girls similar to the Greek system in colleges. It seemed to me the girls with "status" or popularity pledged the most prestigious clubs, ones that their parents favored. I did join a fine club and made good friends in that group, some of whom I am still in touch with today.

Nevertheless, I frequently felt "less than" socially. One of my most painful memories related to the parties given on behalf of graduating senior girls by their parents' friends or family members—luncheons, teas, country club dances. I attended many of them, even saving the invitations in my scrapbooks. No one gave me a party—my mother was too busy working and caring for my father to cultivate "social" friends outside her church. So, I invited all my girlfriends to a going-away-to-college party in our family backyard in August. By then I could give each girl a homemade pennant with her college's name on it as a favor. Only about fifteen of us from my graduating high school class of 465 left the state of Texas for college. I could not wait to get to college in California where no one would know my parents or their backgrounds. Everyone would be treated on merit, not how wealthy their parents were or how high up the social ladder they had climbed.

I now realize I felt emotional turmoil similar to what my father must have felt in his adolescence while he was trying to be accepted as a paraplegic. Although I lacked his disability, I scrapbooked the same kinds of invitations he did, some of which possibly generated painful memories for him as well. Somehow he and I would feel better about ourselves if we had many friends and were liked for who we were.

CHAPTER FIFTEEN

LIFE FOR OUR FAMILY
AFTER I LEFT HOME

After graduating high school and leaving for college in California in 1961, I heard only second-hand accounts of my father's daily life except during periodic visits. My brother, however, lived with our parents through his 1963 high school graduation and nearby in Arlington, Texas, the next four years during college. He stayed in Texas most of the time during the remainder of my father's life and had a better perspective on his aging process than I, who was always far away.

Unable to find a job after graduation, I spent the summer of 1961 sewing a college wardrobe. I left Fort Worth that fall on a 36-hour Greyhound bus ride from Fort Worth to Los Angeles, the way I went to and fro most of my four years at Whittier College. Situated in the Whittier hills southeast of downtown L.A., it was a rolling, green campus with palm and avocado trees, sights I lusted for coming from dry, flat Texas.

My parents picked me up in Whittier the following summer, after dropping off George in New Mexico where he spent another of at least six high school and college summers driving tractors and harvesting wheat for Uncle Ben. I worked that summer as a GS-3 clerk typist at the Federal Aviation Authority (FAA) located at Meacham Field in Fort Worth in the days when we used typewriters (mostly electric) and carbon paper.

A scholarship as well as some insurance money left me by Grandpa Clough allowed me to live in Denmark and see Europe the fall semester of my sophomore year. Traveling all over Europe, studying Scandinavian art and literature, European politics and history, plus living with a Danish family in Virum located several train stops north of Copenhagen were eye-openers for me—learning that others engaged the world somewhat differently than I had been raised to do it. I fell in love with Scandinavian design and made small purchases, even carrying home on a DC6B propeller airplane a floor lamp for my parents. My father and mother continued their routines and local travels while I was away that fall, living for airmail letters from me every week or so. Phone calls were too expensive.

My Copenhagen college friend Alice, who had lived near me in Virum, and I became roommates upon our return to campus in winter 1963. She and her mother, who lived in Tennessee, picked me up in Fort Worth and we drove to California, stopping in Abilene for my sad last visit with Grandma Wyatt, then living with Aunt Verna and suffering from cancer.

After working the summer of 1963, again as a clerk typist, at Housing and Home Finance Agency (HHFA) in Fort Worth, I took a train to meet George in New Mexico where he was working on the wheat farm again. He drove me in his red '55 Plymouth sedan on to California, stopping to explore the abandoned mining town of Jerome, Arizona, today a tourist mecca.

The summer after my junior year I joined a Methodist work team headed to Pakistan. We were tasked with building a wall around Drigh Road Methodist school and church in the hot slums of Karachi. Again, with the last of my grandfather's money and help from my two home churches in Fort Worth, I came up with the $1,500 required for the two-month round-the-world experience. Our team of fifteen students plus advisers stopped at Methodist outposts/missions throughout Asia, the Middle East, and Europe. That trip exposed me to cultures far different from the white-skinned people and tidy landscapes of my ancestral roots in Europe and America.

At Whittier College I participated in various campus activities, was elected secretary of the student body in my junior year and president of the Women Students on campus my senior year. I took 45 units of political science, well beyond what was required for a major, because I found a father-figure and mentor in the form of my professor Dr. Ben Burnett.

That spring before my graduation, I was distraught over a broken love affair. My parents offered to take some of their sparse resources and buy me a plane ticket home for a few days. My bus fare each way was half the price of a plane ticket and I knew what a sacrifice it would be for them. Even though I refused the offer of a ticket, I knew they loved me, something that brought tears to my eyes.

My childhood family was not a demonstrative one, because both parents had been raised in non-emotive homes. As was typical of many families in that era, we all hid our emotions, especially the negative ones. "Sucking it up," as some would say, was the family tradition for both my parents in their childhood homes. Likewise, George and I behaved "properly" and kept anger and sadness to ourselves. We learned from our mother that "when you feel blue, just get busy," exactly what my father also did to cope with his disability. Only in therapy much later was I able to get in touch with some long-hidden, pent-up feelings.

My parents made their second trip to California in 1965 for my graduation. That was the year Republican Senator Margaret Chase Smith gave the commencement address, and former Whittier student body president Richard Nixon and actor Bob Hope were awarded honorary doctorates. My father was thrilled to meet Nixon at the new campus library named for him and collected his autograph on my graduation brochure. I worked a typing job in California that summer while my parents journeyed by themselves to Yellowstone before returning to Fort Worth after two weeks of vacation time. You have to give my mother credit for wanting to see all that she could, even if she did have to do all the driving and cater to my father's challenging needs.

Getting away from Texas to a small liberal arts college in California forced me to question the religious, political and social foundations my parents had provided for me. Anyone going to college in the sixties had to have been challenged by the societal upheavals of that era.

Although I clung to many core values, goals, and interests gleaned from my Southern upbringing, I came to sympathize with and support liberal, antiwar, civil rights causes. Some of my Whittier classmates went to Selma in 1965 for the civil rights march on Montgomery, Alabama. A class in existential psychology challenged my thinking as well. Although I sought out the Christian existentialists like Reinhold Niebuhr rather than the Marxists, by senior year I had moved away from the Methodist trinitarian belief system of my childhood. My study-abroad program in Copenhagen and the trip to Pakistan also showed me a different world.

While my mother kept her more socially liberal views to herself, my father was never vehemently outspoken on any topic, though he had his conservative opinions. He never discussed African Americans, Hispanics, or Native Americans who were outside our social milieu. Nor, to his credit, did he say anything negative about them. African Americans simply lived in their part of town and went to their schools, making it possible for me to grow up open-minded but having no interaction with them until I reached college. There I made my first African American friend, Dottie, with whom I roomed my senior year. Hispanics were treated the same way by my father. Though they attended junior and senior high school with me, I associated socially with only one Hispanic girl whose father worked at Carswell Air Force Base.

My father did on occasion make disparaging remarks about people who had mental health issues, believing those who saw a shrink were weak. Having lived through the Great Depression, both my parents had learned to endure life's hardships—work hard, suffer, get over it, move on. Such issues were hidden or never spoken about by most Southern families. I feel certain he felt the same way about LGBTQ people. Homosexuality was abnormal, not acceptable, not discussed.

Dr. Burnett wrote references that helped nab my fellowship to the University of Michigan where I embarked on an MA degree in international relations. Having recently arrived by bus in Ann Arbor the fall of 1965, I traveled with other graduate students to the American Political Science Association's annual meeting on my first trip to Washington, DC. I wanted to line up some way to get back to the stimulating capital city.

At my father's suggestion, I called on his former student intern at KFJZ radio, Horace Busby, who was President Lyndon Johnson's Cabinet Secretary. During my visit with Busby in the West Wing of the White House, President Johnson came out of a cabinet meeting and headed straight to us. After a photo op, the President inquired why I was there, and Mr. Busby said I was looking for a summer internship at the US Department of State. The President replied, "Well, get her one!" That statement set in motion a background check for a security clearance.

I finished my master's degree with a thesis on the 1956 Hungarian Revolution in early May. Having lived frugally, I had saved enough money from my graduate fellowship to finance a 6-week back-packing trip through Europe, including Yugoslavia and Bulgaria, before moving to Washington to start my paid internship. With three major international trips under my belt by age 23, I was eager to begin work on the Japan desk at the Department of State in late June.

This incredible opportunity catapulted me into my first chosen career field of international relations. My father supplied the key networking contact, a perfect example of "it's not what you know, but who you know." The art of networking, a skill that had been his lifesaver, served me well from the 1970s through the nineties as a career counselor helping clients find jobs. My father passed on this legacy as well to brother George, whose networking skills have served him well in business.

After an exciting, eye-opening summer of intern activities, I walked the halls of State until I found a position as a research assistant in the Near East and North Africa Intelligence and Research Division (INR/RNA). Working in Washington offered more intrigue than embarking on a multi-year PhD program at Michigan. I worked for a year as an assistant to the Iraqi analyst, studying and evaluating classified cables all day. The most fascinating assignment I had was a 3-month detail out to Langley's CIA headquarters where I did intensive research on Mustafa Barzani, then leader of the Kurds in northern Iraq.

In Washington I roomed with two friends from Whittier College, one being my girlfriend Dottie, who was African American. After the three of us were turned down for several apartments, the other girlfriend—who was white like me—and I signed a lease on an apartment near the Cathedral in NW Washington and then moved Dottie in. The only trouble we had with that decision came from an African American maid in our building who chewed Dottie and me out one day: "It's you blacks and whites mixing together that's causing all the trouble in this world!" That was 1967, two years after President Johnson signed the historic civil rights legislation.

I met other African Americans and people from various cultural backgrounds. I remember concern on my parents' part expressed in letters to me that I was spending a lot of time with "Dottie's Negro friends" (i.e., meaning I might actually get involved romantically with a non-white, like some of my girlfriends had done).

The year as a research analyst at the State Department taught me I needed to be working with people more than data. So I quit the State Department and, following my mother's long-standing advice, went into a Master of Arts in Teaching program to obtain secondary certification. At the Antioch-Putney Graduate School of Education's satellite campus in Washington, DC, I taught civics and government half days at Ballou High School in southeast Washington and took evening classes. This adventure turned nerve-wracking during the turbulent 1968 spring when riots occurred around the city following the assassination of Martin Luther King, Jr. After my students saw from our second-floor window someone brandishing a gun, they upended my desk against our classroom door. I managed to get home by bus before the city burned that night. Teaching high school in a marginalized neighborhood in Washington, DC, broadened my perspectives on race, poverty, and injustice. However, I decided teaching high school students was not for me, although I felt I might like training adults.

During the 1966-67 year at the State Department I had met a Foreign Service Officer named David McClintock, who was going through a divorce. We dated while I was doing the Antioch program and I moved with him to Ann Arbor in the fall of 1968 so he could do a PhD program in political science with some of the same professors I had had for my master's degree. Because David, an Arabist, would be posted to the Middle East, I audited related courses and worked as an assistant to a professor doing research on computer-assisted instruction. David and I married in December 1968 at my parents' home on Kenley Street in Fort Worth.

My Father's Retirement Years. In the late 1960s Forrest experienced a cut-back in hours, but why is unknown. My father had hoped to hold on to his job until he could draw Social Security, since there was no pension program at KFJZ. He finally retired in the summer of 1970 at age 61, a year and a half before he could receive Social Security benefits. Whether he was told to take early retirement or he was just ready to go was never discussed.

He told my brother not to consider going into the radio-TV industry because it was "cut-throat" and poorly paid unless you were an anchor newsman or a popular radio or TV personality. Forrest never read any of the mid-century stories by other paralyzed polios so did not realize his plight was similar to their talk of job discrimination. Even if they did land something they could do well, they experienced the failure of getting promoted, passed over by others more able-bodied as the years went by.

Forrest's KFJZ friends threw a retirement party for him in July 1970. They came to the house, bringing lunch and $400 that had been collected. He kept a list of contributors and his usual itemized record of exactly what he spent the money on, just as he had done every day while I was growing up, even if it were only a 35-cent school lunch. I still hear, "Mama, what did you spend today?"

IN "SCOOT BUGGY," 1963

After retiring, Daddy continued several hobbies he had been pursuing over the years. Despite his crippled right hand, he had become a constant photographer after he gave up scrapbooking in 1940. Calling up his left hand's fine motor skills, he made intricate ship and train models. He collected stamps and continued to correspond with relatives to put together our first family genealogy. A record collection of jazz, big band, and "easy-listening" music kept his ears attuned. Always the extrovert, he loved to chit-chat with neighbors in their front yards during nice weather, traveling to their houses in his scoot buggy.

He also turned to "paint-by-numbers," making oil paintings he gave as gifts to friends and relatives and claiming he did 83 such pictures and several original oils. These he could handle with the canvas lying on the desk in front of him and carefully following the lines while holding the brush in his

left hand. He made this 3'x5' painting of a peaceful New England rural scene with barn and deciduous trees in their fall kaleidoscope of colors that hung in my mother's living room for years—his best work. It is a wonder how he managed to do such a big painting on his desk top, for it was not possible for him to work on an easel

PAINT-BY-NUMBERS, 1970S

because of limited major motor strength in his upper body. Excited about his "retirement career," in 1971, he mailed me a small easel and oil paints through the APO while I was living in Amman, Jordan, in the Middle East.

My Middle East Assignments. George married Judy Lesley in 1966 and my parents welcomed their first grandchild in December 1969. David and I travelled to Texas over the holidays before leaving for the Middle East and drove with my parents to visit my brother and his family in Alabama where George was stationed in the Air Force. It was sad for me to think of not seeing my parents for almost two years. They courageously hid their fears about our going to such a remote and possibly dangerous place like Yemen, where David had been assigned and had served a previous tour in the early 1960s.

My husband and I headed to Beirut in February 1970 for his Arabic language refresher course. Having recently finished his doctoral course work and prelim exams, David planned to research and write his dissertation on Yemeni political decision-makers after we arrived in Sanaa, the capital, in May of that year. David was sent back by the State Department to serve as chargé d'affaires. We re-opened the post after it had been closed during the 1967 Arab-Israeli war. Because the Yemenis were not ready to resume full diplomatic relations with the United States, we became the American Interests Section within the Italian Embassy although we physically resided in the old American compound. We were only six Americans and a larger number of Yemeni nationals, some of whom had worked for the embassy before the 1967 closure. Serving as the post's secretary, I used skills my mother had insisted I get.

We called this State-designated hardship assignment our "Peace Corps tour," staying for 21 months. During that time we had our first child, Lesley. I flew over to Kagnew Station, in Asmara, Ethiopia (today, Eritrea), a month before due date to deliver her at the US Army base hospital. Still the post's secretary and not yet willing to entrust my newborn to a local "ayya," I kept Lesley in her bassinet and nursed her at my office desk for a few months. On home leave in February 1972, we took 7-month-old Lesley to meet her Texas grandparents and my husband's California parents

Yemen was a tough but unbelievable experience I would not trade for anything. (See my memoir titled *Arabian Nights and Daze: Living in Yemen with the Foreign Service*, 2010). Sadly, that magical place no longer exists, irreparably damaged by the current Saudi-Houthi war in Yemen. We were the lucky ones to have been there when it felt like we were traveling centuries back in time.

Following home leave, we were posted to Amman, Jordan, where David served as chief of the political section, or number three in the embassy. I found part-time work teaching English to pre-med students at the University of Jordan, learned what life was like at a more typical foreign service post than Yemen had been, and enjoyed watching our young daughter grow.

Jordan was a tense assignment because of the always unpredictable political situation in the Middle East. At that time we were worried about the Palestine Liberation Organization and various anti-Israeli splinter groups that could make our life hazardous. We had several nerve-wracking experiences. (For details, see Chapter three's "Middle East Security" in *Arabian Nights and Daze*.)

—◄\✦/►—

Mildred and Forrest continued to travel in their later years, especially once Forrest retired and they could vacation longer and more often. They first ventured by plane to Hawaii in 1971 for a week of leis, mu-mus, palm trees and Hawaiian music. Tour companies helped them get about.

In 1973 they came to see us in Amman, traveling with Ancel and Adele to London, Paris, Rome, and the Holy Land. They could not have made the trip without Ancel to haul Forrest into and out of hotels and tour vehicles. At that time, airlines could not accommodate people in wheelchairs as easily as today. Their London travel agent recruited an ambulance to speed out on the tarmac to retrieve Daddy from the airplane, process him through customs, and get him into the city. David and I managed to get him via jeep into Petra, the ancient Nabatean carved-sandstone city hidden among the rocks and wadis (arroyos) in southern Jordan. There we stayed overnight in a hotel inside the monument. Fortunately, our Amman house was on a single floor with wide doors and easy for my father's wheelchair to maneuver.

Since my husband was on official business carrying the diplomatic pouch, a US government driver and vehicle took us from Amman to the Allenby (or Hussein) bridge at the Jordan River. We pushed my father in his wheelchair across to Israel. An Israeli-licensed car owned by the US Consulate in Jerusalem met us after we cleared the tedious crossing checkpoint and carried us into the city where we organized several tours for my parents, aunt and uncle. US Ambassador and Mrs. Dean Brown invited the four of them to lunch at their residence in Amman, and they visited a senior Jordanian official's rural irrigated desert farm.

We left Amman in January 1974 for an assignment in Washington and were relieved to get back to the States. At least we knew we would be random targets in the US. Although intrigued by our first-hand experiences, I had decided life overseas was not quite as glamorous as I had anticipated, at least in hardship posts like Yemen and to a lesser extent Jordan.

My parents were pleased about our return to the States as well. In the days prior to easy communication via email and Skype, they had been concerned about our safety and also sad to be so far away from their second grandchild. As in Yemen we communicated by letter and cassette tapes. Maybe Daddy enjoyed making tapes almost as much as he had broadcasting the news. Having taught me to love travel and adventure, he never dreamed I would move half-way around the world to find it.

I was pregnant with Nathan when we visited our families on home leave before settling in Washington. We traveled with my parents to Lubbock, Texas, to visit my brother and family, then posted to Reese AFB where he was a trainer of fighter pilots headed to Vietnam. Daddy loved having all three of his granddaughters sitting on his lap—one at a time that is—memories of bygone days for him.

Six months later, my parents flew to DC the first two weeks after Nathan's birth in July 1974. We had bought a 4-story semi-detached Tudor style house on Cathedral Avenue at the intersection of Massachusetts and Wisconsin. We set up the basement, which was at ground level with a bathroom, where my parents could sleep. We rolled Daddy from the basement up the side yard on an asphalt walkway so he could access the front porch through a side gate and enter the main (2nd) floor with only one step. He stayed on the main floor, which had a bathroom, till bedtime.

How I cried when they left by taxi for the airport. I realized these two children would be primarily my responsibility from then on, and it felt daunting. I thanked the heavens I did not have to earn a living too. I became active in play groups, pre-schools, our Cleveland Park baby-sitting co-op, and instigated the DC Recreation Department's creation of today's Newark Street Park with playground, gardens and tennis courts just behind the second district police station. I also worked (for pay) at my children's Horace Mann after-school program. In 1975 my parents flew back to DC to spend Christmas with us, their first and only time to spend the holiday with us in our home. We were able by then to take them sightseeing, as my mother had never really seen the capital city before.

I was thankful David was able to obtain stateside appointments for the next eight years. In addition to the security issues, we were not enamored with the mandatory entertaining and socializing expected of diplomats overseas. We cherished being able to stay home in the evenings with our two young children.

When Nathan and Lesley were in pre-school and kindergarten, I sought help from the Women's Center in Washington, DC, to determine what I really wanted in a career. Volunteering to lead career and job search workshops, I soon found my calling. Prior to the 1970s, no one talked about having "passion" in a job, an idea that came with the new field of career counseling. *Do What You Love and the Money Will Follow, Feel the Fear and Do It Anyway, What Color is Your Parachute?* are early book titles that inspired job seekers. Match interests with skills and with good networking you can find the job of your dreams. I loved seeing the light bulbs go off when helping job seekers uncover their marketable talents. I showed them how to network to find their niche in the job market, teaching a skill I had learned so well from my father.

Joining the Association of American Foreign Service Women (AAFSW), I supported the group's lobbying efforts to establish a Family Liaison Office (FLO) in the State Department. FLO would help spouses of Foreign Service (FS) personnel find employment abroad and serve the educational needs of FS families and of those in limbo (e.g., the stateside spouses of the Iranian hostages held in Tehran in 1979). At the same time, I was networking with many people to find paid employment. After FLO was set up in 1978, the Foreign-Service-spouse director hired me as the first career coordinator in the new office. Until David's FS retirement in 1982 to begin a new kind of life, I was able to combine my passion for helping people obtain their career dreams with my love for international affairs. That assignment allowed me to visit FLO offices in New Delhi, Bangkok, and Beijing.

I was in a career that my father would have enjoyed had he been physically able. If his disability prevented him from becoming a government official in Washington, then he could satisfy that curiosity through his daughter. Daddy took great pleasure in hearing my stories and visiting me in Washington and Amman. He may not have realized how important his key networking contact was, for Horace Busby had facilitated my 16-year career in the international arena and my meeting the father of my children. I telephoned Busby years later to thank him for his help.

A Move to Abilene and Further Travels. When my mother was promoted in 1976 to GS-6 Clerk-Stenographer with the US Soil Conservation Service, my parents moved to Abilene, Texas, where they had met forty years earlier. They bought a comfortable one-story 3-bedroom, 2-bath house in the south part of Abilene near her sister Verna and her brother C.H. (Bub) and their families. They joined the First Methodist Church. As they were even closer to New Mexico, they continued to enjoy Wyatt family reunions at Gladys and Ben's cabin in Red River through the 1970s.

Giving up Forrest's scoot buggy when they moved to Abilene, they bought a Dodge van equipped with a hydraulic lift so my father could remain in his small indoor electric wheelchair for travel. These devices were necessary when it became too difficult for him to roll a manual chair or scoot himself without help along the board he had used for years to get from seat to seat.

David's and my experiment in weekend country living began in 1976—65 miles west of DC near Amissville, Virginia. On our 27-acre farm we could experience the outdoors in ways that were not possible in DC. Lesley and Nathan loved it too, setting a course for both of them in later life choices. We drove about 90 minutes each way nearly every weekend, cleaned up two abandoned houses, renovating a 600-sq-ft. one for us, cleared three acres ourselves (by hand and bush-hog) and hired a professional company to clear seven more, built a half-acre pond, and pretended we were farming. However, although surrounded by an electric fence, the deer, turtles, and locusts devastated our garden. We made local friends that included a few commuters and others whose ancestors had been there for two centuries. (See my memoir *Thirty Acres More or Less: Restoring a Farm in Virginia,* 2003.)

My parents made one last trip together in the fall of 1981 to visit us in Washington, DC, stopping first at our farm. We joined them in the van for a trip to New York City, where my mother had never been. It was to be a one-day drive through Manhattan on a Sunday and we would stay in easy-access motels in New Jersey to accommodate my father. We visited the World Trade Center and the Metropolitan Museum of Art before the van broke down in Greenwich Village. This mishap forced us to stay two nights in a Manhattan hotel and find a reputable repair shop on a Sunday for a fix on Monday. We ate a meal at an automat diner and showed my mother sights by taxi and subway she never would have managed otherwise. Spontaneity was not usually something my father planned for, and he became anxious initially when the van broke down in an unfamiliar location. However, after David and I sorted everything out, we all had a great time.

While we were all in DC, I invited over for dinner an old classmate of my father's from Tyler, Sarah McClendon, a well-known journalist and White House correspondent under eight presidents. She remembered him from third grade at Gary Elementary through Tyler High School. I first met

Sarah when we were both selected to participate in a Department of Defense evaluation of women's jobs in the US Army at Forts Benning and Stewart in Georgia. My father had told me about her, having seen her grilling various presidents on the nightly news. When she learned who I was, she expressed a view

SARAH MCLENDON AND FORREST, 1981

of Forrest that was likely held by others who knew him. Sarah was amazed to learn from me in 1981 that Forrest had married and had two children. I can still remember her shocked comment: "YOU are Forrest Clough's DAUGHTER!"

Sarah later told a reporter of the *Tyler Courier-Times Telegraph* about the reunion: "He had a wonderful voice" that was instrumental in leading to a radio career. In the interview Sarah made no mention of his being crippled by polio or her surprise when she met me, his daughter. Most of Forrest's peers probably had had the same limited expectations for him as Sarah did. It makes me wonder whether some of the good feelings Forrest received from his many friends were generated more by pity and sorrow for this talented young man than by seeing him as an equal. In those days "cripples" with severe afflictions were simply not expected by normals to achieve the American dream.

The Late Effects of Polio and Respiratory Failure. Described in French medical literature as far back as 1875, the late effects of polio eventually came to be called post-polio sequelae or syndrome (PPS). It refers to the new debilitating symptoms that polio survivors of the epidemic years (1930s-1950s) began having thirty to forty years later. Coined by Dr. David Bodian in 1984, the term "sequelae" refers to the varied late effects of the polio that damaged motor neurons of the brain stem and possibly the spinal cord. "Syndrome" was easier to spell and many use the two words interchangeably. But "syndrome" refers more directly to muscle weakness that may also have pain and fatigue associated with it. It is used by the Social Security Administration to determine disability benefits for those polio survivors who can no longer work.[130]

Polios began to describe their symptoms in a survivors' newsletter, the *Rehabilitation Gazette*[131] in the late 1970s. These included but were not limited to extreme fatigue, muscle weakness, joint and muscle pain, breathing and swallowing difficulty, sleep disorders, increased sensitivity to anesthesia, digestive problems, cold intolerance, and the need to use crutches and wheelchairs again. These symptoms pointed to increased deterioration of both motor and brain-activating neurons,[132] causing renewed grief and disability for polios and their families in their declining years. The *Rehabilitation Gazette,* which later morphed into Post-Polio Health International (PHI),[133] sponsored the first of several conferences in 1981 to look at what had happened to polios over the years. Initial international scientific conferences on PPS were held in Warm Springs, Georgia, in 1984 and 1986, where researchers, clinicians, and the media made PPS a recognized clinical entity.

Figures regarding the number of polio survivors, both paralytic and non-paralytic, and the number of those experiencing PPS vary considerably, likely because of the many undiagnosed cases and the difficulty of diagnosing clinically the late effects of polio (or PPS). In 1987, four years after my father died, the Public Health Service's National Health Interview Survey (NHIS) estimated there were 1.63 million polio survivors in the US, findings far greater than anyone suspected and more than persons with "Parkinson's disease, multiple sclerosis, and spinal cord injury combined."[134] Of those, the survey revealed that 60% of the paralytic and 30% of the non-paralytic were experiencing new symptoms. Dr. Lauro Halstead, himself a polio survivor, drawing from many potential sources for error, estimated the number of polio survivors as of 2006 to be 700,000 with 11.5% (81,000) to 25% (184,000) experiencing new weakness, with or without other symptoms, to some degree.[135] Though the polio population has decreased considerably since then, the percentages of survivors experiencing PPS today likely are similar. Many still do not realize that some of their aging issues may be polio-related.

⸺≽⫯⊰⸺

In the early 1980s my father and I were unaware of post-polio syndrome, since no one had ever used that term to categorize my father's decline. When his muscles began to lose strength at middle age, his doctors in the 1960s told him they had never seen such an "old polio" as he was and had little to compare his symptoms to. They were unable to predict what the future held for him because they had not yet examined the large numbers of PPS patients afflicted in the polio epidemics of the forties and fifties.

By the time my parents moved to Abilene in 1976, in addition to retrofitting the Dodge van with the wheelchair lift, my father required a special mechanism to get into and out of the bathtub. His bath lift chair was connected by hose to the tub's water faucet. A valve on the faucet would allow water to raise the chair up even with the tub's side edge. The chair swiveled 90 degrees to face the side of the tub so that Daddy could slide onto it. He then swiveled the chair back to facing the faucet and turned the faucet valve to allow the seat to drop down to the tub's bottom. As severe as Forrest's paralytic polio and his symptoms of the late effects had been, he indeed would have been diagnosed with PPS if he had been alive in 1987, the year that Congress granted social security disability benefits to those polio survivors severely affected by PPS.[136]

Likely it was his weakened muscles in the respiratory region that finally ended his life at the age of 73 on January 28, 1983. Suffering from a bad cold for several days, he simply did not wake up one morning, dying peacefully in his sleep at home with his wife by his side.

Perhaps the underlying reason for Forrest's decline that last year of his life was the passing of Ancel from stomach cancer in June 1982. His beloved brother, whose legs had carried Forrest many miles during his lifetime, was gone. Forrest had truly lost a part of himself. He commented to his nephew Mike at Ancel's funeral: "This suit I've got on is the one you'll bury me in." He knew the end was near for him as well.

―ゝ＼／⁄―

When David retired from the State Department in the summer of 1982 at the age of fifty, he accepted a political science teaching job in Rome, Georgia. Northwest of Atlanta, Berry College was a place where both of us had been Woodrow Wilson Visiting Fellows while working at the State Department. I gave up my cherished Family Liaison Office job and the possibility of my own pension for what we thought would be an exciting new life for our family of four.

Sadly, my father was never able to visit us the two years we were in Georgia. He died the winter after my State Department career ended and a week before my 40th birthday. Looking back, I am happy Daddy did not have to experience the difficulties of my divorce. It seems that our move to Georgia and my father's death were transition points that ushered in a distinctly new direction for my life.

Eleven years later, in 1995, I followed my heart back to New Mexico and my Wyatt roots, having added that family to my birth name several years earlier. My mother fortunately was able to fly out for one last visit to her birth state to see the new house I had built in Albuquerque. There I met widower Richard Williams, a retired electrical engineering professor and watercolor artist, who became my second husband.

Since this book concerns my father and my relationship with him, I'll not go into my life following the death of my mother in 1997, three months before I met Richard. When I remarried in 1999 I gained a whole new step-family. This last chapter of my life is a happy but different story.

CHAPTER SIXTEEN

FINDING FATHER AND
INTERPRETING HIS STORY

To get a clearer picture of who my paraplegic father was and how he coped in the days prior to disability legislation, I looked at the few narratives I found of polio survivors born before 1930 as well as those afflicted during the epidemics of the 1940s and 1950s. I also had to delve deeper into my relationship with him and discover the positive legacies he bequeathed me as well as admit to a few negative influences from having grown up with a disabled parent.

Comparing Forrest to Other Polio Survivors. Marc Shell, himself a survivor, located only two early-twentieth-century polios, both female children afflicted in the decade after my father was, who documented their experiences in private letters held at Harvard Library.[137] However, I found two polios—William O. Douglas and Alan Marshall—who published books about their personal experiences of having the disease in 1901 and 1908 respectively prior to my father's 1909 bout. Carol Rosenstiel's daughter, Anne Gross, published a book about her mother, who had the disease in 1927. Rosenstiel's polio hit 18 years after Forrest's, nine years after the 1916 New York epidemic, and six years after President Roosevelt's. These three books and several of FDR's biographies plus those of many mid-century polios aided my guessing at what my father's feelings and concerns may have been at many points in his life.

Having an apparently isolated case, Supreme Court Justice William O. Douglas in *Go East, Young Man* documents his polio at age three in 1901 while living in Minnesota.[138] Left with weak and spindly legs, he talks of shame and embarrassment from being called hurtful names by young peers, of his family's expectations that he perform better than the best, if not physically, then academically, and of his need to develop an overachieving Type A personality to free himself from criticism and feelings of failure.[139] Becoming a loner out of shame, he began strengthening his leg muscles through intense hiking in the Yakima hills of the eastern Cascades of Washington where he spent his youth. Hiking and physical endurance challenges in the outdoors became a lifelong passion—pushing himself to the point of exhaustion, pain and often twitching legs. He likely suffered post-polio syndrome before he died in 1980.

In *I Can Jump Puddles* Australian Alan Marshall says he contracted polio in 1908 at age six. He wrote a three-part autobiography, the best known having been made into a TV series by the American Broadcasting Company (ABC) in 1981. Also an isolated case, Marshall lived for months in a men's hospital ward with no other polios.[140] He described how he overcame his disability on an outback bush farm in Victoria province where his father boarded and trained horses for neighbors. He had surgeries and struggled with his braces and crutches but learned to scoot and crawl without these aids in order to traverse the uneven terrain of his rural community. Like my father, his narrative shows no anger. Though he did not like the patronizing attitudes of some adults, he mentions fights with his school mates but never any harassment because of his disability. Determined to be happy despite his lameness, Marshall did manage to ride horses again, even gallop, had some spills, and went on to become a writer.

Both Franklin Roosevelt and Carol Rosenstiel contracted polio in the 1920s after my father did. Struck at age two in 1927, Rosenstiel began writing diaries in her fifties that reflected many of her emotions as she grew up and faced the world as a paraplegic. Her daughter Anne Gross drew heavily from her mother's retrospective notes and her own recollections to write *The Polio Journals: Lessons from My Mother*. Rosenstiel's self-consciousness at her appearance, her drive to be independent and do as much for herself as possible, often spurning offers of assistance, to excel and get approval from her family and friends, and her anger were all emotions similar to those expressed in numerous polio narratives. Her journals illustrate how she hid her disability as much as possible and projected an optimistic, positive face to the world, revealing only her shame, pain, and feelings of social ostracism in her journals.

FDR's biggest challenge as a polio survivor in an inhospitable age came when seeking high public office. No one as severely crippled as he was had ever done so, and social attitudes in the early twentieth century discouraged even an attempt at it. [141] Not only must his prospects have seemed extremely depressing, FDR also had no role models or an organized group of peers to support him. Exposure as "weak" had to have been one of his greatest fears. He had to engineer a massive cover-up if he were to re-enter public life. [142] Fortunately, once back in public life, FDR's leadership and prominence spurred fundraising for the National Foundation for Infantile Paralysis (NFIP) and the March of Dimes. The funds supported many caught in the epidemics of the forties and fifties and drove development, testing, and release of the polio vaccines sooner than might have occurred otherwise, thus saving untold thousands from this dreaded disease.

In Douglas' book I found more anger and fighting back at personal and social challenges to his paralytic state than evidenced publicly by Marshall, FDR, or my father. Gross's narrative about Rosenstiel suggests that her mother expressed her anger and shame only in her journals since a public display of such feelings about her paralysis was unacceptable in her social milieu. Their stories, as well as other narratives, revealed the negative feelings, including tremendous anger many polios felt, something my father never expressed and may never have felt. In any event, expressing anger about most issues in Forrest's family was verboten, with such feelings swept under the carpet. Additionally, I have long speculated that his lack of anger was a result of his never having learned to walk on his own and experience the thrill of self-propulsion— the joy of running, climbing, riding a bike, or swinging from the tree tops. Unlike the active, athletic lads who contracted paralytic polio at such ages as 9, 11, or 16, Forrest did not understand the full extent of what he had lost. No wonder other polio narratives express such anger.

Carol Rosensteil's and FDR's stories were different in one respect from my father's, Douglas,' Marshall's, and most mid-century polios. Their backgrounds were more affluent than the average polio. Rosensteil's family was able to pay her way to Warm Springs on three different occasions and to partake of many therapies and treatments available at the time. Likewise,

FDR's privileged family pulled out every stop to alleviate his suffering. He was able to purchase the Warm Springs resort with half of his family inheritance. Although he generously made its healing waters available to others like him, thousands of survivors during the thirties and forties were never able to go to Warm Springs, my father included, due to limited financial resources—and often, no space, in the small facility. However, once Sister Kenny's methods became the treatment of choice in the forties and fifties, there was less need for such places.

Our Common Polio and Its Late Effects. Among the many aspects of our father-daughter relationship, my bond with my father is also cemented by the common disease of polio. Fortunately, I did not have his paralytic results and have lived a normal active life. However, in recent years it has become clear to me that we also shared some of the debilitating effects of post-polio sequelae (PPS) that was first suggested to me by a chiropractor in the early 1990s. It had never occurred to me that some of my mild but manageable medical problems had anything to do with polio, so I began my own research.

I discovered that even paralytic survivors who had mild cases and a good recovery (as I did) might also be affected.[143] Maybe my chiropractor had been right. Moreover, Dr. David Bodian's research[144] found that the motor neurons in the brain were damaged or destroyed in anyone who contracted or was undiagnosed with polio, also called polio encephalitis,[145] regardless of whether the spinal column neurons were affected. Thus, even non-paralytic survivors can have PPS symptoms.

My father's late effects of polio involved his loss of muscle strength and finally his respiratory system's failure. In my case, my mild scoliosis and weakened right side from polio causes hip pain and the need for regular physical therapy (PT). I have had major sleep problems since my late 30s and use a CPAP (continuous positive airway pressure) machine. I have experienced gut problems, memory issues, cold intolerance, foot neuropathy, restless legs, and osteoporosis, among other things, all of which my neurologist says are my late effects of polio or PPS. (See Appendix B for more details about my experience with PPS.)

My Father's Legacies. Both the good and the bad influences of having been raised by a paraplegic father had to be recognized as I looked back on his life. The positive influences were easy to identify, though startling at first to realize. However, I had to admit that my reluctance initially to include my own story only mimicked his refusal to put any negative emotions to paper that might cast a poor light on him or others. In addition, my writer friends were eager for me to delve into my relationship with him, sharing both the positive and the negative.

Some of my father's dreams and activities have manifested in my own life. For example, what did I major in but political science, the contemporary name for government? My father and I were both active in campus politics at college. We got masters degrees in the same field, both interested in national and international affairs. He was the assistant editor of his high school yearbook, while I was co-editor of mine. I was reporter and editor of my junior high newspaper and considered a college major in journalism. My father was reporter and assistant editor of his college newspaper while obtaining a bachelor's degree in journalism. My father loved history and sparked my interest years ago in genealogy and searching for missing ancestors that I continue today. He also passed on to me his love of travel and of writing as well as his skills at networking and detailed organizing of information and activities that have been invaluable to me.

NATHAN, ANNA, AND LESLEY
IN HYDRA, GREECE, 1981

My father's legacy does not stop with one generation. David and I took our young children to Rome and Greece to visit my stepdaughter Anna who was living in Athens with her mother at the time, so Lesley and Nathan had some exposure to travel prior to our divorce. In the summer of 1991 when they were teenagers, I took them backpacking around Europe and passed on my father's travel legacy. Nathan, over thirty years my junior, was a Peace Corps volunteer in Mali, W. Africa, and had more than 50-something countries under his belt before the age of 40. Lesley spent a summer in Nicaragua and has also made a number of international trips as an adult. Both inherited my father's love of music and are fine writers like their grandfather.

Nathan continues the family genealogy research that his grandfather instigated. Having completed a PhD in Urban Geography at Cal Berkeley, he is an associate professor at Portland State University. Lesley is highly creative with college majors in art and photography and a master's degree in filmmaking and loves being in the out-of-doors. Her career has rotated between national park service work as an environmental education ranger and teaching art to elementary-age children. She currently is a ranger at Bonneville Dam on the Columbia River near Portland.

Dealing with Negative Influences from my Father. Whereas polio at age four months was the defining event that shaped my father's life, it was my unexpected divorce at age 42 when I had to face the most traumatic experience of mine. Two years after my father died, the divorce sent me in new directions I had not planned for. Only then did I begin to see I had my own emotional baggage to deal with, having been raised the child of a disabled parent.

The divorce left me feeling weighted down by heavy logs and I sought professional help for the depression. I embarked on therapy, both individual and family, with several counselors, off and on, over a total of seven years. I was shocked to learn that my childhood had not been normal. In family systems theory, we had all danced around my father, the classic elephant-in-the-room. Although not an alcoholic, he pulled our strings nonetheless—someone we had to take care of. Co-dependency is something my brother and I learned from our parents, and we followed that model, placing as little stress as possible on the family's fragile foundation.

Nonetheless, my forties and early fifties as a single parent and divorcee were growth-filled, fun yet difficult, years of exploration that benefited me greatly. Although I had learned much about engaging the world from my sheltered, safe childhood, I had to reinvent myself, just like my career clients had to do.

The years of reinvention entailed not only the therapy, but also exploration of several non-traditional (for a Southern girl raised Methodist) spiritual paths. I had a breast cancer scare that had me standing up to the doctors and refusing a mastectomy for a 2mm lesion. I completed an interesting on-line PhD program for my counseling credentials. For several years I attended 12-step programs for my co-dependency and wrote a dissertation that focused on folks in 12-step recovery programs. There were several boyfriends, with some relationships brief and one that lasted three years and took me to Johnson City, Tennessee, for a short while.

During my years of "singlehood" and single-parenting of teenagers, I was able to have many discussions with my mother in our visits together about my childhood family. I told her what I had learned in therapy, which had allowed me to get in touch with anger, sadness, and other emotions I had never expressed in my growing up years. My mother listened with empathy and responded with, "But I thought you knew we loved you!" She did admit to me how scared she had felt when I came down with polio—that she might have two people in wheelchairs to care for. How would she have coped?

After my father died, Mama lived another 14 years, moved to Plano, Texas, near my brother, and did considerable stateside and some international traveling. Although a fiscal conservative, she was adamantly pro-choice and switched back to voting Democratic during the Reagan years. She continued to keep to herself any frustrations about the many years of caregiving to the man she loved, but announced very emphatically soon after she was widowed at 67 that she had no interest in taking care of another man. Several older men at church had tried to ask her out.

In retrospect, I see my childhood had its difficulties, but I thank my mother and father for the support they did give. They opened doors for me they had never been able to enter themselves. Of course, much of that had to do with the times, the post-war, pre-Vietnam era of abundance and opportunity. Because of their frugal Depression-era experiences, they wanted their children to have a more comfortable life than they had known as young people, especially my mother. Growing up on a pre-dust-bowl, dry-land wheat farm in New Mexico was spartan for her to say the least. As an elder myself now, I can look back lovingly at the sacrifices made and the support my parents gave me in the best way they knew how.

The Father I Came to Know. Despite his disability, my father traveled widely, perfected a musical instrument, obtained three college degrees, worked in the field of his choice, married, had a family, and lived longer than most others afflicted by polio as severely as he was. He accomplished all this prior to passage of supportive disability legislation and in an age when he would normally have been disregarded at best or cast aside at worst.

The father I knew was wiser and more realistic than the optimistic lad featured in his writings. More conservative than in his youth, he was even less willing to rock the boat, to jeopardize his hard-won gains. His career turned out far different from the glamorous one behind the microphones he had envisioned for himself and that readers of his scrapbooks anticipated. Although during the war years he was able to achieve his on-air broadcasting dream, after his radio colleagues came back from World War II, they resumed their places at the microphones. Though he had covered for them while they were away, he lost his public broadcasting persona. And listeners lost hearing his deep, resonant and trained voice. His colleagues, able-bodied war veterans who had interrupted their careers to fight for home and country, deserved to get their positions back.

Although happy in his family life, his radio career plateaued and leveled his outlook. He felt unappreciated, keeping this sadness to himself, my mother, and possibly his brother. Like many others of his generation, disabled or not, he did his job faithfully, did not ask for or expect much from his employer, and found fulfillment in his life outside of work.

Underneath the upbeat persona he showed the world lay what I believe was a deep-seated fear of being left alone. Certainly, the young Forrest had feared living a solitary adult life with his parents until they became old and infirm. Then what would happen to him? A nursing home at age 50? This fear was likely his primary motivator in life, over and above his normal desire for acceptance, love, sex, family, and a satisfying career. As he grew older, what if something happened to my mother? The fear was always there because he could not physically live alone.

Drawing from my own able-bodied worries, I also suspect he, as a disabled person, had fears of rejection and abandonment tenfold those of normals. Except for the strong-willed and resilient, rejection often leads to isolation and loneliness in addition to one's physical impediments.

My father would have said he had a good life, a happy one, and that he accomplished all that he had wanted given his physical condition. He was indeed blessed. He never had to be institutionalized like others in his generation who were less fortunate. Forrest's family provided not only the physical and financial support but, most importantly, the love and acceptance he needed to thrive. Without this—or his dynamic, positive personality—his life as a paraplegic could never have turned out as brilliantly as it did in the era in which he lived.

This narrative provides a remarkable story about how my father coped with the consequences of paralytic polio in the early twentieth century. It documents the slow march toward the polio vaccines and captures other aspects of American history in the first half of the twentieth century. By mid-century the medical establishment knew far more about how to treat polio, minimize the lasting paralysis, and improve mobility of those afflicted. By then, deaths had dropped from 40% to 5% per year. Because there were so many paralyzed by the polio epidemics of the 1940s and early 1950s, the nation took notice. These epidemics and their paralytic survivors undoubtedly contributed to the push for national legislation to help the disabled. (See Appendix A.)

My family played a multigenerational role in the polio drama that swept this country in the first half of the twentieth century beginning with my father in 1909, who had few resources available to him and his family for treatment. Next came my mother and her 45-year care of my father as well as her participation in the million mothers marches in the early fifties. I joined the family's polio odyssey in 1952 and benefited from then-current treatment methods. Soon after came my father's leadership role in the Texas March of Dimes 1954 campaign that occurred just prior to the roll-out of the first effective vaccines in 1955 and 1962. Although these breakthroughs eradicated polio in the Western world over the next 20-30 years, post-polio sequelae (PPS) was identified in the early 1980s and has affected many survivors, including my father and me. Nonetheless, the remarkable advances over the past 40 years in polio vaccinations worldwide have all but eliminated this disease. Our family has been a century-long witness to America's leadership in addressing and eliminating a once major global public health crisis.

The father I found while researching this book emerged as a hero in my eyes. I only wish I had known more about his early life when he was still alive. Discovery of his heroic journey began with my daughter Lesley's college oral history class in the early nineties when she interviewed my mother to learn her story and that of her life with my father. I was amazed at what she found and soon began interviewing the few relatives and friends still alive who had known my father. In 1997 as my brother and I were downsizing my mother's house and moving her into Assisted Living, I rescued my father's college scrapbooks and other writings from the trash bin, hoping to discover more about his early life. I laughed and cried my way through those scrapbooks for three days and decided then that I had to tell his story. Although there have been many interruptions along the way, I am at last proud to introduce my disabled father and his remarkable story to you.

EPILOGUE

POLIO ERADICATION WORLDWIDE

It has been over sixty years since the Salk and Sabin vaccines were introduced and forty since polio was eradicated in the United States. When I began in earnest this research and writing in 2010, I knew little about eradication activities of a global nature. My family's polio odyssey came full circle over 100 years after my father's 1909 bout when I was invited to a symposium that would update me on current efforts.

NYU's 2014 Innovations in Healthcare Symposium. The Fifth Annual Innovations in Healthcare Symposium at New York University (NYU) medical school was held October 23-24, 2014. Honoring Jonas Salk and Albert Sabin on World Polio Day, the symposium celebrated Jonas Salk's one hundredth birthday, one year short of the 60th anniversary of Salk's inactivated vaccine roll-out. The advances in the worldwide eradication of this devastating disease since 1955 (and Sabin's roll-out in 1961-62) have been nothing short of miraculous.

Again, my opportunity to attend this symposium came about through a friend, one of many professional contacts in my IPhone's address book. Dr. Danielle Ofri and I met over twenty years ago when she worked as a medical doctor on temporary assignment to the Navajo reservation near Farmington, New Mexico. An acclaimed writer as well as internist at Bellevue Hospital, she founded the Bellevue Literary Review in 2001. Lunching with Danielle at an Asian carry-out near Grand Central Station in New York in the spring of 2014, I discussed with her my writing project. She told me a member of her review's board of directors, Dr. David Oshinsky, was organizing a symposium on polio scheduled for the fall, and put me in touch with him via email. The symposium was open to the public and he invited me to attend.

I was excited at the prospect of meeting Dr. Oshinsky, the author of the Pulitzer Prize winning book, *A History of Polio*, which had proved useful in my research. Descendants of key figures involved in the quest to eradicate polio were also on hand: Dr. Peter Salk, son of Jonas and head of the Jonas Salk Legacy Foundation, and his son Michael; Ms. Debbe Sabin, nurse-practitioner (retired) and daughter of Dr. Albert Sabin; and Ms. Francoise Gilot, painter, author, and widow of Jonas Salk. Many doctors, medical researchers and experts on vaccines, the anti-vaccine movement, and efforts to eradicate various infectious diseases also attended.

It is fitting that this conference was held in the NYU Langone Medical Center. In the early part of the last century, highly restrictive quotas against certain minority groups existed with regard to medical school enrollment. Denied admission elsewhere, Drs. Albert Sabin and Jonas Salk, both of Russian Jewish descent, were admitted several years apart into NYU's merit-based system and were granted medical degrees. Each of the doctors developed polio vaccines that were introduced several years apart. Following extensive trials, Salk's killed virus vaccine was declared "safe, successful and potent" in 1955 while Sabin's live attenuated vaccine was finally licensed in 1962, following numerous field trials. These two vaccines that first conquered polio in the US and Western world are currently being used in the effort to eradicate polio worldwide.

My education about the polio vaccine had ended soon after swallowing my live vaccine sugar cube while in high school in the spring of 1961. Since both polio vaccines reduced cases of paralytic polio in the US and the West by 97%, there was no more fear or discussion about polio in the public domain. After the US was declared polio-free in 1979, Europe followed in 2002, and Southeast Asia in 2014. The conference was therefore instructive for me in learning about global polio eradication efforts over the past fifty-plus years.

One of the symposium speakers, Dr. John Sever, MD, PhD, at George Washington University, member of Rotary International and vice chair of the International PolioPlus Committee, stated the CDC (Center for Disease Control in Atlanta), WHO (World Health Organization), UNICEF (United Nations Children's Fund, formerly United Nations International Children's

Emergency Fund), Rotary International, and the Gates Foundation have all been working together on this massive eradication campaign.

Although the March of Dimes through its fundraising drove research that led to development of the vaccines and sponsored vaccinations in the US, it was Rotary International in 1979 that began disseminating vaccines worldwide. Small pox had been eradicated in 1977 and Rotary's leadership wanted to tackle polio next. Rotary had clubs in nearly every country—a million members worldwide—and these members became the natural conduits for education and training of polio vaccine workers.

The Philippines was the first place they went, partnering with the government there, their own Rotary members, WHO, and UNICEF to achieve success. Next they went to the Americas and partnered with PAHO (Pan American Health Organization), taking one country at a time (Bolivia and Haiti in 1981, Costa Rica and Honduras in 1983, and so on). They typically used the live oral vaccine that was cheaper (60 cents per dose), easier to administer (on a sugar cube, no shots), and believed to be more effective. In the late 1990s, officials began using Salk's killed vaccine in conjunction with the live vaccine in the final thrust to render polio impotent globally.

In 1985 Rotary International created the PolioPlus program with a definitive goal of eradicating polio worldwide by 2005, the centenary anniversary of the Rotary organization. In 1988 WHO created its own polio eradication initiative program (GPEI) and joined Rotary in the effort to eliminate the disease. Soon thereafter, UNICEF, the CDC in Atlanta, and the Bill and Melinda Gates Foundation joined the campaign. By October 2014, 2.5 billion people (mostly children) had been vaccinated worldwide.

Initially, Rotary International raised $240 million to purchase vaccine. By October 2014 Rotary had raised over $1.3 billion and a total of $9 billion had been spent in this campaign, with an annual estimated price tag of a billion dollars. The Gates Foundation had been matching all that Rotary raised two to one.

As a result of this massive effort, polio cases made an impressive decline. In 1985 up to 400,000 paralytic polio cases occurred worldwide. In 1988 the figure stood at 350,000. Although Rotary did not meet its 2005 eradication goal, by 2013 the number was down to 420 cases and 359 in 2014. Country by country goals were being met by governments who could take pride in seeing their efforts pay off. For example, by late 2014 India had been polio-free for three years, and officials declared the disease successfully eradicated there, with polio vaccine workers having been tasked to vaccinate against other infectious diseases.

At the 2014 symposium Dr. Jay Wenger, the polio eradication chair of the Bill and Melinda Gates Foundation, hosted a video presentation by Bill Gates and called for more help from the Pakistani government. Preventing attacks on vaccine workers along the Pakistan-Afghanistan border had to be accomplished before the polio vaccination program could make real progress.

In response to Wenger's plea, Dr. Sever pointed out that Pakistani Rotarians were already setting up seven permanent polio vaccine centers along the Pakistan/Afghanistan border to build community goodwill in areas at high risk. They had created health camps (designed to develop trust among the local populace), community workshops, polio guide books written in their languages of Pashtu and Urdu, and enlisted popular celebrities to urge compliance—all part of their education/promotion campaign. They were working with Pakistani police to improve security for healthcare workers, a number of whom had been killed in the line of duty. The Pakistani military had been slowly expanding its reach into Taliban-controlled areas where vaccine resistance is greatest. Workers had used highway checkpoints and border crossings to vaccinate displaced children as their families fled violence. Hopefully, these steps are still in play five years later.

With polio almost conquered, international organizations in 2014 were looking at approximately fourteen other infectious diseases among the poor—endemic, chronic, and disabling diseases (NTD's or neglected tropical diseases). Another symposium speaker, Dr. Peter Hotez, President of the Sabin Vaccine Institute at Baylor College of Medicine in Houston, was trying to find antidotes/cures/vaccines for the bottom billion in the world who are affected by NTD's. These diseases include schistosomiasis (or bilharzia), African sleeping sickness, ascariasis (over 800 million are affected by worms of the Ascaris genus), whip worm, dengue fever, and hookworm to name a few.[146]

Continuing Efforts: 2014-2019. In the years following the 2014 symposium—almost forty years after Rotary's Polio Plus program began its concerted worldwide effort in 1985—the wild poliovirus (WPV) has been eradicated in all but Pakistan and Afghanistan. However, the number of cases of circulating vaccine-derived poliovirus (cVDPV or simply VDPV) has been growing over the last decade and has created a "dangerous new front in the war on polio."[147] It now causes more cases of paralysis per year than the WPV. E.g., 95 cases of VDPV in Africa and Asia versus 88 cases of WPV (all Type I) in Pakistan and Afghanistan had been reported for 2019 as of late October.

In September 2019 two VDPV polio cases emerged in the Philippines, the country's first outbreak in nearly two decades. Zambia, Togo, and Chad reported new VDPV cases in September and October of 2019 as well. Whereas in 2015 there were only 28 cases of VDPV in eight different countries,[148] in 2018 and 2019 combined over 20 countries (210 cases as of late October 2019, all Type II) experienced outbreaks of VDPV.

Why is this happening? These cases often occur in countries where there is current turmoil (for example, in Asia and Africa from Islamic militants, the Saudi-Houthi war in Yemen, the civil unrest in the Democratic Republic of Congo, and the several refugee crises around the world, among other disruptions). VDPV cases are likely to continue to rise where vaccination teams cannot work safely or lack access to vulnerable populations. Rumors abound in some places that workers are spies (some have been killed) and that the vaccine is a Western plot to sterilize Muslim girls. Because the VDPV is causing paralysis among the unvaccinated, some are also afraid to have their children exposed to the vaccine.

What is being done? The World Health Organization's GPEI program launched an ambitious change in routine immunization systems around the world. They introduced the IPV (inactivated, killed poliovirus vaccine) to be injected followed by several doses of the OPV (oral, live polio vaccine). One injection of inactivated trivalent (tIPV, containing Type I, II, and III serotypes or sub-viruses) creates additional immunity when administered along with the several other OPV doses a child must take. As of August 2015, 51% of the global birth cohort was receiving at least one injection of trivalent tIPV in addition to their OPV doses.

In September 2015 the Type II wild poliovirus (WPV) was declared eradicated. However, this dominant Type II virus in the trivalent oral vaccine (tOPV, containing Type I, II, and III serotypes or sub-viruses) has been deemed responsible for 85-90% of VDPV cases, which exhibit rare strains of polio that have mutated from the weakened live virus. The mutation becomes virulent again causing paralysis among unvaccinated children. The Bill and Melinda Gates Foundation is funding research to create new oral vaccines that are "less able to mutate into dangerous forms."[149]

On April 17, 2016, because the Type II WPV had been declared eradicated, the trivalent oral vaccines (tOPV) then being used were replaced on a global basis by the bivalent (bOPV—types I and III) in 155 countries and territories. Done within a two-week period, this was the most "ambitious globally synchronized" project in the history of vaccines. [150] WHO's GPEI plans to use both the oral bOPV and inactivated trivalent IPV through 2020 to try to wipe out both Type I WPV and the increasing numbers of VDPV cases. The WPV type III had its last onset in November 2012 and was declared eliminated in October 2019 by the Global Certification Commission for the Eradication of Poliovirus. It remains to be seen whether the bivalent OPV (with no Type II strain) given in conjunction with the trivalent IPV will be able to eradicate both wild and vaccine-derived poliovirus.[151]

The International PolioPlus campaign to eradicate the poliovirus globally has proved instructive in efforts to address AIDS, HIV, and lately the Ebola virus (EVD). In fact, in Nigeria the Ebola Emergency Operations Center used the staff of the polio eradication program to train Ebola workers. Because Nigeria has a reliable health care infrastructure, the country was able to prevent an Ebola crisis when so many of its West African neighbors were in the throes of the 2014 epidemic, the largest Ebola crisis in history. In 2019, it is the unstable Democratic Republic of the Congo where the Ebola virus is spreading rapidly partly due to deaths of vaccine workers by warring militias.

When infectious diseases such as smallpox, diphtheria-pertussis-and typhus (DPT), measles, and poliomyelitis devastated affluent Western countries, vast resources were marshaled to develop vaccines to fight these horrors. The fight to find a cure for polio also left other legacies identified by Dr. Lauro Halstead.[152] Today's orthopedic rehabilitation programs and the modern intensive care unit (ICU) are the results of tremendous efforts by the US medical establishment to quell polio epidemics. The ICU has been patterned after the aggressive treatment provided bulbar patients in the National Foundation for Infantile Paralysis (NFIP)'s poliomyelitis respiratory centers around the country.

The field of virology was also transformed by lessons learned in the polio campaign that have helped facilitate development of vaccines or antidotes for other diseases. For example, Duke University's Cancer Center is in phase I treatment trials to inject the genetically modified Type I poliovirus directly into glioblastomas (brain tumors) in order to ignite an additional immune response. The neurosurgeons there, hoping to kill or at least slow down the progression of this deadly cancer, received from the Food and Drug Administration "breakthrough therapy designation" to expedite research in May 2016.[153] In July 2018, 21% of patients had survived for three years versus the 3-4% who survive that long using traditional therapies.[154]

Who would have thought years ago that an altered form of the poliovirus might actually become a promising agent in the search for a cancer cure. There are undoubtedly other unknown polio legacies that may surprise us in the future.

APPENDIX A

KEY LEGISLATION GRANTING CERTAIN DISABILITY RIGHTS AND PROTECTIONS

The Architectural Barriers Act (ABA) of 1968 requires that buildings or facilities that were designed, built, or altered with federal dollars or leased by federal agencies be accessible.

The Rehabilitation Act of 1973, as Amended (Rehab Act), prohibits discrimination on the basis of disability in programs conducted by federal agencies, in programs receiving federal financial assistance, in federal employment and in the employment practices of federal contractors. **Section 504** of the Rehab Act is designed to protect the rights of individuals and students with disabilities in programs and activities that receive Federal financial assistance. It was the first disability civil rights law to be enacted in the United States and set the stage for enactment of the Americans with Disabilities Act. The Department of Justice (DOJ) and the Department of Education (DOE)'s Office of Civil Rights (OCR) enforce section 504 in public elementary and secondary schools.

The Individuals with Disabilities Education Act of 1975 (IDEA) guarantees access to a free appropriate public education (FAPE) in the least restrictive environment (LRE) to every child with a disability. Subsequent amendments, as reflected in the IDEA, have led to an increased emphasis on access to the general education curriculum, the provision of services for young children from birth through five, transition planning, and accountability for the achievement of students with disabilities. The IDEA

upholds and protects the rights of infants, toddlers, children, and youth with
disabilities and their families.

The Americans with Disabilities Act of 1990 (ADA) prohibits
discrimination against individuals with disabilities in all areas of public life,
including jobs, schools, transportation, and all public and private places that
are open to the general public. It requires that people with disabilities have
the same rights and opportunities as those provided to individuals on the
basis of race, color, sex, national origin, age, and religion. It guarantees equal
opportunity to the disabled in public accommodations, employment,
transportation, state and local government services, and tele-
communications. The ADA is divided into five titles (or sections) that relate
to different areas of public life. For instance, **The ADA 1990, Title II** law
extends protection against discrimination to the full range of state and local
government services, programs, and activities including public schools
regardless of whether they receive any Federal financial assistance. The
Department of Justice (DOJ) and the Department of Education (DOE)'s
Office of Civil Rights (OCR) share in enforcing ADA's Title II.

**The Americans with Disabilities Act Amendments Act of 2008
(ADAAA)** made a number of significant changes to the definition of
"disability." The changes apply to all titles of the ADA, including Title I
(employment practices of private employers with 15 or more employees,
state and local governments, employment agencies, labor unions, agents of
the employer and joint management labor committees); Title II (programs
and activities of state and local government entities); and Title III (private
entities that are considered places of public accommodation). It also
provides a conforming amendment to Section 504 of the Rehab Act of 1973.

APPENDIX B

MY POST-POLIO SEQUELAE OR SYNDROME (PPS)

Because I came out unscathed from the same disease that paralyzed my father, I never bothered to mention having had polio to anyone before the mid-eighties when I entered counseling. Until then and before doing the research for this book, I believed my polio was a non-event in my life, a childhood illness that thankfully my children would not have to suffer.

However, as knowledge about Post-Polio Sequelae—or the more commonly used word Syndrome—(PPS) spread among medical profess-sionals in the early 1990s, a Tennessee chiropractor suggested my mild scoliosis and some problems with my right hip and S-I (sacroiliac) joint might be related to having had polio. Moving to Albuquerque in 1995, I attended a number of PPS support group meetings at St. Joseph's Hospital. There I saw what other polios were enduring, but felt my problems at that time were minor and simply related to normal aging. The volunteer survivors group disbanded in the late 1990s because their symptoms were getting worse. They could no longer carry on, and I did not want to take on the responsibility of running the organization.

After that, I tried to locate my polio records at City-County hospital, currently called John Peter Smith Hospital, in Fort Worth. Although Heather Wooten's excellent history of polio in Texas claims that many polio records are archived in various libraries around the state, I was told that Fort Worth's individual polio records from 1952 no longer existed. I had hoped to find my discharge records to learn what treatments I had had and an assessment of any lasting disabilities.

I now believe that many of my current medical problems are a consequence of having had polio. For starters, I have muscle weakness in my right leg. Having read childhood polio narratives about shorter legs and smaller limbs, I concluded that my thinner right thigh and calf (by approximately one inch in girth) must be a result of polio. My right leg can only press 40 pounds while my left leg presses 55. My right hip is definitely weaker per manual tests by my physical therapist. A 3/8th-inch heel lift in my left shoe helps with the scoliosis.

Tall, thin and small-boned like my mother, I have lost more than an inch in height. My osteoporosis, inherited from my mother who lost six inches and had many spine fractures as well as a hip break, also seems to be symptomatic of PPS.[155] Dr. Richard Bruno, himself a polio survivor and renowned PPS expert, is director of the International Centre for Polio Education (the new home of the International Post-Polio Task Force). In his 2002 informative "handbook" referred to as the "polio survivor's Bible," Bruno cites a couple of studies showing that women polio survivors "lose bone density at a faster rate than women with disabilities," perhaps as much as 50%.[156] Women polio survivors also lose bone density at a faster rate than those without disabilities. Walking and strengthening muscles increases calcium deposits in the bones. The catch 22 is that hard exercises, stressing bones and muscles, may deplete the polio survivor's remaining motor neurons, forcing more weakness and debilitation.

Thus, I have long worked with a physical therapist who has monitored and adjusted my exercises for home and gym to maintain and improve my strength and balance without overdoing it. She sees definite improvement from all the various types of exercising I do or have done over the years, including tai chi, yoga, walking, hiking, and strength training at the gym. I currently work weekly with a trainer to improve bone strength and balance at OsteoStrong, a national franchise using specialized equipment, and get a yearly infusion of Reclast, a medical intervention for osteoporosis.

In 2015 my Eugene neurologist Dr. Michael Balm, who has a number of PPS patients, confirmed my scoliosis at L-4-L-5 in the lower back is a consequence of polio. He maintains my foot neuropathy, restless legs and long-standing difficulty with sleep—waking up several times each night, unable to go back to sleep often for an hour or two—are also polio-related.

Sleep issues have nagged me since my late thirties (30 years after my polio bout). In my early sixties, I did several overnights in sleep clinics. Diagnosed with "sleep disordered breathing," I was prescribed a CPAP (continuous positive airway pressure) machine to use at night to open up my airways when lying down in bed. Although this device helps my breathing, I continue to have sleep interruptions at night and frequently restless legs for which I have tried various sleep aids or medications over the years. Good sleep is still a work in progress for me.

I do not remember breathing or swallowing problems while hospitalized with polio. However, polios who developed severe scoliosis later in life often have respiratory difficulties as well, according to Dr. Lauro Halstead, also a survivor and retired director of the National Rehabilitation Hospital in Washington, DC:

> Some individuals develop sleep-disordered breathing . . . the most common complaints were waking frequently, followed by snoring and fatigue. These findings were significantly different from a non-polio comparison group.[157]

Although my scoliosis is not severe, my sleep problems, compared to other women my age, are greater than most. I am a snorer as well. Daytime sleepiness is another common symptom, and I occasionally fall asleep, often to the point of embarrassment, during TV programs, lectures, and meetings, anytime I sit still for long and am not engaged in some activity. At this point, I do not have excessive fatigue.

Another problem associated with PPS is word-finding, according to Dr. Bruno.[158] In my senior years I have had to search more often for words that are on the tip of my tongue and only surface later. I believed I might be getting dementia or Alzheimer's and was greatly relieved that this is a common PPS symptom. Less than one percent of the polio survivors ever evaluated by Bruno's Post-Polio Institute got Alzheimer's. According to a study of alumni at Drew University, polios are twelve times less likely to get Alzheimer's than the normal population. One theory by Drew researcher Shanda Davis is that the poliovirus receptor gene found on chromosome 19 shares its DNA with a gene that makes a protein associated with getting Alzheimer's. If you do not inherit the Alzheimer's gene from either parent, you may be able to make more poliovirus receptors and thus get polio as a child, but be unable to manufacture the Alzheimer's gene as an adult.[159]

Difficulty focusing attention, memory lapses and thinking clearly are also PPS symptoms. Besides the dopamine neurons lost with the poliovirus, by age 50 we have all lost over one third of these neurons, and the protein that makes dopamine, the main brain activating neurochemical, has decreased by 70%.[160] Part of the reason I have taken over 20 years to finish this memoir is that I can easily get distracted and onto other projects. I often feel scattered and overwhelmed with too many things "pinging at me" and thus my type A personality feels unproductive, unable to accomplish its goals. The more stressed I am with lack of focus, the more my PPS symptoms surface, especially sleep disturbances and gut problems.

Undue stress and/or reactions to certain foods trigger my belly problems that only began about a decade ago. During that time I have had two stomach ulcers and other digestive issues, something reported by 15% of polio survivors.[161] I watch my diet by focusing on proteins and vegetables rather than carbohydrates. I also drink daily 20-30 ounces of an alkalizing "green drink" (40-plus green grasses in powder form) or alkaline water of 9.5 pH to reduce my stomach acid. Digestive enzymes help me avoid anti-acid medications that destroy bones if overused.

The vagus nerve carries commands from the brain stem neurons, some of which were compromised by polio, to activate muscles in the digestive tract. I have had numerous vagus nerve attacks (often initiated by a sharp pain) over the years in which I have fainted with a rapid drop in blood pressure. These vaso-vagal (syncope) attacks are usually accompanied by hidden hypoglycemia, which can be alleviated when I eat something like a banana. To keep my blood pressure and blood sugar up I work to keep hydrated and have a couple of protein snacks a day between meals.

Other symptoms identified by PPS experts that I exhibit: 1). Cold intolerance in my hands, feet, and body. 2). Pain and tingling on the bottoms of my feet on getting out of bed and putting on shoes in the morning, presumably related to my neuropathy. 3). Rapid heart beating episodes for which I had an atrial ablation several years ago. And, I continue to have atrial fibrillation (irregular heartbeats not necessarily identified with having had polio) for which I take daily medication.

My aging body needs regular exercise and with these various PPS symptoms will undoubtedly demand my attention for the rest of my life. But compared to my father's story and the narratives told by other more severely affected paralytic polios, the residual effects of my polio have been manageable. I hope this will continue to be so.

Identifying PPS and its Relation to Other Diseases. Due to our shrinking numbers, most doctors, including physiatrists, orthopedists, and neurologists, have had little experience with treating post-polios. PPS itself can only be determined by process of elimination of other diseases. However, Dr. Halstead has used a series of muscle and nerve tests on his patients to determine PPS, but these are expensive and not readily available. With no proven way to diagnose PPS, some remain skeptical that PPS even exists.

Dr. Bruno points out that PPS symptoms are similar to those of other enteroviruses such as chronic fatigue syndrome (CFS) and myalgic encephalitis (ME). These enteroviruses have proliferated since the poliovirus was eradicated by the vaccines. He speculates that something had to fill the poliovirus void. There are at least 72 enteroviruses, some of which are autoimmune diseases, that create debilities of fatigue, sleep, memory, cognition, and other issues, which can last for years. Other researchers have speculated that CFS and ME symptoms may be the result of undiagnosed childhood illnesses that affected the brain-activating neurons, including non-paralytic polio.[162]

Of special note is Acute Flaccid Myelitis (AFM), which has been occurring in greater numbers, largely every other year in late summer or fall since first reported in California in 2012. There were 228 cases in the US last year, and 550 in the past decade, far more than in three countries in northern Europe and Canada. Starting with a cold and flu-like symptoms, AFM can cause both temporary and permanent paralysis, and recovery is very slow. Ninety percent of its victims have been children mostly between ages 4 and 6. Scientists suspect AFM is an enterovirus that may be a mutation of a virus discovered more than 55 years ago.[163] [164] Note that 55 years ago was the early 1960s after both polio vaccines were introduced. Another enterovirus to help fill the void?

Will these proliferating enteroviruses have debilitating late effects similar to what polio has had? Perhaps by mid-century the medical profession will know.

Notes

[1] Simi Linton, 107.
[2] Heather Wooten, Appendix A, 182-183. Taken from the National Foundation for Infantile Paralysis/Poliomyelitis, *Annual Statistical Review* (1960), 7.
[3] Wooten, 43-44.
[4] Anne Gross, i.
[5] David Oshinsky, 16.
[6] Lauro Halstead (1998), 1.
[7] John R. Paul, 15; Oshinsky, 10.
[8] Philip M. Parker, 5.
[9] Paul, 17; Oshinsky, 10.
[10] Jane S. Smith, 134; Daniel J. Wilson, 255; Dorland's Medical Dictionary, 1192.
[11] Paul, 22.
[12] Ibid., 32.
[13] Stephanie T. Peters, 9; Paul, 32.
[14] Oshinsky, 11.
[15] Paul, 85.
[16] Ibid., 94.
[17] Ibid., 97.
[18] Ibid., 100.
[19] Oshinsky, 17.
[20] Paul, 39.
[21] Ibid., 32.
[22] Ibid., 69.
[23] Ibid., 64.
[24] Wooten, 18.
[25] Wooten, 18; Paul, 322-324.
[26] Hugh Gallagher, 28.
[27] Peters, 21; Paul, 117.
[28] Gallagher, 29.
[29] Ibid., 29-30.
[30] Halstead (1998), 1.
[31] Wooten, 12.
[32] Smith, 32; Wooten, 12, 181.
[33] Oshinsky, 22.
[34] Paul, 159.
[35] Gallagher, 32.

[36] Ibid., 32-33.
[37] Paul, 190-199.
[38] Wooten, 26-27, 51, 65-66.
[39] Paul, 336.
[40] Ibid., 222.
[41] Wilson, 155-161.
[42] Wooten, 22.
[43] Gallagher, 31.
[44] Ibid.
[45] Norman Gevitz, 19-63.
[46] Linda Cross and Robert Glover, 95.
[47] Mary Hosford Thomas, 14.
[48] Ibid., 30-31.
[49] Darwin Payne, 50.
[50] Thomas,104.
[51] Ibid., 114-115, 119-122.
[52] From a reprint in *Time Magazine* in 2008 of an August 12, 1929, news article in an unknown newspaper.
[53] Payne, 108.
[54] Ibid., 117.
[55] Gallagher, 17, 23; Hazel Rowley, 114.
[56] Gallagher, 18-56.
[57] Wilson, 141-142.
[58] nsidc.org, "Rapid Ice Loss…"
[59] skepticalscience.com.
[60] Payne, 120.
[61] *Dallas Journal*, May 30, 1935.
[62] Joe Nickell, 174-175.
[63] Thomas, 163, Payne, 122.
[64] Payne, 144.
[65] Wooten, 33.
[66] Chris Hansen, 66-67, 144-148.
[67] Wooten, 36-39.
[68] *Dallas Journal*, September 8, 1937.
[69] *The Semi-Weekly Campus*, October 9, 1937.
[70] Peters, 4.
[71] Dorland's, 1172, 1192.
[72] Wilson, 263.
[73] Halstead (1998), 5.
[74] Dorland's, 1192-1193.
[75] Paul, 40.
[76] Oshinsky, 2-23.
[77] Hansen, 132-3, 140, 149, 152, 154-5, 157.
[78] Ibid., 65-66, 138, 145-166.
[79] Ibid., 107-118.

80   Ibid., 166.
81   Ibid., 110-168.
82   Ibid., 152.
83   *Broadcasting*, September 1, 1939.
84   *Advertising Age*, November 6, 1939.
85   *The Fort Worth Press*, January 5, 1940.
86   *Broadcasting*, January 15, 1940.
87   *Broadcasting*, February 1, 1940.
88   Hansen, 166.
89   Ibid., 148-157.
90   William M. Pinkerton and Kirke Simpson, *The Dallas Morning News*, January 20, 1940.
91   *The Fort Worth Star-Telegram* and *The Fort Worth Press*, January 9, 1940.
92   *The Dallas Times-Herald*, February 4, 1940.
93   Hansen, 157, 166-68.
94   Ibid., 6.
95   *The New York Times*, October 28, 1990.
96   Hansen, 168, 173.
97   Kyle Crichton, *Collier's*, November 16, 1940.
98   Payne, 120.
99   Linda Gordon, 5, 11. (See Suzanne Riess's oral history of Lange, Berkeley, 1968.)
100 Dyanna Taylor, "Dorothea Lange," American Masters, *PBS*, 2014.
101 *The Fort Worth Star-Telegram*, June 25, 1949.
102 Wooten, 18.
103 Ibid., 199.
104 Paul, 338, 344.
105 Ibid., 340.
106 Ibid., 335-345.
107 Wooten, 182.
108 Halstead (1998), 2.
109 Dorland's, 1193; Paul, 105.
110 Paul, 225-226.
111 Oshinsky, 126-127.
112 Paul, 373.
113 Ibid., 373-374, 376.
114 Wooten, 100.
115 Paul, 301-323.
116 Wooten, 100.
117 Oshinsky, 188-190.
118 Ibid., 198-200.
119 Peters, 55; Smith, 312.
120 Wooten, 1.
121 Bob Trimble, *The Fort Worth Press*, April 16, 1961.
122 Paul, 379.
123 Smith, 376.

[124] Paul, 454-456.
[125] David Tarrant, 1A and 17A.
[126] Wooten, 17.
[127] Ibid., 57.
[128] Ibid., 185.
[129] Ibid., 122.
[130] Richard L. Bruno, 6, 113-116; www.papolionetwork.org, October 2019 newsletter.
[131] Halstead (2011), 1345.
[132] Ibid., 1346; Bruno, 109-220.
[133] Post-Polio Health International (PHI) is a non-profit organization located in St. Louis, Missouri, and provides a wealth of online information to PPS survivors including newsletters, research articles, directories, etc. See post-polio.org.
[134] Bruno, 6.
[135] Halstead (2011), 1346.
[136] Bruno, 6.
[137] Shell, 120.
[138] Douglas, 31-36.
[139] Bruno, 85, 90, 100-101; William O. Douglas, 31-40.
[140] Alan Marshall, 2-75.
[141] Gallagher, 33.
[142] Wooten, 34.
[143] Halstead (1998), 12, 22.
[144] Bruno, 20-37, 158-159.
[145] Ibid., 36-37, 158.
[146] Notes taken at Fifth Annual Innovations in Healthcare Symposium, October 23-24, 2014, at NYU Medical School and from recent news articles.
[147] McNeil, October 23, 2019.
[148] GPEI, Every Last Child Newsletter, December 18, 2015 and January 20, 2016.
[149] McNeil, October 23, 2019.
[150] GPEI, Every Last Child Newsletter, January 20, 2016.
[151] Victor Racaniello, *Virology Blog*, January 13, 2016.
[152] Wooten, 3.
[153] *CBS, 60 Minutes Overtime*, May 15, 2016.
[154] Annick Desjardin, et al, 150-161.
[155] Bruno, 143-145.
[156] Ibid., 144.
[157] Halstead (1998), 44.
[158] Bruno, 167, 170, 286.
[159] Ibid., 163, 311-312.
[160] Ibid., 169.
[161] Ibid., 200-211.
[162] Ibid., 283-296.
[163] Stobbe, *The Register Guard*, April 3, 2019, A5.
[164] Neergard, *The Register Guard*, October 24, 2019, A3.

BIBLIOGRAPHY

Books

Black, Kathryn. *In the Shadow of Polio*. New York: Addison-Wesley Publishing Co., 1996.

Brown, Daniel James. *The Boys in the Boat: The True Story of an American Team's Journey to Win Gold at the 1936 Olympics*. New York: Penguin Group (Viking), 2013.

Bruno, Richard L. *The Polio Paradox: Understanding and Treating 'Post-Polio Syndrome' and Chronic Fatigue*. New York: Warner Books, 2002.

Byrd, Adm. Richard E. *Alone: The Classic Polar Adventure*. New York: G.P. Putnam's Sons, 1938.

Cross, Linda Brown and Robert W. Glover, *History of Tyler Junior College, 1926-1986*. Tyler, TX: Tyler Junior College, 1985.

Davis, Fred. *Passage Through Crisis: Polio Victims and Their Families*. New Brunswick (US), and London (UK): Transaction Publishers, 1991.

——, *Dorland's Illustrated Medical Dictionary, 24th Edition*. Philadelphia: W.B. Saunders Company, 1965.

Douglas, William O. *Go East, Young Man*. New York: Random House, 1974.

Farrow, Mia. *What Falls Away*. New York: Doubleday, 1997.

Finger, Anne. *Elegy for a Disease: A Personal and Cultural History of Polio*. New York: St. Martin's Press, 2006.

Gallagher, Hugh. *FDR's Splendid Deception*. Arlington, VA: Vandamere Press, 2nd Edition, 1994.

Gevitz, Dr. Norman. *The DO's: Osteopathic Medicine in America*. Baltimore: The Johns Hopkins University Press, 2004.

Gordon, Linda. *Dorothea Lange: A Life Beyond Limits*. New York: W.W. Norton, 2009.

Gould, Tony. *A Summer Plague: Polio and Its Survivors.* New Haven: Yale University Press, 1995.

Gross, Anne K. *The Polio Journals: Lessons from My Mother.* Greenwood Village, CO: Diversity Matters Press, 2011.

Halstead, Lauro S., Ed. *Managing Post-Polio: A Guide to Living Well with Post-Polio Syndrome.* Washington, DC: National Rehabilitation Hospital (NRH Press), 1998.

Hansen, Chris. *Enfant Terrible: The Times and Schemes of General Elliott Roosevelt.* Tucson, AZ: Able Baker Press, 2012.

Kehret, Peg. *Small Steps: The Year I Got Polio.* Morton Grove, IL: Albert Whitman and Co., 1996.

Kluger, Jeffrey. *Splendid Solution: Jonas Salk and the Conquest of Polio.* New York: Berkley Books, 2004.

Kriegel, Leonard. *Falling into Life.* San Francisco: North Point Press, 1991.

Linton, Simi. *Claiming Disability: Knowledge and Identity.* New York: New York University Press, 1998.

Marshall, Alan. *I Can Jump Puddles.* London: Penguin Books, 1955.

Maynard, Frederick M., and Headley, Joan L. *Handbook on the Late Effects of Poliomyelitis for Physicians and Survivors.* St. Louis, MO: Gazette International Networking Institute, 1999.

Mee, Charles L. *A Nearly Normal Life: A Memoir.* New York: Little, Brown, 1999.

Milam, Lorenzo Wilson. *CripZen: A Manual for Survival.* San Diego, CA: MHO and MHO Works, 1993.

Mnookin, Seth. "The Polio Vaccine: From Medical Miracle to Public Health Catastrophe." In *The Panic Virus: A True Story of Medicine, Science, and Fear.* New York: Simon and Schuster, 2011, pp. 39-54.

Nickell, Joe. *Secrets of the Side Shows,* Lexington, KY: The University of Kentucky Press, 2005.

Offit, Paul A. *The Cutter Incident: How America's First Polio Vaccine Led to the Growing Vaccine Crisis.* New Haven, CT: Yale University Press, 2005.

Oshinsky, David. *Polio: An American Story.* New York: Cambridge University Press, 2005.

Parker, Philip M. *Poliomyelitis: Webster's Timeline History 1840-2007.* San Diego: ICON Group International (www.websters-online-dictionary.org), 2009.

Paul, John R. *A History of Poliomyelitis*. New Haven, CT: Yale Studies in the History of Science and Medicine, 1971.

Payne, Darwin. *One Hundred Years on the Hilltop: The Centennial History of Southern Methodist University*. Dallas: DeGolyer Library, Southern Methodist University, 2016.

Pelka, Fred (1997). *The Disability Rights Movement (The ABC-CLIO Companion to)*. ABD-CLIO, Inc., 130 Cremona Drive, P.O. Box 1911, Santa Barbara, CA 93116-1911.

Pepper, William (1843-1898) and Starr, Louis (1849-1925), Ed., *A Practical System of Medicine*, 5-volume set. Philadelphia: Lea Brothers and Co., 1885. Re-published by Reink Books, S-N Books World, Delhi, India, 2018.

Peters, Stephanie True. *Epidemic: The Battle Against Polio*. New York: Marshall Cavendish, Benchmark Books, 2005.

Rogers, Naomi. *Dirt and Disease: Polio Before FDR*. New Brunswick, NJ: Rutgers University Press, 1992.

Rowley, Hazel. *Franklin and Eleanor: An Extraordinary Marriage*. New York: Farrar, Strauss, and Giroux, trademark Picador, 2010.

Sass, Edmund J. with Gottfried, George, and Sorem, Anthony. *Polio's Legacy: An Oral History*. Lanham, MD: University Press of America, Inc., 1996.

Schroeder, Richard. *Texas Signs On: The Early Days of Radio and Television*. College Station: Texas A&M University Press, 1998.

Shell, Marc. *Polio and Its Aftermath: The Paralysis of Culture*. Cambridge, MA: Harvard University Press, 2005.

Shreve, Susan Richards. *Warm Springs: Traces of a Childhood at FDR's Polio Haven*. New York: Houghton-Mifflin Co., A Mariner Book, 2007.

Smith, Jane S. *Patenting the Sun: Polio and the Salk Vaccine*. New York: Doubleday, An Anchor Book, 1990.

Stone, Karen G. *Awakening to disability: Nothing about us without us*. Volcano, CA: Volcano Press, 1997.

Thomas, Mary Martha Hosford. *Southern Methodist University: Founding and Early Years*. Dallas, TX: SMU Press, 1974.

Wilson, Daniel J. *Living with Polio: The Epidemic and Its Survivors*. Chicago: Chicago University Press, 2005.

Wooten, Heather Green. *The Polio Years in Texas: Battling a Terrifying Unknown*. College Station, TX: Texas A&M Press, 2009.

Articles/Newsletters/Blogs

Bristol, Nellie, "Polio Eradication: Nigeria Must Keep its Eye on the Prize," The CSIS Global Health Policy Center, July 24, 2015. http://www.smartglobalhealth.org/blog/

Bruno, Richard L., "Slow Guts and Polio Survivors," The Post-Polio Institute International Centre for Polio Education. http:/www.postpolioinfo.com), no date available.

Byrd, Richard Evelyn, "Exploring the Ice Age in Antarctica," The National Geographic Magazine, Vol. LXVIII, No. 4 (October 1935), pp. 399-474.

Crichton, Kyle, "Mustang Music," Collier's, November 16, 1940.

Desjardins, Annick, et al, "Recurrent Glioblastomas Treated with Recombinant Poliovirus," The New England Journal of Medicine, July 12, 2018. 379:150-161.

Elmer-Dewitt, Philip, "Reliving Polio," Time, March 28, 1994. pp. 54-55.

Fairley, Bill. The Tarrant Chronicles. Three Part Series. The Fort Worth Star-Telegram, December 2000-January 2001. Three articles titled: "Early Radio in Fort Worth." December 20, 2000; "Momentous Days for KFJZ." December 27, 2000, p. 48; "KFJZ Veterans Recall Old Times." January 3, 2001.

Goldstein, Dana and Patel, Jugal. "An Education Wealth Gap: 504 Plans," The New York Times, July 30, 2019.

_____. Global Polio Eradication Initiative (GPEI), "Preparing for the Withdrawal of all Oral Polio Vaccines: Replacing trivalent OPV (tOPV0 with bivalent OPV (bOPV)," Briefing Note, February 2015. Drawn from World Health Organization's GPEI "Polio Eradication and Endgame Strategic Plan 2013-2018."

_____. Global Polio Eradication Initiative—News, 2015-2016.

_____, Global Polio Eradication Initiative—Every Last Child, 2015-2018.

Gold, Daniel M,, "Review: 'Every Last Child,' a Front-Line View of the Polio Crisis in Pakistan," The New York Times, June 2, 2015.

Halstead, Lauro S., MD, "A Brief History of Postpolio Syndrome in the United States," Archives of Physical Medicine and Rehabilitation, August 2011, 92: 1344-9.

LaMarche, Rae, *The Register Guard*. "Polio Is on the Run but the Fight Isn't Over," October 8, 2015. pp. A-7; "Polio Fight Not Yet Over," October 24, 2019, p. A6.

Lovett, Robert W., M.D., "A Plan of Treatment in Infantile Paralysis," *JAMA*, 1916. LXVII(6):421-426.

_____, "Elliott Roosevelt, General and Author Dies at 80," *The New York Times*, October 28, 1990.

McNeil, Jr., Donald G., *The New York Times*. "Polio on the Rise Again in Pakistan, Officials Say," October 13, 2014; "Final Salvos Against Polio," June 8, 2015; "A Milestone in Africa: No Polio Cases in a Year," August 11, 2015; "Polio Paralyzes 2 Children in West Ukraine Outbreak," September 2, 2015; "A Step Closer to the Defeat of Polio: November 23, 2015; "For Polio Vaccines, A worldwide Switch to New Version," April 11, 2016, and in a special report for the *PBS* News Hour, April 16, 2016; "Killing of Mother-Daughter Team Shakes Polio Fighters in Pakistan," January 22, 2018; "Two Strains of Polio Are Gone, but the End of the Disease Is Still Far Off," October 23, 2019.

Milofsky, David, "Cripple's Kid," New York: Bellevue Literary Review, Vol. 8, No. 2, 2008, p. 40.

Neergaard, Lauran, "Study Points to Virus as Culprit in Children's Paralyzing Illness." The Associated Press, in *The Register Guard*, October 24, 2019, p. A3.

Pinkerton, William M. and Simpson, Kirke, "Roosevelt Enters Eighth Year of Presidency with Health Splendid, Hair Sparser, Face Full," *The Fort Worth Star-Telegram*, January 20, 1940.

Racaniello, Vincent, "The Switch from Trivalent to Bivalent Oral Poliovirus Vaccine: Will it Lead to Polio?" Virology Blog: About Viruses and Viral Disease, January 13, 2016.

Stobbe, Mike, "US Officials Alarmed by Kids' Paralyzing Illness." The Associated Press, in *The Register Guard,* April 3, 2019, p. A5.

Tarrant, David, " Two Summer Sundays, One Major Triumph," *The Dallas Morning News*, July 30, 2017, pp. 1A and 17A.

Trimble, Robert, "Latest in Compacts: Voltswagen," *The Fort Worth Press*, April 16, 1961, p. 15.

Videos/Radio/Television/Websites

Beaubien, Jason, "Mutant Strains of PolioVaccine Now Causes More
    Paralysis than Wild Virus," *NPR*, June 28, 2017. Taken from *Goats and
    Soda: Stories of Life in a Changing World*.
Colt, Sara, "The Polio Crusade," American Experience, *PBS*, 2009.
Bruno, Dr. Richard L. HD, PhD, "The Encyclopedia of Polio and Post-Polio
    Sequelae," 2018. Available at Pa. Polio Survivors Network,
    www.papolionetwork.org/encyclopedia or at Dr. Bruno's website,
    www.postpolioinfo.com
Herring, Tony, Mandel, Ken, and Texas Scottish Rite Hospital for Children.
    A Fight to the Finish: Stories of Polio. Texas: Texas Scottish Rite Hospital
    for Children, 1999.
NSIDC (National Snow and Ice Data Center), "All About Sea Ice: Arctic vs.
    Antarctic."
    https://nsidc.org/cryosphere/seaice/characteristics/difference.html
NSIDC, "Rapid Ice Loss in Early April Leads to New Record Low," Arctic
    Sea Ice News and Analysis, May 2, 2019.
    nsidc.org/arcticseaicenews/2019/05/.
Pa. Polio Survivors Network, monthly newsletters,
    www.papolionetwork.org
Post-Polio Health International, St. Louis, MO: www.post-polio.org
Radutsky, Michael, "Using Polio to Kill Cancer: A Producers' Notebook,"
    CBS 60 Minutes Overtime, May 15, 2016.
Skeptical Science, "How Does Arctic Sea Ice Loss Compare to Antarctic
    Sea Ice Gain?" May 2019. www.skepticalscience.com
Roberts, Tom, Carlin, Paul, and Zaidi, Ali Faisal. *Every Last Child,* about
    challenges to polio vaccination efforts in Pakistan. Production by Image
    Nation Abu Dhabi, November 2014.
Taylor, Dyanna, "Dorothea Lange: Grab a Hunk of Lightning," American
    Experience, *PBS*, 2014.
Wagner, Paul, Seavey, Nina Gilden, and The George Washington University.
    A paralyzing fear: The story of polio in America. New York: Public
    Broadcasting Service, 1998.

Acknowledgements

Having spent almost 25 years bringing this project to fruition, I have numerous people to thank for their support, critiques, suggestions, technical expertise, and resources offered. My family were with me all the way: my husband Richard Williams (who died in 2018 and was unable to see this finished product), my children Lesley and Nathan McClintock, my brother George Clough, my aunt Margaret LaPrade, and my cousin Mike Clough. Other supportive cousins were Gana Hill, Jean Graham, and Carol Ireland.

Longtime childhood friends who helped my recollections include Wayne Arrowood, Kaye Brownlow Knowles, and John Higley. Deceased individuals who made major contributions in the 1990s and early 2000's include my mother Mildred Clough, my aunt Adele Clough, and my father's band and radio colleagues Floyd Patterson, Joe Rucker, Johnny Smith, and Dave Naugle. Other family and friends who have been there to urge me onward are Lois Harper, Jon Williams, Paul Williams, Mark Williams, Judy Hubbard, Joyce Leader, and Carla Orcutt. There are too many others to name who have rooted for me along the way.

I especially want to thank my beta readers/editors of recent manuscript drafts for their invaluable critiques that helped me hone the narrative. They are Judy Sawyer, Lealan Swanson, Elizabeth King, Betsy Knapp, Meta Maxwell, Mark Osterloh, Ann Buffington, Jo Beth Wolf, and my son, daughter, and brother.

My writer friends here in Oregon have offered invaluable advice, suggestions, critiques, inspiration, and moral support. They include Lynn Ash, Carol Brownson, Janet Fisher, Kris Jensen, Elizabeth King, and Jennifer Newcomb-Marine, who contributed initial ideas for book cover design.

Before I moved permanently from Albuquerque to Eugene in 2015, I worked over 15 years with my New Mexico writer friends to define and narrow my focus and critique various parts of the narrative. They include

Ella Joan Fenoglio, Judy Fitzpatrick, Gail Rubin, Kay Lamb, Nancy Costea, Gloria Zamora, Kathleen Anderson, Sherri Burr, Sonya Ewan, and Barbara Witemeyer.

Others to thank include my daughters-in-law Hilary Galian for website and design assistance and Lanya McClintock for her refinement of the book's focus and title. Neighbor Don MacNaughton helped with copy editing and bibliography organization. Joan Gosnell, Special Collections Director of Fondren Library at Southern Methodist University, and SMU band director Don Hopkins have shown great interest in this project. Danielle Ofri, who provided the key contact for initiating my attendance at the 2014 NYU Symposium on World Polio Day, read the manuscript and provided an endorsement. Authors Daniel J. Wilson and Heather Green Wooten also kindly read the manuscript and provided endorsements.

Made in the USA
Coppell, TX
08 May 2020

24323045R00193